Home and Work

HOME AND WORK

Housework, Wages, and the Ideology of Labor in the Early Republic

JEANNE BOYDSTON

Oxford University Press
New York Oxford

Oxford University Press

Oxford New York Toronto
Delhi Bombay Calcutta Madras Karachi
Kuala Lumpur Singapore Hong Kong Tokyo
Nairobi Dar es Salaam Cape Town
Melbourne Auckland

and associated companies in
Berlin Ibadan

First published by Oxford University Press, Inc.,
200 Madison Avenue, New York, New York 10016

First issued as an Oxford University Press paperback, 1994

Library of Congress Cataloging-in-Publication Data
Boydston, Jeanne.
Home and work : housework, wages, and the ideology
of labor in the early republic / Jeanne Boydston.
p. cm. Includes bibliographical references and index.
ISBN 0-19-506009-1
ISBN 0-19-508561-2 (PBK)
1. Housewives—United States—History.
2. Wages—Housewives—United States—History.
3. Home economics—United States—History.
4. United States—Economic conditions—To 1865.
I. Title. HD6073.H842U625 1990
331.4'8164046'0973—dc20 90–31349

2 4 6 8 9 7 5 3

Printed in the United States of America
on acid-free paper

Acknowledgments

Perhaps no book belongs to a single author. Certainly this one does not.

In a period in which external funding for research has grown more and more difficult to obtain, I have been fortunate to receive generous financial support for this project. I would like to thank the Danforth Foundation, the Giles Whiting Foundation, the Woodrow Wilson National Fellowship Foundation, the Rutgers University Research Council, and the Graduate School of the University of Wisconsin–Madison. I am especially grateful to the American Association of University Women—not only for the fellowship that supported me through part of graduate school, but for its continuing commitment to the education of women.

Historians generally get the credit for research that is made possible only by the painstaking efforts of superb archivists. Therefore, I would like to acknowledge my very considerable debt to the librarians of the following institutions: the Beinecke Rare Book and Manuscript Library and the Sterling Memorial Library, Yale University; the New York Historical Society; the New York Public Library; the Arthur and Elizabeth Schlesinger Library on the History of Women in America, Radcliffe College; the Sophia Smith Collection Archives, Smith College; and the Stowe-Day Foundation.

Over the decade in which I have been working on this book, it has become, in many ways, the intellectual property of an entire community.

I am especially happy, then, to acknowledge the individuals to whom this book "belongs." Carol F. Karlsen first suggested that I look for the meaning of women's experiences in the history of their labor—starting me on a journey that continues beyond this single volume. She and many others have encouraged me along the way. Nancy F. Cott and David Montgomery helped guide my research through its early stages as a dissertation. From beginning to end—and at critical times in the middle—Elizabeth Blackmar provided the steady strength of her own faith in the project. Lori Ginzberg and I have been doing joint combat with the demon of the "separate spheres" for so long that I find it difficult to name all of her contributions to the final product. To her, and to Mary Kelley, whose daily generosity of spirit embodies feminist scholarship at its very best, I am indebted for the dual pleasures of a rich friendship and a sustaining intellectual exchange. Linda Kerber, Gerda Lerner, Judith McGaw, Phil Scranton, Steve Stern, and Cindy Truelove—all of whom offered valuable critiques of my argument as it lurched through its various stages of development—demonstrate that the community of scholars is alive and well. I would also like to thank the members of the Columbia Seminar on the History of the Working Class for their comments on some aspects of the analysis in its early form, and Gail Cooper for her aid in bringing clarity to the final manuscript. In their unflagging love and patience, as well as in their own respect for the labor that is the subject of this study, Manuel Ayala, Kirsten Harvey, Todd Harvey, Brooke Karlsen, and Joel Steiker have immeasurably enriched both my work and my life. To Joy P. Newmann I owe special appreciation—for the model of her own scholarly work, for the care with which she has read and commented on mine, and for her priceless gifts of laughter and encouragement.

I have benefited particularly from the skilled assistance of Maureen Fitzgerald, Terry Flemming-Murphy, Kathryn Tomasek, and Kathleen Waters; but I would like to acknowledge the contributions of a wider community of students—at Yale, at Rutgers–Camden, and at the University of Wisconsin–Madison—in nourishing my understanding, not only of women's history, but of what research and teaching are all about.

Madison, Wisconsin
April 1990 J.B.

Contents

Introduction

Writing in the first issue of *The Woman's Advocate* in January 1869, Antoinette Brown Blackwell speculated on the challenges faced by America in the latter half of the nineteenth century. Her theme was the theme of many writers in the post–Civil War era—the rebuilding of the nation. As a dedicated woman's rights activist, Blackwell was particularly interested in the civil and political needs of women. What was extraordinary about her reflections, however, even in the context of the woman's rights movement, was that at the head of her agenda was the problem of housework:

> The good, faithful mother is not an idler, and though she may not be herself a money-maker, yet as partner in the matrimonial firm, she is justly fully entitled to an equal share in all profits. The theory that a wife who thus bears her fair share of their joint burdens is yet "*supported*" by her husband, has been the bane of all society. It has made women feel that it is their right to be dependents and non-producers; and it has fostered man's conceit of his own independent sovereignty.[1]

She offered these comments under the title "Industrial Reconstruction."

For most Americans, the matter of housework simply did not figure in the debate over the shape of the postwar American reconstruction—industrial or otherwise. The home, after all, was presumably the antithesis of the economic world—an almost sacred refuge from the ravages of early industrialization and the last resort of all those qualities of human life that were ground down by the heel of competitive materialism. Indeed, the separation of "private" and "public" life—of "home" and "work"—had become over the course of the antebellum period one of the most cherished truisms of American culture. The proposition that "industrial reconstruction" might include the reorganization of family life would have struck most observers as flagrant, and perhaps dangerous, nonsense.

In some respects, Blackwell's comments were atypical even among woman's rights activists. Certainly, in her attention to the economic vulnerability of women in marriage, Blackwell was echoing a concern that had characterized women's rights agitation since its inception. Among the "usurpations on the part of man toward woman" cited in the Seneca Falls manifesto of 1848 had been the protest that, in marriage, "[h]e has taken from her all right in property, even to the wages she earns." The complaint was repeated in the Memorial presented to the 1850 convention in Salem, Ohio, which objected that "[a]ll that she has, becomes legally his, and he can collect and dispose of the profits of her labor without her consent, as he sees fit, and she can own nothing, have nothing, which is not regarded by the law as belonging to the husband." Speaking the following year at a woman's rights convention in Worcester, Massachusetts, Lucy Stone gave these sentiments their most pointed expression. She observed that "[i]n the household [woman] is either a ceaseless drudge, or a blank."[2]

Yet Blackwell's objections to the economic organization of family life and to the general invisibility of women's contribution to "the matrimonial firm" also signalled a departure from these earlier analyses of the economic vulnerability of women in marriage. They had tended to center on women's rights to their own wages and to separate property, either brought into the marriage or accumulated through wages. By inserting *housework* into the discussion, however, Blackwell was significantly broadening the terms of the debate. In linking the economic vulnerability of wives specifically to the *unwaged* character of housework, she pointed to the enormous importance that wages had assumed in determining the status of different forms of work in America, and to the implications of that development for workers whose labor remained outside of the wage standard.

For the historian, Blackwell's comments raise as many questions as they answer: Was a wife in mid–nineteenth-century America a full economic partner in "the matrimonial firm"—or was she, in fact, "supported" by her husband? What were the origins of "the theory" that wives were "dependents"? Who believed it? And what did the emergence of such a "theory" have to do with the problems of industrialization? How did wives themselves experience their work? What are we to make of Blackwell's own apparent ambivalence—her contradictory assertions that wives *do* bear their "fair share" of labor within the household and yet that they expect to be "non-producers"?

Antoinette Brown Blackwell was not the only feminist thinker in the post–Civil War ear to take up such questions. As Dolores Hayden has documented in her study *The Grand Domestic Revolution* (1981), between the Civil War and the Depression a growing number of women perceived housework, and especially its social invisibility in an industrialized society, as a core mechanism of gender inequality. Furthermore, they identified "a complete transformation of the spatial design and material culture of American homes, neighborhoods, and cities" as the central agenda of feminism.[3]

Hayden's study begins at the Civil War, but, as she recognizes, the transformations that would bring the problem of housework front and center among feminists originated earlier, in the gradual emergence in the United States of an industrial economy. Over the course of a two-hundred-year period, women's domestic labor had gradually lost its footing as a recognized aspect of economic life in America. The image of the colonial goodwife, valued for her contribution to household prosperity, had been replaced by the image of the wife and mother as a "dependent" and a "non-producer," as Blackwell so aptly put it. With the departure of any general social acknowledgement of her material value to the family had gone the traditional basis of a wife's claim to some voice in the distribution of economic resources and to social status as a "productive" member of society. To be sure, new grounds for such claims had emerged,[4] but increasingly over the late eighteenth and early nineteenth centuries they rested on notions of women's nurturant capacities as a mother—a category that seemed to set her outside of the main arena of action of nineteenth-century America: the struggle for economic power. Stone had not been far off. In industrial America, the housewife seemed to be "a blank."

The study that follows is a history of housework in the United States prior to the Civil War. More particularly, it is a history of women's unpaid domestic labor as a central force in the emergence of an industrialized society in the northeastern United States. My interest in the subject originated in my perception that, although women's domestic labor had certainly changed between the founding of the colonies and the early years of the republic, antebellum housewives were not only working, but were working very hard indeed, and that their labors were contributing in substantial ways to the survival and material prosperity of their households. At the same time, it seemed clear to me that the society these women live in—and, in many respects, the women themselves—had come to doubt, even to deny, the economic value of their labors, perceiving as Blackwell suggests that the "support" of the family came entirely from wages, and especially from the wages of the husband. Clarifying both the nature of the changes that had occurred and the origins of the paradoxical status of housework in the antebellum period seemed to me essential to understanding the intimate relationship between the gender and labor systems that characterized industrializing America. That relationship is the real subject of this study.

It is also the subject of a discussion that has resurfaced periodically since the early days of the contemporary women's movement—largely in the form of a debate (at times a virtual battle royal) over the adequacy of traditional Marxist frameworks for analyzing the role of the family, and specifically the role of unpaid labor within the family, in the rise of industrial capitalism.

Marx described capitalism as an economic system directed to the creation—not of subsistence, or additional goods, or even simply of wealth—but of wealth to produce more wealth, to produce more wealth, ad infinitum. That is to say, he identified the product of capitalism as the reproduction of capital itself. Thus, for Marx, the critical characteristic of capitalism was in the way capitalists produce new capital (the capitalist "mode of production"), which he found to be a distinctive organization of labor. First, workers are deprived of control of the tools necessary to make goods that might be exchanged for the essentials of survival. Rather than by exchanging goods they have made themselves, they are forced to secure their subsistence by exchanging their *labor power* (now expended on someone else's tools) for cash to purchase what they need. Thus, labor itself is bought and sold and becomes a commodity. Second, the owners of the means of production bring the workers together in large-scale labor units, where their individual work can be specialized and their total output increased. Finally, because workers now have no other options for survival, they are forced to accept remuneration for their labor according to a wage system that is based, not on the value of what their labor power has created, but on the (lower) cost of keeping the labor force alive. In this way, the capitalist is able to retain a portion of the value actually created by the workers. Converted from goods into money, this "surplus value" becomes available for reconversion as new capital. Industrial capitalism is simply a specific instance of this model, one in which the mode of production includes the use of machinery as well as collectivization and a wage system.

Marx himself discussed the position of unpaid labor in this analysis only fragmentarily, and most scholars who have relied on his framework have concluded that unpaid domestic labor exists outside of the capitalist mode of production. That is, since it *is* unwaged, housework by definition does not enter into the wage-for-labor power exchange that is characteristic of the process of producing new capital. Where housework has been useful to industrial capitalism, according to this analysis, is in the *reproduction* of conditions necessary for the creation of capital—primarily, in keeping the paid labor force alive and tractable from day to day, year to year, and generation to generation.

But if this has been the orthodox view, it has not been without its challengers. From very early on in the contemporary women's movement, feminists like Juliet Mitchell, Selma James, and Mariarosa Dalla Costa insisted that the traditional analysis did not address the gender dynamics that inform the operation of economic systems. As early as 1969, Margaret Benston noted the complex relationship of gender and labor under capitalism, where a specific labor form (housework) seems to define the group "women"—"women" being the "special category" of workers with exclusive structural responsibility for the activities that do not enter the cash marketplace.[5]

In 1974, Wally Seccombe offered his highly controversial revision of the Marxist analysis. Rejecting the contention that housework has no formal value, Seccombe argued that the housewife produces the labor power of the wage earner, and that the wage therefore represents, in part, *her labor*. It was precisely in its unwaged character that Seccombe found the importance of housework to capitalism: the invisibility of domestic labor, he claimed, is a "structural pre-requisite" to the mystification of the wage that is necessary to the creation of surplus value.[6]

Seccombe's analysis came under immediate attack. While Margaret Coulson, Branka Magas, and Hilary Wainwright contended that "value" was a meaningless term in the absence of a direct market exchange, Jean Gardiner raised the problem of measuring the value of domestic labor. She took particular issue with Seccombe's assumption that "the value of the wife's services is equal to the value she receives from her husband's wage packet." As Gardiner pointed out, this correspondence implies "that the economic relationship between husband and wife is one of equal exchange," and thus obscures "the power relations within the family."[7]

In her now-classic article "The Traffic in Women: Notes on the Political Economy of Sex," Gayle Rubin melded these strains of analysis into a powerful statement of the limitations of traditional Marxist theory for the study of women. Rubin herself found comparatively unimportant the discussion of whether or not housework was, strictly speaking, "productive." She argued: "Housework may not be 'productive,' in the sense of directly producing surplus value and capital, and yet be a crucial element in the production of surplus value and capital." She criticized Marx for his failure to account adequately for the "historical and moral element" in a society's determination of the value of labor—an element, she rightly pointed out, that Marx recognized but left largely "unexamined." As a result, his analysis ignored the "long tradition . . . of forms of masculinity and femininity" capitalism was heir to from the beginning—ignored, indeed, "The entire domain of sex, sexuality, and sex oppression" embedded in the processes of capitalism.[8]

Among the gender systems embedded in the operation of industrial capitalism has been the tendency to conceive of the world as divided into two sex-linked spheres, sometimes described as a dichotomy between "private" and "public," sometimes between "leisure" and "labor," and sometimes between "home" and "work." Too often, as Michele Rosaldo argued some years ago, scholars have accepted these dichotomies as accurate reflections of the material organization of society. In her own review of the anthropological evidence concerning the existence and nature of opposed-sphere dichotomies, Rosaldo discovered that "domestic/public constitutes an ideological rather than objective and necessary set of terms." Unexamined for its ideological content, she noted, "a model based upon the opposition of two spheres merely reflects the prevailing gender belief system; its *assumes*—where it should rather help to illuminate and explain—too much about how gender really works." In words reminiscent of critiques of the traditional Marxist approach, she concluded: "It now appears to me that woman's place in human social life is not in any direct sense a product of the things she does (or even less a function of what, biologically, she is) but of the meaning her activities *acquire* through concrete social interactions."[9]

More recently, historian Linda K. Kerber has echoed these criticisms. As Kerber notes, the model of "male" and "female" (or "public" and "private") spheres has been extremely useful to American women's historians, initially providing a way of conceptualizing the limitations placed on women in society, and later permitting the exploration of a richly textured separate female culture. But, because it is essentially metaphorical, the model of opposed spheres has also remained "vulnerable to sloppy use." Metaphor too easily serves as description, obscuring "more complex questions about the social relations of the sexes," and veiling the possibility that "the language of separate spheres itself is a rhetorical construction which responded to changing social and economic reality."[10]

These criticisms may be usefully focused on Marx's analysis of capitalism, and particularly on his comparative inattention to the role of unpaid domestic labor in the process of capitalist production. The distinction Marx drew between "productive" and "reproductive" labor closely mirrored the divided-sphere gender *ideology* of the world he wrote in—a world that found considerable solace in the belief that the values and behaviors of the home had escaped economic contamination.

In her examination of the paradigm of spheres, Kerber notes that the criticisms of the opposed-sphere model have been growing among women's historians for the last decade. Little of this discussion has yet found its way into evaluations of the history of housework, however. Indeed, historians have tended to simply concur with the nineteenth-century conclusion that industrial capitalism removes economic production from the household and relocates it in large-scale, profit-directed factories. The chief historical effect of industrial capitalism on housework has thus been to exclude it from the economy.

Prior to industrialization, according to this view, material life was fully integrated in the individual household; production, distribution (both internally and between and among families), and reproduction (not merely bearing children, but the larger project of surviving from one generation to the next) constituted a single, largely undifferentiated process. Presumably, industrialization fractured that unity. By removing production from the household, it created a society of two almost polar-opposite zones: one (the workplace) economic in nature and focused on production, the other (the home) noneconomic in nature and focused on reproduction. Housework was the labor of the latter zone.

Either explicitly or by implication, most analyses of the history of housework go a bit farther. Not only was domestic labor structurally and generically excluded from the economy, but its new sphere was a shrunken relic of its preindustrial past. Since the growth of cash markets required a society geared to purchasing rather than to home manufacturing, and since, in any event, few families in an "industrial" society are able to control all of the resources necessary to be self-sufficient, a sizeable chunk of the labor formerly undertaken by wives presumably vanished from the household: increasingly, bread came from bakers, yarn from textile mills, and eggs, cheese, and butter (foodstuffs the colonial goodwife had been responsible for) from specialized producers. According to this view, even women's childbearing and child-rearing duties underwent a marked transformation. Mothers might dote on their children, but there were fewer children, and raising them involved little occupational training in the home. Especially in bourgeois families, where goods and services could be easily purchased, housework became a largely managerial function. Indeed, the wife's freedom from actual labor became a badge of class status.

This version of the industrial transformations of housework has emerged more by deduction than by direct examination—a deficiency in the research which women's historians have begun to redress only in the last decade. During that time, various monographs not specifically on the history of housework have nonetheless brought new attention to the roles of women in the household, and to the importance of those roles to the larger social and economic history of the United States. Examining the history of paid domestic service in pre–Civil War America, Faye E. Dudden's *Serving Women* (1983) identified changes in the relationships of mistresses and "helps" that are strongly reminiscent of the growing tensions between "bosses" and "workers" outside the household during the same period. Both Laurel Thatcher Ulrich's *Good Wives* (1982) and Joan M. Jensen's *Loosening the Bonds* (1986) helped to restore to the historical record a more detailed understanding both of the daily labor of housewives in colonial and pre–Civil War America and of the importance of that labor in the larger social and economic systems of the community. Jensen's work, in particular, offered an important challenge to the belief that household production vanished with the advent of early industrialization.[11]

During the same period, at least four full-length studies specifically of the history of housework under conditions of industrialization have appeared: Susan Strasser's *Never Done* (1982), Ruth Schwartz Cowan's *More Work for Mother* (1983), Annegret S. Ogden's *The Great American Housewife* (1986), and Glenna Mathews' *"Just a Housewife"* (1987). As their titles suggest, each of these works has been essentially iconoclastic, calling in some way for a reevaluation of traditional views of women's unpaid labor in the home. Moreover, each has closely associated changes in the experience of housework with the rise of industrial capitalism—

the first two books analyzing the technological history of housework, the latter two focusing primarily on changing images of the housewife in American culture.[12]

Of these recent studies of the history of housework, however, only Cowan has proposed a fundamental revision of the traditional view of the impact of industrialization on housework. Specifically, she contended that "industrialization occurred just as rapidly within our homes as outside of them." Noting the attraction of the popular imagination to a vision of the home as an ideal retreat from industrialization, Cowan argued that although "there are three significant senses in which housework differs from market work (in being—most commonly—unpaid labor, performed in isolated workplaces, by unspecialized workers)," there are also "three significant senses in which the two work forms resemble each other (in utilizing nonhuman—or nonanimal—energy sources, which create dependency on a network of social and economic institutions and are accompanied by alienation from the tools that make the labor possible)." Viewed from this perspective, she suggested, housework is more precisely understood, not as nonindustrialized labor, but as labor that has been "incompletely industrialized or . . . industrialized in a somewhat different manner" than market work. Cowan's caution against accepting the popular image of the home as a realm distinct from the realm of work echoes a growing rejection among women's historians of two-sphere analyses of social life.[13]

In the study that follows, I have attempted to retain what is useful in the traditional Marxist framework and to incorporate the insights and conclusions of recent studies in the history of gender. Although Marx did not consider unpaid domestic labor a part of the capitalist mode of production, his discussion of the process through which surplus is created did not necessarily exclude it. Marx analyzed the wage as a specific type of what he called the capitalist "price-form"; the wage being the price of labor power sold as a commodity. Marx argued that prices are misleading under capitalism: seeming to express an objective economic value, they in fact express "social custom" and the historic and contemporary "social relation" prevailing among members of a society. As Marx noted, the result of this "qualitative contradiction" in the capitalist price-form is that "price ceases altogether to express value. . . . Hence a thing can, formally speaking, have a price without having a value."[14]

As an instance of the price-form, the wage also suffers from this "qualitative contradiction." That is to say, the wage presents itself as a mathematically fair gauge of the "magnitude of value" created in a given amount of labor, when what it actually measures is an historic and current social relationship between employer and employee—usually, the minimum that a capitalist can pay without endangering the survival of his labor force. Thus, a particular labor form can, in a formal sense, have a wage without having a value.

What Marx did not consider—but what follows logically from his discussion of the contradictory nature of the price-form—is that a thing can also, formally speaking, have a value without having a price; or, to put it another way, a labor form can also have a value without having a wage. The possibility exists both in the nonobjective nature of the wage, and (especially) in the historic character of the capitalist wage *system*. Wages, understood simply as payment for labor in money, long predated industrial capitalism. It was only with the emergence of a wage system—that is, the widespread acceptance of money as a fair measure of the value of labor—that labor power itself could become a commodity. That system developed on the foundations of earlier, preindustrial social and economic organizations and reflected their relations. Among the historic relations that structured the nature of the capitalist wage system was gender. As evaluation of the role of unpaid domestic labor under conditions of industrial capitalistism must begin, then, with this distinction between the socially created relations of gender and the objective characteristics of labor.

It is not a simple or easy distinction to draw. As a number of scholars have pointed out, in virtually every recorded human society, gender has functioned as a central category through which experience is mediated. Conceptions of gender permeate social life, and symbols of gender both delineate and depict primary relations of power, purity, and status.[15] Nonetheless do they shape our perception of what constitutes work, of who is working, and of the value of that labor.[16]

This point has been underscored by recent anthropological and sociological research, which indicates that the social status of women's labor is seldom a direct reflection of the actual subsistence worth of that labor. Studies of various nonindustrial societies—ranging from the Iroquois of early America to the ¡Kung of contemporary southwest Africa—have suggested that the status of women as laborers is less a function of the subsistence value they create than it is of their ability to control the products of that work. And that ability appears to be closely linked to gender, especially as expressed in the operation of kinship groups. So long as the kin group is organized, both literally and symbolically, in a way that acknowledges women's claims to the products of their labor, women appear to be able to maintain visibility as workers.[17]

The implication of these findings is that it may be less the advent of commodity production per se, as the Marxist analysis would suggest, than the advent of commodity production in conjunction with a parallel process of the reorganization of gender, that makes domestic workers seem marginal to the economy. Conceiving of the issue in this way does not utterly dissociate material life from belief systems. A copious literature has now demonstrated the complex dialectical relationship between these two, particularly under conditions of industrial capitalism. As early as 1976, Heidi Hartmann pointed to the pervasive influence of gender systems in structuring the early industrial paid-labor market. Hartmann argued that it was not only, perhaps not even primarily, the actions of employers that resulted in the weak position of women in the paid-labor force, but more importantly the actions of male workers and husbands, who considered their prerogatives as *men* to be at stake. Drawing an analytical distinction between the organization of production and the organization of gender, as Hartmann and others suggest, may enable us to sort out more clearly the dynamics of the marginalization of women as workers. In the case of the present study, it may permit us to observe the process through which housework came to be perceived as removed from social production.[18]

In what follows, I have attempted to keep two questions in the forefront of analysis: What were the objective characteristics and material value of housework at various times as the United States moved toward and through the process of early industrialization; and how did the gender culture of America before the Civil War affect the perception of the characteristics and material value of housework? In examining the latter issue, I have focused particularly on gender patterns in the household and on their impact on the larger social claim women were able to stake to the products of their own labor. Because industrialization came earliest to the northeastern United States, my focus is on that region, stretching from New York northward and eastward through New England.

In Chapter I, I examined the conditions in the early British and Dutch colonies in North America that gave rise to a recognition of the economic importance of women's domestic labor, and trace the changes in social life that had undercut that visibility by the middle of the eighteenth century. Chapter II focuses on the years between the Revolution and the War of 1812—the decades when the states of the Northeast began to lurch toward more fully realized regional market relations. Chapter III provides an overview of that transition, examining especially the changing work and ideological roles of men. Chapters IV, V, and VI provide a detailed analysis of antebellum housework: what it consisted of, how it was changing, and its importance in the emergence of an industrial economy. In Chapter VII, I explore the ideological history of housework over this same period, arguing that the growing social invisibility of labor women performed for their own families made housework in many ways the prototype for the restructuring of the social relations of labor under conditions of early industrialization.

Home and Work

Chapter I

An "Œconomical Society"

The colonial household has long held a revered place in American history. Both in the scholarly literature and in the popular imagination, it has served as the touchstone of a simpler and somehow more straightforward way of life—an America before industrialization, cities, and frantic job schedules; where work and leisure alternated in easy rhythms, and where the struggle for survival was made agreeable by an ethos of family cooperation. The mother at her spinning wheel, children scattering feed to the chickens, a daughter carrying kindling to the hearth in preparation for a day's baking, the father with his older sons in the fields, girdling trees, plowing the land, or mending a fallen fence—the sense of harmony and shared enterprise of this vision of the colonial family has remained compelling for Americans across a span of almost three hundred years.

In its early years, the field of women's history both reflected and reinforced this celebration of preindustrial America. Much of the scholarship of the 1960s and 1970s focused on the problem of the origins and implications of the nineteenth-century "cult of true womanhood," a set of ideological conventions that narrowly associated women with the household and with political subordination and economic dependence. Identifying the emergence of this domestic female ideal with the rise of industrialization, women's historians concluded that the status of nineteenth-century women represented a decline from the status of women in the colonial era. They explained this shift in terms of the later disappearance of the colonial household. In the earlier period, they theorized, the family- and subsistence-based organization of material life had rendered women's household labor essential to survival. With economic significance had come social significance. "In family production," one analysis suggested, "each member contributed work of equal importance to the group's survival. . . . Under such conditions . . . the woman's reproductive work, as well as her productive work, was valued."[1] But those conditions had presumably vanished with the advent of early industrialization. The rise of commercial markets and manufacturing in the late eighteenth and early nineteenth centuries had spelled the end of the corporate colonial household. With the removal of productive labor from the family to the factory, historians argued, women lost the basis for earlier claims to economic and social standing. In the demise of the self-sufficient household lay the decline of women's status.

Although no one has challenged the economic importance of colonial women's labor, a substantial body of recent work has called into question these earlier attempts to presume a high social status for women based on the role of their labor in the "self-sufficient" colonial household. In the wake of a decade-long debate over the nature of the American transition to industrialization, most historians now consider it unlikely that self-sufficiency ever characterized colonial settlement. Merchant capital was the driving force behind the European colonization of North America, and most European settlers arrived in North America with robust commercial aspirations. Even had they wanted to maintain self-sufficiency, few families had the resources to survive apart from the dense webs of trading, bartering, buying, and selling that characterized colonial American communities.[2]

Women's historians in particular have abated their enthusiasm for the colonial past. In an early essay disputing the "golden age" theory, Mary Beth Norton drew on anthropological studies from around the world to observe that "the mere fact that a woman's economic contribution to the household is significant is not sufficient to give her a voice in matters that might otherwise be deemed to fall within the masculine sphere." Norton returned to the subject in her subsequent full-length study of women in the eighteenth century, arguing:

> Modern historians can accurately point to the essential economic function of women within a colonial household, but the facts evident from hindsight bear little relationship to eighteenth-century subjective attitudes. In spite of the paeans to notable womanhood, the role of the household mistress in the family's welfare was understood only on the most basic level.

Norton concluded that "[s]uch minimal recognition did not translate itself into an awareness that women contributed to the wider society."[3]

Norton's opening salvo against the "golden age" theory was seconded by Laurel Thatcher Ulrich's close study of colonial women's lives, *Good Wives: Image and Reality in the Lives of Women in Northern New England, 1650–1750*. Arguing that "survival" is, at best, "a minimal concept" that has never adequately explained gender relations, Ulrich asserted that the really striking differences between the lives of colonial women and women who lived in later periods lay less in the objective economic necessity of the labor they performed than in "the forms of social organization which linked economic responsibilities to family responsibilities and which tied each woman's household to the larger world of her village or town."[4] The point was not what colonial women had done, but where that work was positioned in the patterns of daily community interaction.

Good Wives signaled a valuable shift in the study of colonial women's domestic labor, a shift away from seeing housework merely as a stalking horse for abstract questions of female status and toward a greater emphasis on the nature of the work itself, especially as it was constituted in the social organization of daily life in northern New England. But conceptual problems remained. The new localism emerged at some sacrifice to a broader regional perspective. Deeply embedded in the dense social networks of the colonial village, housework appeared to stand apart from the unfolding economic history of New England, neither shaping nor being shaped by the transformation of the colonial Northeast from a series of outposts on the Atlantic Ocean into an elaborate, market-oriented regional economy. Most problematic for the long history of domestic labor, the matter of change over time was not addressed. Unexplained were the numerous signs that, early on at least, housework *was* viewed as central to economic life—a recognition that had faded by the close of the colonial period.

Clearly, the theory of a "golden age" of preindustrial labor will not account for that change. As Mary Beth Norton's study of Revolutionary-era American women makes clear, the status of colonial housework was declining in the Northeast as early as the mid-eighteenth century, well *in advance* of the industrial transformation. However we are to account for the diminishing status of women's most characteristic labor in the colonial period, industrialization alone will not do. Certainly, industrialization would severely disrupt both the work and the social relations of household labor, but the foundations for that disruption had been laid earlier, in the fabric and evolution of colonial life itself, and especially in the changing relations of gender and labor over the course of the preindustrial period.

The debate over the "golden age" theory has generally been cast in terms of whether or not economic status translates into political and social status: to put it another way, whether doing important work brings one rewards and prerogatives as an important member of the community. In the northeastern British American colonies, the answer to this question was clearly no. The Europe the settlers had come from was a society deeply defined by patriarchy. English Puritanism, in particular, was a pervasively patriarchal belief system, and the social institutions that it fostered—families, religious congregations, civic governments—were all conceived and understood (as the Puritans also conceived and understood history and creation) not merely as male-dominated, but, more precisely, as dominated by the person and figure of the *father* (ultimately, the figure of God-the-father). Virtually all relations of power vested superior legitimacy in the decisions of men—merely a logical reflection of the natural order, William Secker thought, since "Our Ribs were not ordained to be our Rulers"—and virtually all male roles (including that of husband) were understood in terms of the authority and presumed sagacity and experience of the father. It was on this basis—as fathers, both the sires of future generations and the sources of those generations' material settlements—that men claimed social and political preeminence. In the settled Puritan community, for a woman "to transgress the will and appointment" of her husband, pastor, or magistrate was tantamount to transgressing the fifth commandment to honor one's father.[5]

Although it would later become a key commercial and cultural hub for the Northeast, New York was founded under Dutch laws and customs that allowed women, both single and married, a margin of comparative autonomy in matters of property ownership, inheritance, and the making of contracts. Like England, however, the Netherlands was a male-dominated society, and in the New Netherlands, as in New England, religious, magisterial, and social authority was vested in men. Moreover, perhaps in part because the culture of colonial New York was influenced throughout the seventeenth century by contact with the Puritans to the north, once New York became an English colony in 1664, Dutch customs more supportive of female autonomy appear to have faded rather quickly.[6]

In order to understand the complex dynamics of gender and labor in the northeastern colonies, it may be necessary to transpose the elements of the question: to ask, not whether economic status determined social and political status, but rather whether social and political status determined economic status. Here, too, in important ways, the answer is a clear no. While women in the early colonies were undoubtedly deemed to be both the social and the political inferiors of men, this subordination did not function to deny entirely women's important contributions as economic agents. Not only did women work, but they were *recognized* as workers, and the value of that labor—both to their households and to their communities—was openly and repeatedly acknowledged. Certainly, Puritan husbands, by and large, did not countenance women's usurpation of customary male occupations. John Winthrop set it down as fact that Ann Hopkins of Connecticut could have avoided insanity had she only "attended her household affairs . . . and not meddle[d] in such things as are proper for men."[7] Equally certainly, formal acknowledgements of the economic valorization of women's domestic labor did not lead to discernible political or social power for colonial women. Nevertheless, the economic valorization of wives as workers and the social, religious, and economic subordination of wives as females were not perceived to be mutually exclusive concepts. Samuel Willard captured the paradox of women's position when he instructed that "the Husband is to be acknowledged to hold a *Superiority*, which the Wife is practically to allow; yet in respect of all others in the Œconomical Society, she is invested with an Authority over them by God; and her husband is to allow it to her."[8]

Seventeenth-century Europe was still a society in which, as Alexander Niccoles indicated in 1615, a man could anticipate having in a wife not only a companion and a source of comfort, but also "a servant for profite."[9] The English immigrants whose culture would so dominate American experience carried this view with them to the colonies. Certainly, the labor of women in the northeastern English colonies was largely gender-prescribed: in a rough spatial division of labor, men worked in the fields, while women attended to the work within or more immediately in the vicinity of the household. But a gender division of labor did not mean that women were expected to be less productive than men. Ministers praised the woman who "looketh well to the ways of her household. . . . " When John Cotton referred to women as "a necessary good" in human society, he very probably meant the material as well as the psychological support their presence supplied. Indeed, a woman's work in "managing . . . domestical and household affairs" in general and, more specifically, "at the wash-house . . . at the needle, at the wheel, [and] at the spindle" were considered to constitute "her *trade.*" And she was expected to ply it. As Essex's Mary Boutwell learned in 1640, women as well as men could be and were brought to court on charges of "not working but living idly."[10] In the New Netherlands, meanwhile, married women proved "a servant for profite" to their husbands through numerous commercial operations. Able to make contracts in their own right, married women were licensed to run taverns and inns, vended produce and manufactured goods in city markets, taught school alongside their husbands, and, in some cases, carried on extensive independent trading operations.[11]

The importance of wives' work in and for their families was recognized in a variety of ways in the early northeastern colonies. Advising friends still in England on the necessary provisions for settlement, men included in their lists specific enumerations of the "household implements" of women's work: "1 iron pot, 1 kettle, 1 frying pan, 1 gridiron, 2 skillets, 1 spit, wooden platters, dishes, spoons, trenchers." Once in the colonies, moreover, the settlers attached concrete significance to the difference that a woman's work could make in the founding and operation of a successful homestead. In a 1639 land division proposal, Sudbury, Massachusetts, inhabitants recommended that land be distributed according to a formula that allotted 6 acres for a man, 6½ acres for his wife, and 1½ acres for each child. As well as an inducement to marry (and populate the community), the allotment to the wife expressed colonists' belief that the addition of her labor more than doubled the viable economic size of a farm.[12]

That belief was specifically affirmed in men's wills, where husbands sometimes publicly recorded their gratitude to the "loveing wife" whose "care and diligence [had helped] to get and save what god hath blessed us with. . . ." When husbands failed to acknowledge the value of their wives' labor, colonial courts had the option of rectifying the error—as did the Plymouth Court when it moved to protect widows' dower rights on the grounds that a wife's "diligence and industry" were indispensable to "the getting of the [family] Estate."[13]

This was not the only occasion on which institutions of colonial government gave formal recognition to the value of women's domestic labor. Plymouth Colony deemed dairying (largely women's work) important enough to the colonial economy to justify making an official inventory of the equitable distribution of milk-producing animals in 1627. In 1630, the Massachusetts Court of Assistants allotted early male settlers whose families had not yet arrived twenty shillings "to buy . . . helpe to washe, brewe, & bake." Seemingly of the opinion that men lacked either the time or the skills (or both) to do this work themselves, the Court also evidently concluded that men could not well do without it.[14]

Wrapping up their regular business in 1645, the Massachusetts Court of Elections offered a rare and intriguing glimpse of the ways gender and labor intersected in the colonial Northeast. In separate orders, the Court reimbursed Richard Sherman "19s for lodging 3 of ye deputies & ye Gov[e]rn[o]rs men" and "ye wife of Rich[a]rd Sherman 13⅓s . . . as a gratuity for her cares & paines ys Co[u]rt about o[u]r dyet. . . ." Whether the Shermans operated a regular boarding establishment is unclear and, for our purposes, unimportant. What is significant is that Richard Sherman and his wife were remunerated *separately*—the Court recognizing his distinct contribution in making available the property that he owned, and her distinct contribution in preparing the Court's food. Moreover, in affixing a monetary value to each, the Court recognized *both* claims as essentially economic.[15]

Neither the nature of the claims nor the values awarded were identical, of course. Richard Sherman's claim was based on his right in the ownership of property, not in direct labor; indeed, it is a safe guess that any direct labor provided in connection with the lodging (preparing linens or cleaning, for example) was his wife's. That separate labor was not identified in the Court's action, but was, instead, submerged in his rights of ownership. Her claim, meanwhile, was based largely on the provision of direct labor: her work in the preparation of food. And *that* claim, valued at only about seventy percent of his, was deemed inferior. The Court clearly attached a greater value to the man's rights in property ownership than to the woman's rights in labor.

The example of the Shermans raises the question of whether women's work was valued only when it led to a direct market exchange. That this was not the case is suggested by a series of orders passed by the General Court of Massachusetts in 1646 as it sought to standardize punishments for various crimes in the colony. The Court levied "double damage" against any person convicted of destroying timber, coal, corn, hay, straw, hemp, or flax—all but the last commonly considered the products of men's work. At the same time, the Court set an award of *triple* damages for the destruction of fruit trees, linen or woolen goods, gardens, or stacked wood; all but the last of these was generally associated with women's household labor, but none was necessarily associated with market production. However one explains the specific discrepancy between the two categories of damages, the comparatively severe penalties set for the destruction of the products of women's work attest to the Court's understanding both that the products (fruit from orchards, vegetables from gardens) were important to family well-being and that producing them required labor. In particular, in setting higher damages for the destruction of linen goods than for the destruction of unworked flax, the Court affirmed the *value added* by women's labor.[16]

The inequities of the 1645 awards to Richard Sherman and his wife expressed the limits of the recognition accorded to women's work even in the early years of settlement. That decision may also have reflected changes that were already underway by mid-century and which would be well established in the culture of the colonial Northeast by the middle of the next century. Certainly, various signs indicate that even by the middle decades of the seventeenth century the public recognition of the value of women's labor had begun to wane. In his 1653 will, Boston merchant Robert Keayne was careful to secure to his wife her full "widow's thirds" of the estate. Significantly, however, he acknowledged her claim exclusively on the grounds of her having been a "dear and loving wife" rather than on her labor in helping to accumulate the estate. Keayne added, moreover, that "if she desire to have a cow or two, a piece of plate or two, or any other part of the household stuff besides what I have given her as a legacy," she must purchase it. Beyond her dower rights, Anne Keayne's relationship to the estate was that of a stranger.[17]

In his will, Robert Keayne took pains to try to ensure amity between his wife and his son. Various historians have suggested that as the century wore on, this pattern became more and more common, with husbands including elaborate protections for the support of their widows as regular components of their wills. Alexander Keyssar speculates that these provisos reflected an economic competition in which sons challenged their widowed mothers' right to any part of the accumulated family holdings. Sermons from the late seventeenth and early eighteenth centuries support this speculation. Regularly associating "widowhood" with "poverty," ministers implied that the cause of widows' hardships lay, at least in part, in sons' "readiness to *Slight* their mothers" and to deny women's "Serviceableness" in the family enterprise.[18]

Sermons from this period indicate that the ministers perceived themselves to be women's defenders, but the manner of their defense revealed important shifts in the grounds on which a woman might claim both respect and a share of the family's material holdings. Increasingly through the early decades of the eighteenth century, ministers described wives in a way that emphasized their *freedom* from labor and that framed their contribution to the family in emotional and psychological (rather than economic) terms. Benjamin Colman dwelt on wives' "Retiredness from *the Cares & Snares of the World*." Contending that widows should be treated well, Increase Mather found his justification in the argument that their husbands had been "*Useful Men*." Dropping earlier formulations that praised wives as "fellow labourers," Thomas Foxcroft maintained that women deserved respect based on their "wise Advices, their faithful Admonitions, their holy Examples, their devout Prayers, and *Labours of Love*."[19]

The polite literature from England that was distributed and read throughout New England reinforced this new emphasis. Savile's *Advice to a Daughter*, a popular example of the genre, implied that women's only responsibilities were to preserve marital peace and family honor. Mary Beth Norton has pointed particularly to the influence of Samuel Richardson's novel *Clarissa* in establishing a cultural example for young womanhood. Affirming "Modesty & Sweetness" as the hallmarks of the female temperament, the Clarissa model denied any evidence of labor in women's lives. The opposite of Clarissa was "Masculina": "her Voice loud & manlike, her Discourse Rough & indelicate [,] her dress sluttish, & she strides along, when she walks. . . . " Disheveled, assertive, and athletic, "Masculina" associated activity with manliness and suggested by implication that the true female betrayed no sign of toil.[20]

Although the polite literature generally presented "Clarissa" as a positive role model for women, this image of womanhood was not secure from all criticism: even as they praised women for their delicacy, eighteenth-century observers admonished women for not working hard enough. A poem by Nicholas Noyes, included in Cotton Mather's 1703 eulogy of Mistress Mary Brown of Salem, took up this theme:

> *O Parents*, Pity the fond *Sons* of Men,
> And your fair *Daughters* well adorn for them.
> With *Useful Knowledge* fraight their Tender Souls;
> Why should they *Empty* be, but *Noisy Fools*?
> Teach them the Skill an House to *Guide & Feed*,
> And with Kind Mates an *Easy* Life to lead.
> *Goodness* to them, and all *Good Humour* Show;
> The Pious Parents Shap'd their MARY so.[21]

In the more raucous popular press, meanwhile, women's presumed idleness had become the stuff of overtly misogynist satire. Over the course of the first half of the eighteenth century, wives became a favorite object of ridicule in colonial newspapers, which portrayed them as lazy, vain, and "want[ing] sense, / And every kind of duty." The best a man might hope for was a wife who was "prudent," it seemed. What he was more likely to get was a self-indulgent child who would quickly become a parasite on the household economy: "She's married now," taunted a typical newspaper barb of the 1750s, "and spends her time / more trifling than a baby."[22]

Even when women were described as hard at work, moreover, their very industry could easily be made into an illustration of foolishness. The author of a letter to *The New York Mercury* in 1758 began by praising his wife as "an irreconcileable enemy to Idleness." But the compliment was tongue-in-cheek, for he soon made it clear that her activity was mindless, frivolous, and without any real value to the household: "We have twice as many fire-skreens as chimneys," he observed dryly, "and three flourished quilts for every bed. Half the rooms are adorned with a kind of futile pictures which imitate tapestry. . . . [S]he has boxes filled with knit garters and braided shoes. She has twenty coverns for side-saddles embroidered with silver flowers, and has curtains wrought with gold in various figures, which she resolves some time or other to hang up. . . ." Even when her fancy fell upon an activity which might indeed be useful—spinning—she insisted that it be done on inefficiently small wheels, protesting "that great wheels are not fit for Gentlewomen. . . ." But eighteenth-century attacks on women as economic leeches were not directed exclusively at women in wealthy households, who might have been considered to be ladies of comparative leisure. As Christine Stansell's description of sexual mores in late–eighteenth-century New York City suggests, the assumption that females were economic vampires could be applied to hard-working women in great economic need as easily as to the wives of the wealthy.[23]

There survived in the late colonial era an exception to this portrait of female economic silliness: the image of the "notable" housewife, praised and valued for her skill at management and her cleverness at making ends meet. The "notable" housewife was a descendant of the virtuous woman described in Proverbs 31, the woman whose "candle goeth not out by night": "She seeketh wool, and flax, and worketh willingly with her hands," "bringeth her food from afar," "riseth also while it is yet night, and giveth meat to her household"; "with the fruit of her hands she planteth a vineyard," and "[s]he layeth her hands to the spindle, and her hands hold the distaff." Yet the good woman of Proverbs and the "notable" colonial housewife were not quite the same. The wife of Proverbs is a bustling woman-about-the-community whose "works praise her in the gates." In contrast, as Laurel Thatcher Ulrich has pointed out, colonial women were deemed most "notable" when least noticed. They were expected to be pious, obedient, and industrious, but scarcely visible. At least prescriptively, the "notable housewife" was something of a contradiction in terms: the worker whose very claim to importance depended in part on the unseen nature of her labor.[24]

What is particularly puzzling about these changing attitudes toward women's labor contributions is that they were not paralleled by changes in the work itself. Throughout the colonial period, precisely what a given woman did depended on the overall age, wealth, and membership of her household and on whether she lived in a more- or less-rural area. Within these parameters, however, neither the actual labor involved in housewifery nor the economic value of that labor to the household appears to have varied significantly between 1650 and 1750.

At the end of this period, as at the beginning, most households were agricultural. They were not self-sufficient; in almost all places and at almost all times, some goods were purchased on the market and many were acquired through trading. As early as 1633, an order of the General Court of Massachusetts mentioned "carpenters, sawers, masons, clapboard ryvers, bricklayers, tylars, joyners, wheelwrights, [and] mowers" as among the various specialized workers a family might depend on. But the market was of comparatively minor importance and payment was often in kind; indeed, cash was rare enough in early Massachusetts that the Court was prompted to order that

> after the last day of this month [October, 1640] no man shalbee compelled to satisfye any debt, legacy, fine, or any paym[en]t in money, but satisfaction shalbee accepted in corne, cattle, fish, or other com[m]odities, at such rates as this Courte shall set down from time to time. . . .

Of necessity, families pieced together their livelihoods by combining an internal system of home production with external systems of both borrowing and barter. In the process, the primary category of labor organization was gender.[25]

On farms, men were responsible for providing grain and fuel and the permanent structures of the homestead. They managed the pastures and the out-buildings; made some of the equipment used by themselves and their wives; saw to the care and maintenance of their own tools; and supervised the work of older sons and male servants. Women were responsible for providing fruits, vegetables, dairy products, and fowl; for manufacturing various goods needed by the family; for managing the distribution of goods in the household; for the daily care of the house proper, the home lot, and much of their own equipment; and for training and supervising infants, older daughters, and female servants.[26]

In the business of meeting their separate obligations to the family, both men and women grew food for the family, engaged in commerce and manufacturing, and provided maintenance services. A woman might bake her own bread, or trade cheese for it. She might herself spin the yarn for the family's clothes, or she might knit scarves for a neighbor more skilled at the wheel than she. Similarly, her husband might manufacture harnesses himself, or borrow a harness from a neighbor whose cow grazed in his pasture. He might raise grain for his family's bread, or he might barter for it. Even among men who were no longer farmers, barter, as opposed to cash, was a common form of payment. When Thomas Cooper agreed to build a meetinghouse for Springfield, Massachusetts, he received "fouer score pounds as money . . . which is to be paid in wheate, peas, porke, wampam, debtes, [and] labor."[27] The mode one worked in counted for far less than one's final success in providing the goods and services needed. This organization characterized household economies early in the colonial period and it persisted into the mid–eighteenth century.

In 1750, as in 1650, then, country women washed and cleaned, kept chickens for eggs, meat, and feathers, tended small barnyard animals, foraged for berries, fished, clammed, and kept kitchen gardens. They helped slaughter animals and preserve meat, milked cows, made cheese, butter, cider, wine, and beer. They sewed and knitted, quilted and spun, and prepared all of the food for family consumption, collecting and chopping kindling and spending long (and dangerous) hours coaxing cooking fires to just the right temperature. Women often used these same activities as the basis for networks of barter and sale. Sarah Edwardes of Springfield, Massachusetts, sold and bartered the milk her cows produced. Alice Apsley of Ft. Saybrook, Connecticut, developed a small business selling the medicinal herbs and onions she grew in her garden.[28]

Diaries surviving from the mid–eighteenth century demonstrate the continuing importance of rural wives to the economic systems that supported their families. Mary Cooper lived on a farm near Oyster Bay, Long Island. It was an agricultural community, but one with strong ties to the urban markets of New York and New Haven and New London, Connecticut. Covering the years from 1763 to 1773, Cooper's diary chronicles a life of hard and almost constant labor—labor that led her, in July of 1769, to reflect: "This day is forty years sinc[e] I left my father's house and come here, and here have I seene littel els but harde labour and sorrow. . . ."[29]

Much of Cooper's work involved the daily maintenance of her house and family. The single job most frequently mentioned in her diary is cooking: cooking for her family, cooking for her friends, cooking for relatives and visitors, sometimes even cooking for overnight boarders. It was work that seldom gave her any pleasure. "O, I am dirty and tired allmost to death cooking for so many peopel," she wrote on March 7, 1769, "freted almost to death." Equally onerous, however, were the cleaning, washing, and ironing required by a household of four with a steady stream of guests. Longing to "prepare" herself for the Sabbath, Cooper instead spent December 24 of 1768 "drying and ironing my cloths til allmost brake of day."[30]

Although she purchased various items for her family's use—dye, cotton, scissors, nails, and molasses, for example—Mary Cooper produced both food and goods for her household. She picked apples, cherries, blackberries, quince, and peaches. What was not served immediately was cut up and dried or made into preserves or sweetmeats for later use; in good years, she kept up a lively business selling surplus cherries to neighbors. Meanwhile, she also salted beef, kept bees for honey, made wine, sausage, and pickles, and grew herbs. Although the diary does not record that Mary Cooper herself did the family spinning, she did comb flax. Among her other home manufactures were candles, soap, and clothing.[31]

In addition to her husband and herself, Cooper's household included six children (two of whom survived to adulthood), four slaves, and innumerable visitors. The entries in Cooper's diary often use the plural pronoun—"Wee are much hurred drying appels," she noted on October 11, 1768, and recorded a few days later that "[w]e are cleaning the house"—reflecting her ability to delegate part of her work to others, as time or the limits of her own skills dictated. Her daughters spun, for example, and also helped clean and pick berries. The Coopers' slaves appear to have worked primarily in the fields, although a female, Frances, combed wool and may have assisted with the washing. Occasionally, the need for additional skills prompted Cooper to hire outside workers. In October of 1768 and again in March of 1769, she employed a seamstress to help with her sewing. She regularly sent her weaving out to a professional weaver and she hired a workman to construct a new hive for her honey bees.[32]

Like women a hundred years earlier, Mary Cooper was involved in an intricate network of neighborly swapping. She frequently went to friends' homes to assist in the delivery of a child or to help tend the sick, and her diary indicates that, in turn, neighbors sometimes came to her aid, helping to pull flax or giving her some of the fish they had caught. On occasion, Cooper borrowed equipment from friends or relatives. Making preserves in October of 1772, she recorded that she was "very buise and mighty angrey becaus the cittel [kettle] is sent for before I have don my quinces."[33]

One might speculate that the mid–eighteenth-century satires of housewives were directed less to the Mary Coopers of the colonial world than to the growing population of city women, whose work lives were more directly altered by the development of urban markets—and especially the women of more prosperous urban families. Certainly there were important differences between the economies of rural and urban households. In general, both men and women in town were likely to engage in more trade and less agriculture and household manufacture than their rural counterparts. More particularly, the nature and division of husbands' and wives' respective contributions to the household economy was changed in the city: increasingly, urban husbands made their contribution in the form of wages (or credit) to facilitate the acquisition of family provisions. Wives, meanwhile, assumed a greater responsibility for actually obtaining the goods needed by the family. In addition to the foodstuffs traditionally considered a part of women's contribution (vegetables, fruits, and fowl, either from their own yards or from trade), urban women began to assume responsibility for shopping or scavenging for the grain and wood that, in an earlier period, their husbands would have supplied. This new distribution of work did not lighten the load of urban women, however. Trips to the wharf and to nearby villages to make purchases and to establish buying and trading contacts merely substituted for trips to the woods in search of wild berries and roots.

All colonial women were expected to be able to assume their husbands' responsibilities as need arose. Farm wives had to speak for absent husbands, discipline sons and male servants and assign them chores, and work in the fields as needed—although these tasks remained designated as "men's" work regardless of how often a woman did them. These "deputy husband" functions may have expanded in urban environments, where men were more likely to be absent from the home for long periods of time. The wives of sea-going men assumed virtually all of their husbands' customary daily responsibilities. Where men's wage work took place in the dwelling itself, wives were often expected to integrate into their own schedules substantial aspects of their husbands' occupations. The wife of a cobbler often stitched the uppers of the shoes he sold, and the man who turned his best room into a storefront or his home into an inn generally anticipated, as Benjamin Franklin noted, that his wife would "assist . . . by tending shop."[34]

Given these redistributions of specific tasks, however, the approach to family survival that marked rural households was largely preserved in the organization of mid–eighteenth-century urban homes. Women remained responsible for cooking, cleaning, fire-tending, food storage, the manufacture of a wide range of household items, the care of household linens and clothing, and child rearing, while their husbands still provided direct labor to the family in the form of household repairs, some domestic manufacture (mending shoes, for example, or woodworking), and perhaps some shopping. Even among more prosperous families, few women enjoyed any great leisure, or even found their labors reduced to mere supervisory work. As Laurel Thatcher Ulrich has pointed out, even the "pretty gentlewomen" of the colonial period "had few of the privileges, yet most of the responsibilities, of gentility."[35] This is well illustrated in the life of Esther Burr, whose journal provides one of the few surviving detailed records of a woman's daily life and work in the mid–eighteenth century.

Written as a series of letters to her friend Sarah Prince, Burr's journal covers the last three years of her life, 1754 to 1757, by which time she had long since moved away from her family in Northampton, Massachusetts, and was living with her husband and children in northern New Jersey (first in Newark and later at Princeton). Since Burr's husband was a minister and a college president, the particular shape of her work differed in some respects from that of the wife of a cobbler or merchant. Like Mary Cooper, Esther Burr had help with her work. Although her children were too young to be useful (Sally was born in 1754 and Aaron in 1756), Esther's sisters were sometimes present to assist her, and the family had at least one household slave, Harry, and an occasional hired woman—with the result that Burr seldom had to do her own cooking. But the presence of additional household labor did not make Esther Burr a woman of leisure. She remained the primary child-care provider and nurse for her family and she herself continued to perform much of the other housework, a point she underscored as she recorded her work for Sarah Prince: "So busy about some Tayloring that I must beg to be excused. You must know that I am the Taylor." Sometimes with help, sometimes without it, she was also the cleaner, the ironer, and the seamstress. On one occasion she described herself as "all up in Arms a cleaning House, white-washing, rubing Tables, cleaning silver, China and Glass, etc.," work that left her, she commented, "almost tired out of my sense." At other times she merely noted to Sarah that she was "So very busy that I cant get time to write."[36]

The journal makes it clear that Burr was involved in the household manufacture of a number of articles, particularly yarn, clothing, and quilts. But Burr also purchased much of what her family needed—a cash-based aspect of her domestic labor that she referred to as her "business." Much of this work was conducted at some distance from her home. Her "cuntry business, such as speak[ing] for Winter Tirneps, Apples, and syder, and butter," generally required that she ride out from town to buy food from more-rural neighbors. For major purchases—heavy clothing or furniture, for example—Burr found it necessary either to travel to New York herself or to request a friend in New York or Boston to act as her agent.[37]

Like other urban women, Esther Burr bore heavy responsibilities as a "deputy husband," either providing for and entertaining her husband's associates (or boarding the college's students), or visiting "the Widow, the fatherless and the sick" in her husband's congregation. Unsurprisingly, since the numbers of guests in her home at one time could easily exceed thirty, she found entertaining "Tedious" and exhausting, although it was "visiting" that she considered "the heardest [hardest] work that I do." Neither, as Burr well understood, was optional. Both were required by her husband's employment.[38]

To argue that even prosperous women worked hard in the mid-eighteenth century is not to suggest that housework was unaffected by the economic status of the household. The most obvious differences by economic level were probably not so much in the types of labor performed or in the overall importance of that labor to the material survival of the family, but in the specific tasks, in the time allotted to each, and in the total time spent working. For example, although virtually all women bore some responsibilities as "deputy husbands," the nature of that work undoubtedly varied with the overall resources of the family: poor women hired out to work in an employer's fields as part of a family unit; women in "middling" households tended shop; wives of more prosperous men entertained guests associated with their husbands' work.

There were some forms of work the wife in a poor family performed regularly but her counterpart in a higher economic class undertook only sporadically if at all. In the country, poor wives earned a few shillings or in-kind payment weeding gardens or gathering vegetables; in the towns, they took in wash or worked in other women's homes sewing, washing, or ironing. It was not uncommon for wives in middling households to add to the family resources through barter or trade, but this was generally through the exchange or sale of goods (yarn, cheese, butter, eggs, or poultry) rather than of labor. In both types of exchanges, women in wealthy households were far more likely to be the purchasers than the vendors. Middling and poor families were also distinguished from their wealthier counterparts by the greater likelihood that they would take in paying boarders. Elite families often had extra people in the household, creating extra work for the wife, but they generally did not accept payment for the service.[39]

Wives in middling families spent more time in some tasks than did either their poorer or their wealthier counterparts. With fuller larders and more extensive equipment than poor women, they devoted a greater effort to food preparation and preservation. Lacking the servants who might be present in elite households, middling women tended to do this work themselves, sometimes delegating parts of it to daughters or young women hired from the neighborhood as "helps." While all women spent time acquiring the family's food, poor wives, whose household economies required that they piece together an elaborate combination of production, purchase, trade, and scavenging, were likely to spend a disproportionate share of their time in the labor of physically acquiring the family's necessities, while their husbands (day laborers, mariners, mercenaries, poorer artisans, and the wandering unemployed) made their contribution in whatever cash they could earn and sometimes in the savings realized from their physical absence.

Some of both the similarities and the differences in women's household labor—between country life and city life and (to some extent) between households of greater and lesser wealth—are made concrete in a comparison of Burr and Cooper. Both women cleaned, washed, ironed, made and mended clothing, preserved food, and manufactured necessary items for the family's use. Both women supervised other household workers. Both were personally involved in the rearing of their children. Both spent exhausting hours providing for visitors in the household. Yet the contrasts between the two women's lives are striking. Burr spent far more time shopping than did Mary Cooper—and did almost none of the work that so determined Cooper's daily schedule, cooking. Neither was she engaged in the extensive horticulture that helped shape Cooper's work life.

Among the most dramatic differences between the two diaries is not the work performed, however, but rather the two women's consciousness of themselves as laborers. Mary Cooper loathed much of what she did, and apparently rarely received direct recognition for it. Nevertheless, she understood well enough that what she was engaged in was indeed "harde labour." This was less clear to Esther Burr, who seemed at times reluctant to claim her labor as real work, noting instead at the end of one busy Thursday in October of 1755 that she felt "*as if* I had been heard [hard] at work all day."[40] By the mid–eighteenth century—well before the beginnings of industrialization in North America—the denigration of women's household labor was becoming an established cultural practice for some *women* as well as for men.

The changing perception of housewifery appears to have reflected changes in the larger social and economic context, rather than changes in the nature and economic value of housework itself. A variety of early conditions had created a cultural setting favorable to the recognition of housewifery's economic contribution. More specifically, early conditions had preserved and fostered a cultural context in which women's social subordination did not determine their economic status. As the colonial period wore on, those conditions disappeared. Increasingly, men's claim to social superiority was based on a claim to an exclusively *male* economic agency. In this context, the likelihood that women's domestic labor would be counted on a par with the work of their husbands declined. Many of the changes were material in origin, but the key shifts were ideological. By the eve of the Revolutionary crisis, colonists had largely ceased to *perceive* housewifery as a part of the real economy.

To some degree, the visibility of wives' domestic labor in the early settlements may be attributed to the Puritan definition of *economy*, which traced its origins to the Greek *oikos*, "the household." Reflecting this concept, Puritan minister William Perkins gave his 1631 sermon "Œconomie" the subtitle "Or, Household-Government: A Short Survey of the Right Manner of Erecting and Ordering a Family, according to the Scriptures." All labor that contributed to the material viability of family life—whether it was growing food or cooking it, tending livestock or tending children—was "economic." Within the household, as Samuel Willard had declared, woman was "invested with an Authority . . . ; and her husband is to allow it to her. . . ."[41]

Although it fit rather closely, this emphasis on the household as the origin of economic life should not be interpreted as a simple and direct reflection of how Puritans actually organized material affairs; as we have seen, families were not utterly self-sufficient. Nonetheless, traditionally the Puritan household had been formed and was operated as a joining of two types of resources: the tools and skills in housewifery of the bride and the lands and skills at husbandry of the groom. Both components were understood to be essential to household success.

The valuing of women's work was undoubtedly encouraged by the underrepresentation of women in the early settlements, and by the fact that many women who did participate in the migration died during their first years in North America. Their relative scarcity may well have created a psychological atmosphere in which women's domestic work assumed a more visible family and community significance than would otherwise have been the case.[42]

The importance that the Protestants who settled the northeastern colonies attached to the institution of the family reinforced this psychological and communal visibility. When Puritans described the family as "the very *First Society*," they meant politically and religiously, as well as materially: God had chosen "to lay the foundations both of State and Church, in a family. . . . " Because of its central position as a model for all social relations, the seventeenth-century nuclear family was not private, especially among the Puritans. To be sure, New England settlers had always shown a proclivity for the nuclear family form: within a few short years, Plymouth Colony had done away with its communal organization because "the yong men . . . did repine that they should . . . worke for other mens wives and children. . . . And for mens wives to be commanded to doe service for other men . . . , they deemed it a kind of slaverie. . . . "[43] Nevertheless, the household was subject to intervention and restructuring whenever its operations or its composition appeared to deviate from the social goal. In 1642, for example, the Massachusetts Court created a panel of men in each town to correct "the great neglect of many parents & masters in training up their children in learning, & labor, & other implyments which may be proffitable to the common wealth. . . . " An important consequence of this permeability of household boundaries was the nonprivatization of housework. Indeed, Laurel Thatcher Ulrich has suggested that housewifery was so fully perceived as part of the community domain that if courts failed to give satisfaction against a stingy housewife, her neighbors might make redress on their own: Patience Denison of Ipswich, Massachusetts, successfully prosecuted her servant for giving household goods away to the poor, but the community's sentiments were sufficiently strong on the side of the servant to give Denison a lasting fear of her.[44]

At the same time, the Puritan belief in the "calling" underscored qualities of contribution and service, rather than profit, as the distinguishing traits of culturally recognizable labor. Based on the belief that, just as each person had a religious "calling" from God, each individual had a "calling" to an appropriate sphere of labor, the concept infused secular work with an ethical dimension: the goal of labor was to be useful to the larger purposes of creation, as expressed in the commonweal of the society. "Œconomy," then, was the process of "stewarding" (or conserving and enriching) material resources to the end that the general welfare of both household and community was strengthened. There was nothing in this definition that denied—and much that emphasized—the importance of housewifery to material life.

Other conditions supported this general cultural visibility. In the fundamentally barter-based economy of the early settlements, husbands' and wives' work were understandable in the same economic terms. To be sure, men sometimes dealt in acres while much of women's work was counted out in stitches and cupsful, but both often dealt in bushels and pecks. More to the point, men and women were engaged in comparable and interdependent systems of production: both brought raw materials into the household, both spent long hours processing raw materials into usable goods, and both conducted the exchanges necessary to supplement the family's own resources. Men raised the grain that women brewed into beer; women manufactured the clothing that men wore into the fields.[45] Moreover, the local, informal scale of trade preserved the similarity of transactions outside of the household: for both men and women, labor was valued in both money and in-kind exchange.

The exception to this rough parallelism may have lain in the production of tools. Men and women both manufactured at least some of their own equipment, but men also manufactured a good many of the tools that women depended on in order to do their work. Men carved the wooden bowls and stirring spoons used to prepare food, for example; laid the fireplaces used in cooking; and made the lye for soap; while, with the possible exception of brushes and cordage, women manufactured few if any of the tools used by men in their husbandry. In this sense, women experienced a special practical and daily dependence on men, particularly at times (the period of early settlement) and in places (rural areas) where trading for provisions was especially difficult.

Over the course of the late seventeenth and early eighteenth centuries, transformations of colonial life not immediately related to the economic function of women's domestic labor served to slowly undermine the visibility of housework. Among these transformations were a growing sense of constriction in material opportunity and the emergence of essentially commercial habits of mind. These shifts in the culture of colonial society heightened the association of *men* with the symbols of economic activity and profoundly weakened the ability of women to lay claim to the status of "worker."

From roughly 1670 onward, the colonials perceived their material opportunities as increasingly restricted. There was some basis for this perception. Although immigration to New England began to drop off after about 1660, and although recurrent epidemics took high tolls throughout the colonial period, the first generations of settlers had set in motion a cycle of relatively large and long-lived households that was reflected in an impressive rate of population growth. By 1700 the European population of the northern colonies had reached 144,000; by 1775, it stood at over a million and a quarter. The crowding caused by this demographic pattern was intensified by the effect of periodic wars with the native Americans, which shut down—or at least gave pause to—the Europeans' drift inland. King Philip's War (1675–1676) accomplished this end so successfully that it was fully a quarter of a century before all of the outlying English towns destroyed in the conflict were resettled.[46]

Much of the increased population density was in the older large towns and cities, where it made itself felt in a generally decreased standard of living and in a more stratified economic structure. In Essex, Massachusetts, the number of households that were transient increased by 56 percent between 1740 and 1750 and by 116 percent in the next decade. Between 1687 and the eve of the Revolutionary War, the percentage of Boston's adult male population who were propertyless more than doubled, to 29 percent; while the wealthiest 5 percent of males increased their share of the total wealth from 26 percent to 44 percent.[47]

The countryside was not secure from these pressures. New England farmland had never been of superior quality. By 1686, in communities like Windsor, Connecticut, "only marginal land [remained] to be brought under cultivation"; by the early eighteenth century, most of the land in many towns was "worn." In western Massachusetts the number of transient households increased by as much as 76 percent between 1740 and 1750, and by as much as 248 percent between 1750 and 1760. By 1771, propertyless men comprised almost a third of the adult male population in some communities.[48]

These figures represented the results of processes that began in the late seventeenth century and have been documented for virtually every colonial New England town so far studied by historians: a growing shortage of both town and family lands, culminating by the third generation in delayed access to land, differential inheritance among sons by order of birth, the settlement of some sons on land purchased outside of the community and others in trades, and out-migration. In at least some places, however, a mentality of hoarding seems to have preceded actual insufficiency. An average rural colonial family required only about forty acres to live. The original grant to Dedham, Massachusetts (to use that community as an example), was sixty-four thousand acres—enough to support sixteen hundred families. Less than fifteen percent of that land had been distributed when Dedham closed admission to the status of proprietor in 1656.[49]

Fear found many causes. In his study of Andover, Massachusetts, Philip Greven has suggested that the decline of open-field farming, the rise of individually owned but nonconsolidated holdings, and concern that time and population growth would blur the collective memory of boundary decisions all combined to create, within fifteen years of the town's founding, anxiety about property titles and land ownership. These worries had other origins as well. The colonies' land-tenure systems (based on a corporate form not strictly allowable under their charters) were vulnerable to challenge by England—a possibility that loomed large after the Restoration in 1660 and did finally occur in the 1680s. At the same time, settlers' claims to the lands of native Americans were often legally tenuous, at best.[50]

The shortage and depletion of the land, in combination with ongoing population growth, helped foster an increased cash dependency in the northeastern colonies. This transformation can be easily exaggerated. The colonists were not changed overnight from a community of simple peasants to a society of entrepreneurs. In the first place, they had never been simple peasants. The New Netherlands, in particular, had been settled as a commercial center, and as we have seen, the colonies to its north had been active in trade since their founding. On the other hand, on the eve of the Revolution, New England and the colony of New York were far from committed to the commercial way of life. On the contrary, most of the population continued to engage in semisubsistence farming. Even the wheat for Boston's burgeoning population, for example, was the surplus from essentially family-based farms in the surrounding area. Although a variety of English-made goods made their way into colonial households, between 1700 and 1760 English settlers in North America consumed only about eighteen shillings' worth of imported goods per person per year—a figure that includes both urban and rural areas and also includes goods consumed by English soldiers stationed in the colonies. Most of what northeasterners lived on was still produced either in their own homes by their own families or by their immediate neighbors.[51]

If not market-dependent, however, between roughly 1700 and 1765, both rural and urban northeasterners do appear to have become much more market-conscious, finding ways to accommodate traditional activities to the new potential of expanding commercial networks. With over sixteen thousand inhabitants by 1743, Boston exerted a powerful influence over the economic lives of surrounding communities: "[T]here are above one thousand able bodied Men in towns not far from Boston," complained one *Evening Post* writer in 1748, "who have wholly left off Labour . . . to buy up, at any Rate, Cattle, Sheep, Calves, Fowles, etc., (dead or alive) to sell out at an exceptional Price in Boston." Even frontier towns like Northampton, Massachusetts, and Kent, Connecticut, claimed enough merchants and craftsmen for these to be identifiable groups in the community. Indeed, Kent had been founded in the spirit of commerce. In contrast to earlier-settled towns, which had pursued programs of gradual distribution of lands to inhabitants, the lands of Kent (established in 1738) were sold off in one-thousand-acre parcels, mainly to absentee speculators.[52]

Land pressures also increased market contact. In the mid–eighteenth century, Franklin's "Father Abraham" advised farmers who wished to prosper to "plough deep" to "have corn to sell and to keep." It was advice worth taking. In Northampton, by the 1740s, fathers who wanted to see their sons settled on farms were forced into the market, for additional land had to be purchased, and as historian Patricia Tracy has observed, "[o]nly those fathers who had advanced beyond subsistence level had the capital to buy farms. . . . " Advancing beyond subsistence level often meant undertaking some form of commercial labor. As one observer remarked, there was scarcely a husbandman who did not want "besides his Farm . . . to be fingering of Trade. . . . " Sometimes farming had to be abandoned altogether: a quarter of third-generation Andover, Massachusetts, sons were settled in trades. Some sons went without a settlement and supplied the ranks of the landless agricultural workers dependent on the wages paid by their more prosperous neighbors.[53]

The growth of organized markets affected the status of money as an exchange medium. As late as 1704, and in a community as trade-oriented as New Haven, exchange occurred in a visibly mixed mode: "*Pay*," as Madame Knight explained in her journal, "is Grain, Pork, Beef, etc. . . . *mony* is pieces of eight, Ryalls, or Boston or Bay shillings . . . or Good hard money, as sometimes silver coin is termed. . . . " Over the next half-century—and long beyond it—barter would remain essential to the daily lives of most households. Doctors took payment in "pigeons, cranberries, bees wax, considerable wood, turnips, bricks [or] turkeys," and artisans and shopkeepers accepted both goods and services for their labor, either paid immediately or deferred through the elaborate credit systems that characterized colonial exchanges. Yet money was making inroads into both the conduct and the perception of economic life. Massachusetts' 1747 decision that the value of its paper currency should be adjusted as needed to fit the availability of "provisions and other necessaries of life" indicated the growing importance of money in exchanges directed to simple survival. By 1748 it would be said of New England that "[a] man who has money . . . is everything, and wanting that he's a mere nothing. . . . " The statement was undoubtedly an exaggeration, but it reflected a heightened awareness of money as a means to both economic and social success.[54]

This consciousness was evident both in internal tensions and in the colonies' dealings with England. Colonial merchants agitated for tight money; rural folks replied that "the Country inhabitants . . . would be ruined" by such policies. England revoked the power of colonial legislatures to authorize currency and asserted Parliament's right to remove specie from the colonies through taxation; the colonists retorted that England meant to reduce "the Inhabitants . . . to the necessity of primitive Times . . . , of going to Market . . . with Rum[,] Sugar[,] Melasses[,] Ozenbrigs[,] &c &c instead of Money. . . . "[55]

It is in the context of these larger social patterns that the changing evaluation of housework must be traced and interpreted. Population growth, land speculation, anxieties over property titles, the increasing familiarity of money in market relations—none of these fundamentally affected the economic role or importance of women's domestic labor. What they did accomplish, however, was a widespread dissociation of wives and wives' work from the symbols of economic value.

The first of these symbols was property itself. Although they had recognized women's contribution to the accumulation of family properties, most of even the early European settlers had considered ownership rights to reside almost exclusively with males. Women became legitimate owners of property only by exception: in the event of a husband's death, for example, or if a family had no male heirs, or by special legal instrument. Even the common-law custom of the "widow's thirds" provided for outright ownership only of personal property; the widow's rights to a third of the real property was for her lifetime *use* only. In the atmosphere of shortage that prevailed in the latter part of the seventeenth century, even this limited recognition of women's property rights was challenged. In effect, men acted both to consolidate the actual ownership of property in their own hands and to strengthen the linkage of property ownership with manhood. In a study of witchcraft in seventeenth-century New England, Carol F. Karlsen has discovered that many of the accused were women without brothers or sons—that is to say, increasingly, as the period wore on, a woman who either had or stood to inherit property found herself in danger of being accused as a witch. Similarly, both Alexander Keyssar and Patricia Tracy have concluded that early-eighteenth-century husbands expressed a growing concern in their wills that their widows needed to be protected against the greed of sons, whose resentment at their mothers' lifetime claim on a part of the estate might be manifested in mistreatment.[56]

These developments were accompanied by an increasing cultural aversion to images of women actively engaged in business. The few female innkeepers and merchants notwithstanding, the witchcraft trials had brought to the surface deeply held Puritan associations of woman with Eve: vain, domineering, greedy for what was not hers to possess. With the world outside the household ready "to traduce for, *A Witch*, Every *Old Woman*, whose Temper with her usage is not eminently Good," the kind of assertiveness required for visible economic enterprise carried with it palpable danger. In 1692–1693, Massachusetts spinsters faced enough public hostility for the General Court to deem it necessary to legislate their right to try to earn a living.[57]

Meanwhile, the land shortage clearly interrupted the traditional process of household formation. As sons waited longer to be settled on their own land, the northern colonies experienced something of the reversal of the earlier shortage of wives: a *practical* shortage of marriageable men. The situation was reflected in the ages at first marriage, which rose from the late seventeenth century on. In the emphasis that this situation placed on the groom's contribution to household formation, it encouraged the belief (noted by the clergy) that families maintained material viability solely "at Mens Estate."[58]

It was in the context of this growing emphasis on the centrality of men's contribution to family formation, and on men's superior social claim to economic resources, that the early–eighteenth-century clergy undertook their defense of women. Against the image of Eve, the ministers attempted to pose the image of Mary, long-suffering mother of Christ. It was an argument for the social rehabilitation of women, but only at the expense of their claim to social recognition as workers. If women's economic visibility had marked them as witches, their emotional contribution to the family might now mark them as good mothers and wives.

At the same time, the developing reliance on money weakened the visible parallels between men's and women's work and reinforced the apparent contrasts between their contributions to household life. Colonial women as a group had never had as much access to money as colonial men had. A wife's trade networks were likely to remain informal and local and to involve simple exchanges among known values. There was relatively little need for the equating function that is one of the important attributes of a monetized system. Equally important, the money wives did earn was not theirs, in fact or in social perception. A wife conducted economic activities (running a business or contracting for goods and services) only under the husband's aegis and as his surrogate—that is, in her role as "deputy husband." Whatever gain she realized was legally his, as if the husband himself had performed the labor leading to it. This ideological fiction was encouraged by the growing use of money, which dissolved the specific identity both of the worker (as a woman) and of the product (as one traditionally produced by women).

Laurel Thatcher Ulrich has argued that, by the eighteenth century, the husband who let his wife control her own cash earnings was the exception, and a cause for general amazement among his peers. But the cultural dissociation of women from cash-earning appears to have been underway by the late seventeenth century. Wives maintained some visibility as "workers" well through the turn of the century: in his 1692 "Ornaments for the Daughters of Zion," Cotton Mather still described them as "labouring bees" in the family. But even in 1692 Mather was far from clear that most women really did anything very useful, and he apparently accepted it as a matter of fact that women's activities were distinct from the cash-earning enterprise of the household: "it is as *often so*, that you have little more Worldly Business, than to spend (I should rather say, to Save) what others *Get*, and to *Dress* and *Feed* . . . the Little Birds, which you are *Dams* unto." For emphasis, he added: "And those of you, that are *Women of Quality* are excused from very much of *this* trouble, too."[59]

Mather's allusion to "women of quality" was inaccurate as a simple description of the labor of any but a tiny fraction of women in the northeastern colonies. It was nonetheless a resonant and powerful image that gained credence through the conjunction of two strands of colonial belief. On the one hand, European culture had traditionally conceived of women as vain, irresponsible, and dependent creatures. On the other hand, the colonials were disposed to view England as a nation of pampered aristocrats. Propagating new standards of bourgeois womanhood, the influx of polite literature from England encouraged the colonials to identify women especially with the corruptions and indolence of wealth. Both aspects of this identification—the belief that women were by nature undependable and the special association of women with English decadence—would flourish in the later eighteenth century, as colonial men from all economic ranks began to articulate a revolutionary ideology of civic republicanism that explicitly joined political status to economic status, excluding women from both. At the time Mather spoke, however, the two strands functioned together on a more covert level, subtly strengthening a general inclination to discount the significance of women's economic endeavors.

These specific changes in women's experiences and status were aspects of a larger ideological transformation throughout the last half of the colonial period: the emergence of a new cultural understanding of what constituted "economic" and what constituted "non-economic" terrain. Eventually, the core cultural definition of "economy" itself—the household—would change. In the meantime, the events of the late seventeenth and early eighteenth centuries served to chip away at many of the ideological supports of the traditional "œconomical" society. The disengagement of individual households from a tight communal identity, and so from the concept of the general good, began almost at once in the northeastern settlements. In Sudbury, for example, the conflict between common and private lands brought the town to the verge of a split only thirteen years after its founding. Nor were the heads of household arrayed on the side of private property willing to submit to that customary arbiter of social conflict, the church. The pastor was requested not to "meddle." It was suggested that he would be better off confining himself to "the conversion and building up of souls."[60]

The fear of scarcity that set in toward the end of the seventeenth century exacerbated this drift toward individualism. Rather than protecting the general good against the wayward impulses of its members, the town structure increasingly served to protect the private households that comprised it against the possible claims of outsiders. By the mid–eighteenth century, "warnings out" (not expulsions, but official disclaimers of community obligation for support) were common tools of civic security in both older and newer settlements, and their rate of use was increasing.[61]

This growing independence of individual households was probably echoed in a number of ways in the perceptions and conditions of women's labor. The breakdown of the original fervor and homogeneity of the Puritan community resulted in a population less willing to submit to scrutiny of their interior family lives. Certainly, as early as 1666, John Barret of Wells, Maine, felt confident of his own dominion: charged with abusing his wife, he replied coolly, "What hath any man to do with it . . . ?" Fueled by the patriarchalism that had always informed Puritanism, but that now increasingly assumed the individualistic qualities also appearing in other aspects of New England life, such assertiveness by husbands diminished the social permeability of the household and literally "privatized" the life and labor of the wife.[62]

At the same time, the incursion of markets and cash relations into daily life helped undercut the association of "stewardship" and "service" with economic activity. Markets connected individual households in ways that were often outside of—and not necessarily consonant with—the good of the immediate community. Men might argue, as they had in Northampton, Massachusetts, as early as 1668, that in trade "is the advance of people"; but increasingly it was a population of individuals rather than a strongly bound community that constituted the definition of "a people." As the cultural definition of economic labor became more individualistic, it also became narrower. Increasingly, labor that was not directed to cash markets seemed questionable as a form of "economic" activity. Indeed, by the mid–eighteenth century, Jared Eliot suggested that monetary incentive was what distinguished work from sloth: the absence of the prospect of a profit, he insisted, "tends to enervate and abate the Vigour and Zeal," rendering the worker "Indolent." Far from strengthening the spirit, labor without profit, it seems, had become a threat to the character.[63]

Historian J. E. Crowley has suggested that these tensions between the private good and the commonweal were at the heart of the religious revivalism that spread through the colonies in the 1740s. The Great Awakening, he argues, redefined "service" as "an attitude of mind," thus "providing a religious context for the secularization of the social ethics of the calling." That is, the revivals constituted a social ritual that sanctioned the separation of the spiritual and the occupational aspects of the concept of one's "calling." Employment was thus placed outside of the realm of religious concerns, and "service" outside of the realm of material relations. The emerging formulation of "economy" as an extra-household activity encouraged the perception that the work that went on within the household—especially if it was work that did not at some point realize an external cash value—was not a part of the material ordering of social life. As Franklin's famous maxim—"a penny saved is a penny earned"—suggests, the twin functions of conserving and enriching (the traditional basis of the household economy generally and of housewifery specifically) continued to matter in the eighteenth-century definition of economy, but they mattered chiefly in monetary terms. Economic life, while still based in the family unit, was coming to be seen as an activity shaped by individual interest, characterized by market contact and money-making (the "penny"), and focused on extra-household activity—none of which well fitted the work of housewifery. In this context, the patriarchal presumptions of colonial households assumed a new meaning: to be a "keeper at home," as John Cotton had instructed women, was not merely to recognize one's subordination to one's husband, but to surrender to him all claim to economic activity in the family enterprise.[64] By the eve of the Revolutionary crisis, social and political position had indeed become determinative of the economic status of women.

Chapter II

"A New Source of Profit and Support"

The Revolutionary War era brought to the Northeast the first of those abrupt reversals that have periodically characterized the status of housework ever since: having been impugned in the 1740s as virtual parasites on the family economy, by the 1760s and 1770s women suddenly found themselves and their work in the household elevated to a position of social and political preeminence. In the turmoil of the coming conflict, the *Boston Evening Post* declared in 1769, women would challenge men "in contributing to the preservation and prosperity of their country. . . . " The *Post* cited approvingly a sermon that claimed that in the discharge of their daily labor women possessed the power to "recover to this country the full and free enjoyment of all our rights, properties, and privileges. . . . " Even after the outbreak of the war, statesmen like John Adams would agree that the success of the rebellion depended in large part on women's economic efforts in their households.[1]

However heady the language, this recognition of the importance of women's domestic labor would not survive the Revolutionary crisis. Americans would continue to associate political independence with economic agency. Indeed, the Revolutionary experience served to reinforce that connection. But in the new republic, this conflation of political and economic agency would be reserved for the work that men did—paid work that was more and more often pursued outside of the household.

The shift is illustrated by a 1789 petition of the associated tradesmen and manufacturers of Boston requesting favorable tariff treatment from Congress. Using language that was virtually identical to that of the *Evening Post* twenty years earlier, the Boston group now argued that "on the revival of our mechanical arts and manufactures depend the wealth and prosperity of the Northern States. . . ." As men asserted a unique association with wage-earning and with the health of the economy, the tributes to women's work would be replaced by a narrower emphasis on their responsibilities as child-rearers and as the shapers of the next generation. In this roller coaster of changing perceptions were the first signs of a new and distinctly industrial culture of gender in the northeastern United States, a culture in which "labor" would become synonymous with wages, and wages synonymous with manhood.[2]

The origins of the Revolutionary-era celebration of women's work are not immediately apparent. It was a sentiment that emerged in part in the context of prewar boycotts and nonimportation agreements, a coincidence that might suggest that housework underwent a wartime conversion and was newly valued for its productivity simply because it became newly productive. Such a conclusion fails to withstand careful scrutiny, however. Most of the affected goods were not items traditionally produced by women, and they were not items that women suddenly began to produce during the war. The important shortages were in hardware, farming equipment, household utensils, livestock, and grain, the products of men's labor.

Equally important, colonial housewives had not ceased home production in the *pre*boycott years. Much of the new attention paid to women's work was focused on the production of yarn and homespun cloth—labor that had persisted at a sufficiently high level through the early eighteenth century to raise complaints from British agents in 1715 that the manufacture of homespun had "decreased the importation of [English cloth by the New England] provinces above £50,000 [sterling] per annum." By 1748, when newspapers were heartily disparaging the importance of women's work, New England's cloth production was adequate to "clothe themselves and their neighbors." To be sure, long after the war, Tench Coxe would declare that "a great advance" in manufactures had occurred between 1774 and 1782. In the main, however, the wartime expansion seems to have taken place in manufactures other than those carried on by women in their homes, and particularly in the production of steel, powder, salt, paper, glass, pottery, and some articles of ironware. Women may have been producing *more* cloth during the Revolutionary period, but it was not so much the activity itself as the notice the activity attracted that was different.[3]

Nor should the wartime attention paid to women as producers be understood to reflect the movement of women into traditionally male fields, such as farming. Many women did take over the management of family farms when their husbands went to fight. But taking over men's work was not new to women during the Revolution. In their "deputy husband" role, colonial women had traditionally performed aspects of the labor that theoretically belonged to men—with little noticeable effect on their status as workers. Furthermore, Mary Beth Norton's analysis of Loyalist women who filed postwar claims for property losses suggests that many women did not assume additional "male" responsibilities during the war. Of 468 women who filed, only 71 were able to provide sufficiently detailed information to be awarded compensation for their losses in the colonies. The critical data missing from their claims concerned such matters as property value, debts, and shop accounts—precisely the information we would expect them to have known had they assumed active management of their family estates during the hostilities. There is no reason to think that these women's experiences differed significantly from those of their "rebel" counterparts; as Norton points out, "the 468 claimants included white women of all descriptions, from every colony and all social and economic levels. . . ."[4]

The broad reevaluation of the importance of women's domestic work arose less from the *economic* than from the *social* relations of housework during the Revolution. In a variety of ways and for various reasons, the contribution made to material life by women in the course of their regular domestic labor again became *visible* to their families, their communities, and themselves. As it did, the culture's definition of "economic labor" once more expanded to include housework.

Although it was largely for the rights of private property that the colonists fought, the ethos of the Revolutionary years represented a striking return to mid–seventeenth-century values of the "common weal" and to the right of the community to pass judgement on individual behavior. When storekeepers hoarded goods, for example, the patriot mobs simply stormed their shops and took what they wanted. For the moment, individual enterprise had been subsumed by the corporate good.[5]

This renewed communalism increasingly associated households with the business of the larger community, an association that undermined the tendency to see men as the whole of the household labor system. Attempting to stabilize household economies during the war (and probably to limit household dependence on the community), the town of Enfield, Connecticut, expressed its concern for the families of soldiers by assuming control of the men's pay: their wages were deposited in a fund from which money could be withdrawn only with the permission of the town.[6]

This permeability of the household was further enhanced by the general patriotic fervor of the times. During the period of the nonimportation agreements, individual household consumption patterns became a matter of absorbing community interest. Hearing of a home where tea was being hoarded, the good citizens of Poughkeepsie determined what they considered to be a fair price and helped themselves to the family larder. Wives who refused to serve boycotted goods earned lavish attention and approval from journalists and the clergy. Those who did not, earned an equally public scorn. Although it was only with difficulty that a wife separated herself from her husband's political views, in the management of her household she might establish the outlines of an autonomous social identity.[7]

At the same time, the Revolution moved the point of consumption of many of the products of women's labor out of the individual household. Providing quilts, socks, mufflers, bandages, biscuit, and nursing care for one's husband was a personal economic relation. Provisioning the same man in his capacity as a Continental soldier visibly served the economic interests of the community, the state, the region, and the nation. Indeed, both formally and informally, women were the shadow "quartermaster corps" of the Revolution. This role was reflected in official acts of the new governments. As historian Linda Kerber has pointed out, Revolutionary laws regulating production for the army were sometimes framed in both the male and the female pronouns, rather than (as had been the custom in colonial legislation) in the generic "he." The shift in language signaled the revived cultural understanding that women working in their households were important participants in the economy.[8]

The deterioration of money as an exchange medium, and consequently as an index of economic worth, supported this cultural shift. As specie grew short and the value of Continental bills plummeted to a ratio of 100:1 (paper dollars to gold or silver) by 1780, labor once more became the currency of fact. Abigail Adams wrote frequently to her husband about the worthlessness of money, noting in 1777 that it "is lookd upon of very little value, and you can scarcly purchase any article now but by Barter." Indeed, economic life began to be measured by both official and unofficial tables of barter equivalence. Of particular significance for the economic visibility of women, the exchange values were often expressed in terms of traditionally female products. For example, all but two of the barter equivalences for payment of a 1782 New Hampshire tax were given in quantities of textile goods, traditionally women's products. The remaining exchange standards were men's "neat leather shoes" and "good felt hats"—in the manufacture of both of which women often had a hand.[9]

As labor process overwhelmed political and social structures, the definition of "economy" itself underwent a temporary change. Boycotts underscored the importance of labor aimed at avoiding the purchase of goods and made that work a respectable as well as necessary part of wartime considerations. Not only must dependence on English imports be terminated for political ends, but the money that might be spent paying for those goods must go to the prosecution of the war. As John Adams wrote to Abigail in 1774: "Frugality must be our Support. Our Expences, in this Journey, will be very great. . . ." Meanwhile, upheavals in trading patterns and the shortage of sound money helped create conditions that emphasized the value of *labor contribution* (rather than property ownership) in determining economic activity. These dislocations also recreated a similarity in men's and women's work by returning men's work to the barter nexus where women's labor had, in great part, remained. The *Providence Gazette* was accurate when it affirmed that the colonies must "depend greatly upon the female sex for the introduction of œconomy among us"—for the stretching, skimping, and substituting that enabled the colonies to survive their own revolution was an economic process far more familiar to women than to men.[10]

By the late 1780s, nevertheless, little remained to suggest that, for a time, northeasterners had considered women's economic efforts to be at the very heart of the struggle for political independence. As John Adams had predicted, the founders of the new nation knew "better than to repeal our Masculine systems." In most of the new states, women were excluded from political participation on direct grounds: suffrage was limited to males.[11] Once again, economic contribution did not reap formal political rewards. Indeed, very nearly the reverse was true. In the context of the emergent ideology of civic republicanism, women's exclusion from the franchise bore heavily on their status as economic agents. Although domestic labor would remain crucial to the economy of the Northeast—both to its individual households and communities and to the developing regional economy—the political culture of the early republic reinforced late colonial tendencies to denigrate the contributions of women to material life.

In many respects, the world in which northeastern households operated and attempted to become viable after the Revolutionary War remained essentially rural, and many of the old ways and resources still constituted the wherewithal of family survival: a good settlement of land, a knowledge of farming and housewifery, and a trading network for materials and services to circulate through the community.[12]

At the same time, much had changed in the former colonies by the end of the eighteenth century—changes that eroded the conditions under which housework had become visible and valued during the Revolution. Chief among these was the reemergence of the cash-based market. The expansion of overseas commerce encouraged population growth in the port cities, increased the complexity of their dependence on markets, fed the coastal carrying trade, and gradually drew even rural households to the cash market. There were other changes as well. Although it would be several decades before capitalized manufacturing was established with any great permanence in the Northeast, observers noted that almost every neighborhood had its mechanical genius who was looking for a better way to make nails or duck cloth or paper. Many communities boasted operational, if small, manufactories. Traditional forms of home industry both persisted and increased during this period. Ironically, however, household manufacture often supported the incursions of cash into the household economy, since such production not only added to the supplies of the family but, in some instances, "yield[ed] a considerable surplus for the use of other parts of the union."[13]

These often small and slow changes did not result in a family economy that was cash-based. An enormous amount of domestic labor was still required to convert the raw materials of a household into a living maintenance. The shifts did increase and give a more elaborate shape to the ways the market touched family life, however. First, a growing variety of services was obtained from outside the household. In addition to a doctor, two school teachers, and hired agricultural workers, for example, author Samuel Goodrich recalled that his parents' comparatively prosperous turn-of-the-century rural Connecticut household had drawn upon no fewer than eleven types of specialized laborers: a butcher, a tanner, a fuller, a flax spinner, a wool spinner, a carpenter, a weaver, a tailor, a shoemaker, mantua-makers, and milliners. Although Goodrich remembered the transactions as having occurred mainly in barter—"meat, vegetables, and other articles of use"—their nature was probably more complex. Travelling through New England in the post-Revolutionary period, Englishman Joseph Hadfield remarked on the flaxseed operator who charged "one quart or a sixth part of the produce for making it." At the same time, late–eighteenth-century diaries are filled with entries denoting cash transactions: "Received of Abigail Lyman the sum of forty-three dollars & 2 shillings. In full of all demands for one year['s] service ending this day," and "Mr. Savage made the irons for our loome. I paid him 4 shillings in cash." Probably most common were transactions that combined barter and cash relations: "he . . . has got a good place . . . ," one writer explained, "10/a day & found that is in cloaths [,] bed[,] fo[o]d & washing."[14]

Growing market contact reshaped both a family's work and its purchase patterns. Although most households still drew upon the same set of basic resources that had characterized colonial households—land, labor, cash, credit, and barter—the combinations were becoming more elaborate and the role of cash was expanding. Even full-time farmers worked with an eye to the market. By the late eighteenth century, Massachusetts agriculture had become sufficiently commercial to support a lively traffic between country and city, with "professional teamsters" carrying "wool, butter, [and] cheese" to the city, and returning with loads of "salt, molasses, dry goods, [and] rum" to stock the country stores; while farmers "took a trip or two yearly to market, carrying their own produce, beef, pork, or whatever they had to sell, and returning with articles for home consumption or for merchants." According to J. P. Brissot, many rural men were doubly linked to the market, working as "both cultivators and artisans; one is a tanner, another a shoemaker, another sells goods; but all are farmers." Other men (perhaps a third of the adult male population in some rural areas) owned no land and were entirely wage earners. Most of these men probably worked as hired agricultural laborers, but some of them were the butchers, weavers, and peddlers who came to homes like Samuel Goodrich's.[15]

In the cities, cash became even more central to decisions concerning family welfare. Visiting in Boston in 1797, Abigail Brackett Lyman wrote that her husband was "much engaged . . . in making money" and commented: "[W]hen the former stopes we must all retreat. For you know there is no way of living in this town without Cash." William Bentley argued that it was the lure of cash that siphoned people off the land into late–eighteenth-century cities: "10 families enter Salem, for one that retires into the Country, with this difference that the families which come from the country are commonly young enterprising tradesmen, while those which retire are generally possessed of a competence, which they hope to enjoy more at their ease or with less expence & hazard." Although some men involved themselves in the operation of small family garden plots or in the raising of hogs and chickens, most urban husbands made the bulk of their contribution to the household in the form of cash-earning—from commerce, unskilled manual labor, craftwork, or shopkeeping. In these capacities, they provided their families either with cash directly or with credit contacts that could function as cash for the purpose of obtaining raw materials.[16]

Cash-earning was not confined to men, however. In poor urban households, wives often engaged in regular or near-regular wage employment. Some married black women and probably a smaller portion of married white women hired out as domestic servants and washerwomen, earning meals and a shilling or two in cash each day. Women became midwives and "doctresses" to their neighborhoods. When she had the skill, a woman might go out as a seamstress. Other women worked at piece-rate both in and out of urban manufactories. As early as 1788, Brissot commented on the number of mariners' wives who took employment in Boston's cordage industry during "the long voyages of their sea-faring husbands." Some wives from poor urban households took up more or less permanent and regular occupations as hucksters, circulating through streets and market areas, selling everything from coffee, chocolate, and muffins to "roots, berries, herbs, . . . birds, fish [or] clams" they had collected on the beaches and outskirts of the city.[17]

Wives of urban artisans, marketmen, and shopkeepers were also aggressively present in cash and credit work. Because the larger resources of their households often enabled them to keep a garden, a few animals, or some fowl, these women sometimes went to the market as "green-women," vending their own fruit, vegetables, butter, and eggs. Like New York's Mary Simpson, a woman might open a small shop to sell "cookies, pies, and sweetmeats of her own manufacture. . . . " Sometimes women operated small businesses in sundries, retailing needles, pins, and combs. From these means, along with the husband's income, a family might save enough money to purchase or rent a larger dwelling. This in turn became additional capital for the wife's work; a residence could either be converted into a full-fledged inn or boardinghouse, or could be used for taking in a "private" boarder or two, for whom the wife cleaned, cooked, and sometimes washed.[18]

In addition to the money they earned in their own right, women who were married to artisans or small shopkeepers frequently participated in their husbands' businesses. Anna Bryant Smith of Portsmouth, Maine, waited on customers and helped purchase the stock for her husband's shop. She was, she confided to her diary, both "Maid about house, & Cleark in the store." The wife of Andrew Paff, a butcher in Catharine Market in New York City, "brought down his breakfast, and while he was eating she would attend [the customers]"; when Andrew was finished, she packed up the breakfast utensils and pushed them home in the wheelbarrow her husband used to carry meat to the market each morning. It was not uncommon for the wives of butchers to help slaughter and cut the meat for the market. Similarly, wives of cobblers routinely bound and closed the shoes their husbands made.[19]

Rural life enabled a family to provide more of its own goods and services and so took some of the pressure off the cash and credit cycles that drove late–eighteenth-century urban households. At the same time, the evidence points overwhelmingly to the involvement of country women in market-based operations. Rural wives spun and wove and made lace, hats, and handkerchiefs, either for sale or on account to a local shopkeeper. Some women did spinning for the manufactories that were beginning to dot the countryside. Particularly if their families lived close to a larger town or city, wives might travel to the urban market to sell their own fruit, vegetables, eggs, butter, cheese, or milk. Long Island egg-women commonly paid their ferry passage to Manhattan with a percentage of their produce. In the country, as in the city, wives hired out their skills at spinning, weaving, baking, and cleaning to other households.[20]

Women's household manufacturing was not always for a local market. Living in Creekvale, New York, in 1815, Mary Ann Archbald's family purchased "a spinning machine for wool [perhaps a jenny] to spin with 16 threads at once." In addition to "blankets & cloth for the family," Archbald produced "five handsom fine pieces for sale." But an overstocked local market required that "we must send it off to N[ew] York." Wethersfield, Connecticut, women cultivated the onions known as "Wethersfield Reds," which were sold up and down the East Coast and shipped as far away as the West Indies.[21]

In Maine, Martha Moore Ballard's household responsibilities illustrate the important involvement of rural women in cash transactions. Ballard's husband was a farmer, surveyor, and sawmill operator, and Ballard herself was a midwife. In many ways, the patterns of her work resembled those that had characterized the lives of colonial women. While much of her labor occurred within her household, both as a midwife and as a housewife Ballard also engaged in exchanges that took her beyond the boundaries of her family. In both roles, Martha

Ballard sometimes conducted her transactions in the barter system of the colonial period. When she hired Mr. Hallowell to mend her pewter in December of 1785, Ballard paid him three pecks of corn. When she served as midwife to the birth of the Williams' child, she received in payment "6 gallons rhum, 2 lbs. coffee, 5 lbs. sugar and some tobacco and 1 ¼ bush. salt."[22]

But Ballard was also actively involved in cash exchanges. Her diary indicates that she often received money for her services as a midwife: seven shillings for service and medicine for Mrs. Springer, six shillings, eightpence for the difficult delivery of the Sewall's third child, six shillings for the delivery of the Brown's daughter. Ballard made money in other ways, too. In the summer of 1803, for example, she earned six shillings, sevenpence baking and two shillings shocking stalks for a neighbor. Ballard also paid money out: thirteen shillings for a spinning wheel, two shillings, ninepence for textile cards, six shillings for "some cambrick," three shillings for a bushel of apples, and two shillings for having her wash done.[23] The importance of these transactions to Ballard is indicated by her careful periodic tallies: "In 1794, I received 20 lbs., 10 shillings, 9 pence. In 1[7]95, I received 18 lbs, 7 shillings, 7 ½ pence. In 1796, I received 19 lbs., 8 shillings, 6 ½ pence. In 1797, I received 20 lbs,. 7 shillings, 4 ½ pence."[24]

Ballard kept equally close track of the cash she *spent* for various goods and services: "In 1794 I paid 19 lbs., 11 shillings, 9 pence. In 1795 I paid 14 lbs., 14 shillings, 4 pence. In 1796 I paid 15 lbs., 7 shillings, 1 ½ pence. In 1797 I paid 20 lbs., 6 shillings, 8 ½ pence." The expenditures were not incidental to her household's overall economy. Like her husband's earnings, Ballard's helped to purchase the tools, food, raw materials, and finished goods her family required: brooms, coffee, a handkerchief, knives and forks, needles, pins, fabric, the services of a weaver, a cloth-dresser, a chair-bottomer, and several household workers.[25]

Whether obtained through the labor of the husband or the wife, however, purchased goods and services did not constitute the whole of the household economy. Raw grain was not bread; a length of cloth was not a shirt; and a fish was not a broth to feed a family. There was still the business of converting what came into the household into a stable system of consumables. Martha Moore Ballard manufactured candles, soap, pickles, and sausage, and brewed beer. She hatcheled and combed flax, carded cotton, picked and pulled wool, and spun shoe thread. She made blankets, quilts, leggings, nightcaps, mittens, and hose.[26]

Moore also kept a garden where she produced much of her family's food: onions, beans, corn, cabbage, and winter squash. She kept currant bushes, apple trees, and a strawberry patch, and gathered wild strawberries. Her turkeys and chickens yielded, not only meat and eggs for the table, but also feathers for stuffing mattresses and pillows. From the cows she tended came milk, cheese, and butter.[27]

Other women documented similar activities. On October 10, 1807, Mary Ann Archbald noted that, "after being bussy for some time," she "had just got all the family clad in cloth of my own spinning." Archbald's letters from rural New York to friends and family in Scotland also record that she picked and preserved apples, tended a garden, raised chickens, and preserved "meat of every kind" for her family's consumption. Learning housewifery from her mother in the 1790s, Elizabeth Fuller of Princeton, Massachusetts, made pies, sausages, and cheese; picked, broke, and carded fibers; spun yarn, wove cloth, sewed and quilted clothing, and made candles. Her mother worked with her in all these activities and also made clothing and manufactured soap. Other women produced sugar, syrup, butter, bread, pickles, lard, mittens and hosiery, quilts, carpets, bedding and household linens, cider, and beer for their families.[28]

By manufacturing directly for their families, women enabled their households to increase their independence from the cash market. The monetary importance of this work was occasionally made explicit in the letters of turn-of-the-century Americans. Mary Archbald wrote to her cousin in Scotland that, in New York, her spinning and weaving were "more thrift than it was at home as wool and woolen cloath of all kinds is high priced & of a bad quality." John Pintard (who considered $1,000 a year "a slender stipend" and whose household included hired domestic servants) noted that the coat his daughter was making him "will be better than those purchased at the sale stores, & less than half price. . . . What an immense difference in expenditure."[29]

As had been the case in the colonial period, a household's overall economic standing determined the specific shape of a woman's labor. The amount and types of family-directed home production engaged in by a given woman depended on the amounts and types of resources available in her household. Whether she lived in the city or the country, a poor woman was unlikely to have at hand the quantities of raw materials necessary to spur extensive home manufacture or food-preservation activities. At the same time, poor families stood in especially urgent need of the benefits of this type of purchase-avoidance work. Those benefits were realized through scavenging rather than manufacturing. In the city, women needed a sharp eye for discarded items, and a knack for the skillful intermeshing of the help available from charity institutions. From the former might come rocks to build a fire grate, wood or fat to burn, bits of food, old clothing, furniture, or tools; from the latter, a woman might obtain firewood, food, coupons for food, or even cash. Rural women foraged for berries and wood chips, cut pine knots to burn in place of candles, dragged trees out of the forest to serve as clotheslines, and provided the "hand unknown" that stripped many a fruit tree in the autumn.[30]

Wives in elite urban households—women whose husbands were professionals or successful merchants, for example—appear to have done less household manufacturing than the wives of farmers, tradesmen, and mechanics. Still, they were not entirely outside of this system of home industry. At the turn of the century, Abigail Brackett Lyman counted among her responsibilities both plain and fancy sewing, tailoring, and making butter. Writing to his elder daughter from New York City in the second decade of the nineteenth century, John Pintard portrayed a wife and younger daughter who sewed, tailored, preserved food, cooked, and baked.[31]

With the exception of wives in very wealthy families, turn-of-the-century women in all places and of all groups in the Northeast also provided much of the daily maintenance required to keep a household operating. Most women cooked for their families—sometimes with help, often without it. Even Mary Ann Archbald, who declared that "there is nothing I like so ill as cooking," and counted herself fortunate to have daughters who did most of the kitchen work, was unable to avoid doing some of the cooking herself. To women also fell the daily labor of trimming the candles, tending the fires, cleaning the house, and washing, ironing, mending and putting away clothes and linens, as well as much of the basic care of the dwelling proper. To draw an illustration from the economic extreme, Pintard took it as a matter of course that his wife and daughter would lime the basement, attend to basic carpentry and to the whitewashing of the fences, and clear and clean "the yards and borders." When needed, Mary Ann Archbald also served as the family veterinarian, resuscitating sick livestock.[32]

Different women organized their work differently. Like Archbald, Martha Moore Ballard appears to have delegated much of the clothes washing, cleaning, and cooking to others, either her daughters or paid help. She noted on January 4, 1793: "I have washt the first washing I have done without help this several years." But even Ballard did not escape the routine labor of maintaining a household: she cut firewood, built fences, baked, bleached, mended, shoveled snow, scoured flatware, and scoured rooms. Like those of most other women of her period, Ballard's contributions to her family combined cash-earning with unpaid labor that mediated between household interests and the cash market while also keeping the family nourished and functioning from day to day.[33]

Despite the enormous size of the workload undertaken by turn-of-the-century women as part of their obligations to their households, and despite the persisting importance of that work to family well-being, by the opening of the nineteenth century, prescriptive literature addressed to women accorded a vastly diminished role to their work in the household economy. The "Genius of Liberty" that had once resided in women's material contributions to home and state now "hover[ed] triumphant" over their role as child-rearers. "Let us then figure to ourselves the accomplished woman," suggested the speaker at Columbia's 1795 commencement, "surrounded by a sprightly band, from the babe that imbibed the nutritive fluid, to the generous youth just ripening into manhood . . . ":

> Let us contemplate the mother distributing the mental nourishment to the fond smiling circle, by means proportionate to their different powers of reception, watching the gradual openings of their minds, and studying their various turns of temper; see, under her cultivating hand, reason assuming the reins of government, and knowledge increasing gradually to her beloved pupils. . . . Already may we see the lovely daughters of Columbia asserting the importance of their sex. . . .

"While you thus keep our country virtuous," the speaker declared, "you maintain its independence."[34]

Designated by historians "the ideology of Republican motherhood," this emphasis on women's role in child-rearing had some roots in demography. The new nation was a nation of children: in 1800, 34.6 percent of the population was nine years old or younger, and visitors to New England frequently commented on the importance that parents attached to their children—an importance that Brissot found "almost idolatrous." In rural areas, and especially among families who owned their own land, the rearing of children past infancy was still accomplished mainly by the parent of the same sex. Mary Ann Archbald's letters describe this world of sex-segregated labor—her husband and son working in the fields, "riding home firewood, filling the icehouse with ice &c[.]," while she and her daughters tended the chickens, cooked, spun, and preserved food. Nevertheless, there are indications that these patterns had begun to change. In her study of attitudes toward child-rearing in the late eighteenth century, historian Ruth Bloch has discovered a shift in the depiction of fathers in published prescriptive literature; by 1800, fathers had not only lost their earlier role as the primary instructors of children, but had begun to disappear from the literature altogether.[35]

What is of chief significance to the history of housework, however, is that Republican motherhood emphasized women's child-rearing responsibilities almost to the exclusion of the remainder of their work—a vision of domestic labor which was sharply at odds with the reality of their lives. While their letters and diaries suggest that some wealthy women may have focused their time and attention largely on the rearing of their children, for most women, as historian Lisa Norling has pointed out, "[c]hildcare was just one task, no more or less important, among many."[36]

The full significance of the ideology of Republican motherhood for the visibility of women's labor is evident only in the context of the rise of the political culture of civic republicanism in eighteenth-century America. To the extent that historians have assessed the meaning of civic republicanism for women (beyond the emergence of the ideology of Republican motherhood), they have focused their attention on the impact of the Revolution in expanding women's legal rights to property.[37] More telling, if more diffuse, was that the ideology of civic republicanism revived a rationale for denying women's significance as economic agents. In this sense, civic republicanism was a transitional gender ideology, bridging the old notions of rural patriarchy and nineteenth-century industrial ideologies of the male breadwinner.

Even the strongest supporters of republicanism in seventeenth- and eighteenth-century England and British North America feared for the safety of a form of government that depended on the potentially capricious will of its people. The survival of the republic was presumed to require a number of specific attributes in its citizens—among them, a commitment to the commonweal, industriousness, virtue, and a love of equality. But the most critical characteristic of the republican citizenry, and the one all the others rested on, was its economic independence: citizens of the republic must not be susceptible either to bribery, to threats, or to promises of wealth. Indeed, "citizenship" in the new Republic was directly contingent upon economic standing. Not only did the federal constitution privilege the rights of property ownership, but even the most liberal of the new state constitutions (that of Pennsylvania) included economically based restrictions on voting.[38]

Some level of property ownership had been a common qualification for formal political participation in the colonies, but the political culture of civic republicanism elevated the association of political and economic identities to a new level of social importance and invested it with a new social urgency—with profound implications for the gender culture of the new nation. European and colonial culture had traditionally defined females as economic dependents, not only on the basis of actual individual dependence, but categorically, on the grounds that females as a group were irresponsible and required male political and economic supervision. Embracing this presumption about women, who were routinely included in the lists of categorical dependents, civic republicanism reinvigorated traditional Euro-American patriarchalism.

At the same time, civic republicanism supported the growing cultural predisposition in the colonies and new Republic, not simply to conceive of women as economic dependents, but to deny that they contributed to the household economy at all. Indeed, this dimension of civic republicanism may in part account for its broad attractiveness to men in the eighteenth-century colonies. In a technical sense, economic independence was evidenced by property ownership or the payment of taxes. In a more diffuse cultural sense, however, economic independence was evidenced by the presence of economic *dependents*. The true citizen of the Republic was the man upon whom others depended; his economic obligations to subordinates both expressing and solidifying his commitment to the common good of the Republic. To the extent that household members asserted autonomous economic identities, the household head's claim to the status of citizen was undermined. Conversely, to the extent that males laid exclusive claim to economic agency within their households, they buttressed their position in the new political order.

The diminishing recognition accorded to women's domestic labor other than child-rearing was part of a more general revolution in perceptions in the early national period. That revolution occurred simultaneously on two fronts. On one hand, cash-earning became more and more closely identified with economic activity; unpaid labor, or labor did not bring cash profit, became marginal to the definition of economic agency. At the same time, husbands became more and more closely associated with cash-earning. While these changes certainly reflected the early stages of the transformation to industrial capitalism, what they did not accurately reflect was the full range of activities necessary to provide for family survival. In particular, they obscured the considerable portion of that labor—paid and unpaid—that was being provided by wives.

Some of the timetables that would lead to this end had been in place since long before the Revolution and (the celebrations of housework during the war notwithstanding) had been further ratified by it. The communal rhetoric of wartime, which had helped reveal the labor dynamics inside the family, had been in direct contradiction to the values the colonies contended for, particularly private property and freedom from unwanted intrusion into economic affairs. Unsurprisingly, the ethos of community surveillance did not long outlast the war. To the contrary, by the latter years of the conflict, speculation in money and land were on the rise, watchdog committees were having a difficult time implementing wage and price guidelines, and many citizens were utterly disenchanted with emergency confiscations of food and clothing. Linda Kerber has speculated that, if anything, the household disruptions fostered by the war encouraged a new conservatism—a tendency to idealize the sanctity of the individual home.[39]

The visibility of women's unpaid labor during the Revolutionary period had also been supported by the temporary failure of money as a meaningful index of economic worth. Those conditions persisted for a time after the war. Separation from Great Britain had come at the price of tens of millions of dollars in foreign loans and, by 1779, an internal issue of paper money of almost two million dollars. By the eve of the ratification of the Constitution, both state and Continental currencies were depreciating wildly; the resumed importation of English goods was succeeding in draining off the nation's specie; and the international credit of the new nation seemed on the edge of collapse.[40]

The Federalist response to these problems was a large-scale involvement of the national government in the fiscal life of the society: the assumption by the federal government of state war debts, the funding of the old currency, the minting of new currency, and the development of new sources of national revenue. These strategies amounted to a federal policy emphasis on "active wealth, or, in other words, moneyed capital." It was an important step in the creation of a culture in which only paid labor was comprehended as a part of the economy.[41]

Nowhere is this intrusion of the Federal government into the discourse on "economy" more evident than in Alexander Hamilton's 1791 "Report on Manufactures." Less a survey of existing manufacturing in the United States than an argument for extensive future capital investment, the "Report" constituted a monumental redefinition of the concept of "manufacturing" in American economic culture, and in that, of "economy" itself. Traditionally, "manufacturing" had been a term with multiple references. In the correspondence leading to the "Report," for example, Peter Colt of Hartford, Connecticut, had felt compelled to clarify which forms of manufacturing he was discussing: "The Manufactures of this State naturally present themselves to our view under the following Heads," he wrote:

> Those carried on in Families merely for the consumption of those Families;—those carried on in the like manner for the purpose of barter or sale; & those carried on by tradesmen, single persons, or Companies for Supplying the wants of others, or for the general purpose of merchandize, or Commerce.

Written in 1791, Colt's description fitted well with the concept of "manufacturing" as Martha Moore Ballard or Mary Ann Archbald would have understood it.[42]

To a degree, this same spectrum of meaning was evident in Hamilton's "Report"—but with an important difference. Hamilton was interested in Colt's first category, family-directed manufacturing, solely as an early and imperfect stage of development, deserving of mention only because it had the potential to evolve to that "degree of maturity" in which manufacturing is geared toward exchange outside of the household. But even barter exchange outside of the household was depicted as a flawed form of commerce. Although Hamilton ostensibly wished only to demonstrate that manufacturing could be as useful as farming in enhancing the "maintenance . . . of citizens," his overriding interest was in "the total produce and revenue of society," with produce and revenue here deemed virtually indistinguishable. Only goods that created revenue were included in Hamilton's conception of "the total produce . . . of society." What attracted Hamilton about manufacturing was its potential as a component of a cash market network; that is, as it conformed to Colt's third definition. Gradually, over the course of the document, "manufacturing" became synonymous with "capitalized manufacturing"—manufacturing "for the general purpose of merchandize," in Colt's lexicon. Ultimately, Hamilton attributed a "superiority of . . . productiveness" to labor whose product was, not subsistence, but circulating revenue.[43]

The implications of this line of argument for women's domestic work were evident throughout Hamilton's "Report." The labor that a woman spent in manufacture for her family was gradually set in opposition to "productive" work: "The husbandman himself," Hamilton insisted, "experiences a new source of profit and support, from the increased industry of his wife and daughters, invited and stimulated by the demands of the neighboring manufactories." Echoing the rationale of the 1751 Boston Society for Encouraging Industry and Employing the

Poor—that "our own women and children . . . are now in great measure idle"—Hamilton concluded that "[i]t is worthy of particular remark that, in general, women and children are rendered more useful . . . by manufacturing establishments, than they would otherwise be." The denial of the value of women's domestic labor was once more being enlarged into a denial of the social usefulness of women themselves.[44]

This ideological separation of women's non–market-based labor from "productive" labor evolved throughout the last decade of the eighteenth century, and the first several of the nineteenth. In his 1792 "Reflections on the State of the Union," for example, Tench Coxe in effect defined "agriculture" as farming for the market, not as land-based household subsistence, and so was able to conclude that women played no part in rural economic life: "The objection, that manufactures take the people from agriculture," he insisted, "is not solid . . . since women, children, horses, water and fire, all work at manufactures, and perform four-fifths of the labour . . . ." Coxe's implication that the labor of women was comparable to that of fire and water—forces of nature—would reappear as a central theme in nineteenth-century views of housework; but for the moment the important feature of his writing was its association of ideas of the useful and productive with the cash market. In his 1787 "Address to the Society for the Encouragement of Manufactures and the Useful Arts," for example, Coxe focused entirely on goods "*in our own markets*." When he published the speech in 1794, he appended his opinion that among the great values in manufacturing was the advantage that "women, valetudinarians, and old men, could be employed; . . . the portions of time of housewives and young women which were not occupied in family affairs, could be profitably filled up." Although he did acknowledge the existence of women's family responsibilities, Coxe considered that work meager enough to leave women with a substantial amount of free time. It would be almost half a century before the relative valuations of work implied in this passage would become dominant enough to create clearly differentiated gender languages—consistent distinctions between men's paid work and women's "family affairs." But analyses like Coxe's helped formulate them. In the process would be lost the voices of women who, like Martha Moore Ballard, continued to insist that "[a] woman's work is never done, as the song says, and happy is she whos[e] strength holds out to the end of the rais [rays]."[45]

The new economic discourse was not limited to individuals directly concerned with the market or with the encouragement of capitalized manufacturing, however. In 1793, John Cosens Ogden, pastor of Concord, New Hampshire, addressed his congregation on the subject of women's education. Well within the clerical tradition of female prescriptive literature, Ogden's sermon affirmed that "home is the mother's province" and based its proposal for female education on that assumption. What distinguished this exposition from its predecessors, however, was that the domestic labor that interested Ogden was solely the part that was destined for the market, "those useful and necessary branches of industry which are peculiar to their sex . . . [and which] furnish . . . a source of wealth and profit." The value of a woman's spinning was that "[b]y this she is furnished with a means to open a merchandize." The value of her gardening was that she might come to know the market value of land. Women's traditional work-swapping and bartering, meanwhile, were functional chiefly for what they might teach about commerce, "which gives her the productions of distant regions." Strikingly absent from this encomium of the "useful and necessary" was the non-market-based labor of housework. In fifty pages, there was scarcely a mention of baking, cooking, cleaning, sewing, or even child-rearing. Only work that earned cash and further access to the cash market was "visible."[46]

Also of interest in Ogden's sermon was the recurrence of the theme, touched on by Coxe, that, while men must learn their business and cultivate their abilities, women's work comes to them naturally. "The peculiar nature of the occupations of women," Ogden observed, "gives them every necessary art, at a much earlier period in life than men can obtain a knowledge of the laborious and extensive business that naturally falls to their share." Somewhat contradictorily in a tract on female education, little education seemed necessary, for women's skills were reduced to being a function simply of age and gender. Ultimately, the tract undercut its own argument. After all is said, the wife remained simply "one of those guardian angels, who . . . attend around the good in this world."[47]

The growing invisibility of the economic value of women's domestic work in the late eighteenth and early nineteenth centuries was not merely a function of the power of prescriptive literature, however. The daily experiences of family life also created the conditions necessary for the new ideologies of capital and market value to take root.

While some merchants had windfall profits from the expansion of trading opportunities immediately after the Revolution and later during the Napoleonic Wars, for many families these were times of general disorientation punctuated by periods of severe distress. The growing importance of cash to the family did not make household economies fully market based, but it did measurably increase household sensitivity to the vagaries of the market. And vagaries aplenty there were. Prices rose steadily: a bushel of Indian corn that cost 67 cents in 1786 cost $1.08 in 1800 and $2.00 in 1813. Potatoes went from 17 cents a bushel in 1784, to 36 cents a bushel in 1800, to 62 cents a bushel in 1813. Molasses tripled in cost between 1785 and 1813, and salt doubled. The cost of wood rose by 1,100 percent. Currency finally stabilized, but access to it was not evenly distributed throughout the society. The banking system Alexander Hamilton had encouraged was not designed to meet rural needs. Even in urban areas, the proportion of wealth controlled by the bottom sixty percent of the population dropped between 1771 and 1790 to less than five percent.[48]

Market fluctuations were particularly hard on urban families, to which the husband's contribution was more exclusively in cash. Dips in commerce, such as those that characterized the credit crises of the late 1780s and the embargo of 1807, meant widespread under- and unemployment among mariners, laborers, and mechanics, in whose households half the family resources might thus be slashed off at a single stroke. Their vulnerability was not confined to periods of crisis, however. As Matthew L. Davis noted at the time, by the close of the eighteenth century,

> the necessaries of life had progressively risen . . . in many particulars beyond what was ever remembered before. . . . [T]he rise of mechanical labour had by no means been equal. . . . The one had risen in many instances, an hundred per cent. While the other, generally speaking, had not risen more than twenty-five to thirty. The rent of houses had also nearly doubled. . . .[49]

The observation is generally borne out by available wage data: wages were not keeping pace with the prices of goods the wages were supposed to cover.[50]

The pressure on cash resources was not confined to the households of journeymen and laborers, however. By 1801, master bakers in New York City were protesting that cost increases had completely offset their profits. Meanwhile, master shoemakers struggled to stay even with the costs of production by denying wage hikes to their employees; and chandlers, soap makers, and textile manufacturers repeatedly petitioned Congress to hold down the costs of their raw materials. Caught between two systems of exchange, domestic merchants also felt the pinch. As John Mix, Jr., of New Haven explained the problem: "[T]he retailer in general sells his goods for Produce; therefore he will not give us our

Price, in Cash[.] [W]e are oblidged to . . . Barter . . . for articles which we are oblidged to make a very great discount to get them Into money again . . . for we Cannot Purchase one Oz of Stock without money[.]"[51]

In the countryside as well as the city, there were signs of a growing anxiety over the impact of the market on the household economy. Although farm prices rose through the early part of the period, they leveled off in the mid 1790s and did not improve significantly after that time. Meanwhile, farm costs climbed—the cost of land and farm wages, particularly. Visitors to the Northeast found farmers complaining bitterly about their growing tax burden, which, in the experience of one couple who had come to the United States to escape starvation, meant there was "little difference between this country and Ireland." One measure of the growing market-dependence of rural households may be farmers' willingness to travel longer and longer distances to sell their goods. Another may be the new practice, in towns like Augusta, Maine, and Princeton, Massachusetts, of paying ministers' salaries entirely in cash. Since the clergy also received land for farming as part of their original settlement in a community, the conversion to currency may have reflected an increased need for cash even in land-based household economies.[52]

Given this pressure on the cash-based dimension of household economies and the special republican association of men with cash, it is not surprising that as mechanics, shopkeepers, and small manufacturers began to articulate the survival problems faced by their households, they framed their protests and memorials in language that depicted male cash-earning as the *whole* of the economic system. By 1801, for example, the mechanics and merchants of New York City and Providence would suggest that not only did the general "prosperity of a State" depend exclusively on the market activities within it, but that "the industry of its inhabitants [and] their usefulness to each other" consisted solely in the degree of their engagement in market activities. The echoes of Hamilton were growing strong.[53]

Embedded in this assertion of the primacy of market-based labor was an assertion, shared across a broad class spectrum, that waged work represented the entire labor system of the household, and that that waged labor was exclusively men's. The Journeymen Hatters of New York complained "[t]hat your petitioners . . . did expect, by their industry and attention to that art, to gain an honest livelihood for themselves and families. . . ." The seamen who met at City Hall in 1808 sought "wages which may enable them to support their families," and the journeymen cordwainers tried in 1809 for conspiracy and unlawful combination argued "that the wage rates contended for . . . were reasonable, and no higher than to afford them a bare maintenance" for their households.[54]

Although the absence of agricultural combinations during this time makes it somewhat more difficult to trace, a similar perspective began to mark discussions of rural life. "Farming" was construed to be a market activity, and only the portion of the farm labor that contributed products directly to the market was included in this category. Coxe had suggested as much in his 1782 "Reflections on the State of the Union." In the same year, Crevecoeur published *Letters from an American Farmer*, which also depicted the rural household as market-dependent: "100 bushels [of wheat] being but a common quantity for an industrious family to sell. . . . " By the early 1790s, agricultural tracts had begun to make this changing concept of the farm explicit. In his essay *Rural Economy* (printed in the United States in 1792), Arthur Young dismissed the "frugality" that lay at the heart of subsistence farming as "but a narrow idea." He argued instead for a concept of a "rural economy" that was both rationalized and fully market-based—a "system of GENERAL MANAGEMENT" in which prices and acres planted were carefully calculated to realize the greatest profit possible. By the end of the century, rural produce dealers in New York markets petitioned for altered regulations on the grounds that their cash earnings, which were being interrupted, were "the support" of their families.[55]

It was not only men for whom an awareness of the impact of the market led to a conflation of "cash income" and subsistence. Women's private diaries and letters suggest that they also discounted their contribution to the economic needs of their families.[56] During this period, for example, some wives began to draw a distinction between the labor of cooking, cleaning, and washing, and the other work they performed—particularly work that created goods associated with the market, whether the goods were actually sold or not. The former was often clustered together, undifferentiated, under the category "housework": "Ma began to spin . . . [I] do the housework," for example, and "I finished knitting . . . and mended Dickey's stockings. . . . Hannah did housework, the other girls turning cotton sheets and other mending."[57]

Some women failed altogether to see the value of their own economic contribution. Lydia Almy, of Salem, Massachusetts, who wove, attended to livestock, made cider, carted wood, tanned skins, took in boarders, and sometimes worked in the fields, nevertheless recorded in her diary that she was "in no way due any thing towards earning my liveing which seems rather to distress my mind knowing that my dear husband [a mariner] must be exposed to wind and weather and many hardships whilst I am provided for in the best manner." Separated from her husband, Henry, by the War of 1812, New Englander Mary Lee wrote, "I know not why the wife should not work *a little* as well as the husband *labour so hard.*" She begged him to "return to me and give me the delightful occupation of attending you"—apparently a different category of activity from his "labour." From very early on in her daughter's life, moreover, Lee inculcated in the child a similar consciousness of the superiority of men's cash-based labor. "I have lately hit upon a method to make her feel her dependence on you," Mary informed her husband:

> I had noticed that she understood the use of money, and one day when she wanted some cracker . . . I gave it to her and then asked if she knew who gave it to her. She, of course, answered—mama—I told her "yes, but who do you think gives it to mama?" This puzzled her and I told her "papa"—then enumerated the clothes, etc. purchased for her and me—she was highly delighted, and now never mentions buying anything without recollecting, and saying "papa buy."

She declared herself "very much pleased with the success of it."[58]

The War of 1812, which is generally considered the end boundary of this period, provides a measure of how deeply the cultural meanings of "labor," "manufacturing," and "the economy" had altered over the first quarter-century of United States history. By and large, the second war with England did not spark the positive reconsideration of the value and status of domestic labor that had been one of the hallmarks of the Revolution. There was, to be sure, some renewed discussion of the importance of home manufacturing. One writer insisted that "[o]ur most dashing bucks are proud to boast a *homespun coat*; and the prudent house-wife delighted exhibits her newly made table linen, sheets, carpets, &c." Agricultural societies awarded premiums for the largest quantities and finest qualities of homespun yarn. The importance of these homemade articles to their communities seems to have been chiefly symbolic, however, and alongside discussions of their merit ran a parallel but more deadly earnest argument for the development of commercial manufactories. The main cry during this period was less for *home*spun than for *mill*-spun goods, and the truly patriotic act was not so much to *make* as to *buy* American.[59]

The prewar assaults on United States shipping offered a particularly good opportunity to couple the encouragement of capitalized manufactures to the patriotic cause. In 1811, Vermont's governor,

Jonas Galusha, justified the special treatment of manufactories in the preceding session of the legislature on the grounds that "an object so beneficial in the system of economy & so favorable to *our real independence*, will ever be kept in view and fostered by every prudent legislature." By 1812, the editor of *Niles Weekly Register* quipped that the construction of cotton manufactories running eighty thousand spindles near Providence, Rhode Island, was simply "the practical operation" of the policies of England and France. In "the establishment of numerous manufactories," in "the many, many thousand spindles, now in motion," was "*the treasure at home*." In the encouragement of the manufacturing interest lay the road to "entire independence."[60]

The failure of the War of 1812 to generate a renewed recognition of the value of housework was not the result of a market so fully developed as to remove productivity from the household. Capitalized manufacturing was still in its early stages. The products it provided to families were useful and often necessary. Wethersfield, Connecticut, women used their onions to purchase store credit toward cloth, food, and ribbon. Theodora Orcutt of Whateley, Massachusetts, kept a running account with shopkeeper Wells, trading her yarn for beef, pork, cheese, and occasionally, even cash. As the continuing volume of women's household manufacture indicates, however, the goods of the marketplace were neither of a quantity nor of a nature to offset the bulk of the wife's work. Even among city dwellers, women still produced an array of essential goods and services for their families. Moreover, much of that production was still geared toward the market. Visiting the United States shortly after the War of 1812, Adam Hodgson was "surprised to find to how great an extent this species of manufactures is carried, and how rapidly the events of the last two years have increased it."[61]

In an earlier period, the recognition of women's market work had been associated with an appreciation of housework generally—in part because the Revolution had also led to a temporary weakening of the privacy of the household. What had been visible and of concern to the community was not solely women's paid work, but also their daily decisions within the family. By the turn of the century this connection had been severed. As Ogden's sermon on female education demonstrated, if women's market-oriented labor was emphasized out of a belief in the superiority of cash systems over barter and subsistence work, that emphasis could operate to denigrate, rather than reveal, the importance of other forms of domestic labor.

The War of 1812 did not foster the sense of community and of the commonweal that had helped break down the boundaries of household privacy—and thus expose the importance of family-directed labor—during the Revolution. There were no foreign troops stationed at the door, and no large populations of enemy sympathizers abroad in the town, to create a mentality of embattlement and mutual scrutiny. The meaning of community itself had also traveled a long way from Puritan days. Western lands had opened up and the population was pouring out of old communities—and away from old community ties—to occupy them.

Perhaps most important, the conditions of the War of 1812 did not interrupt either the growing stature of money as the dominant index of economic value or the perception that family survival depended primarily on the wage. Banking and transportation networks were sufficiently developed to permit a switch from overseas to interregional trade. The results were successful enough to double the specie holdings of some New England banks, maintaining the value of the currency and forestalling the large-scale return to barter systems that had characterized the Revolutionary period. Shortages occurred, but they were temporary, and the workers who were left unemployed by the embargo were largely absorbed by manufacturing. By and large, Americans were not turned back on their own resources to rediscover the role of unpaid labor in subsistence. Indeed, by 1820, wage earners comprised 21 percent of the paid work force.

The experiences of 1776 and 1812 suggest that the cultural impact of a war on the position of women—in this case, on the recognition of women's work—depends on the nature of the society at war and on the particular characteristics of that war. The patriots of the Revolutionary period had begun the transition to industrial capitalism, but that transition was uneven and was, moreover, still in its earliest phases. The Americans were still a preindustrial people, yearning, as Robert Gross has pointed out, to resurrect the past. The old ways of perceiving economic life, including housework, remained vital enough to be reenlivened by the exigencies of conflict. This was no longer the case by the outbreak of the War of 1812. The full development of the wage system still lay in the future. But the patriots of the second war with England were people who believed that their household economies and their identity as a nation depended on growing cash markets and capitalized manufacturing, and their energies were largely directed to working out the terms of a new economic order. As one facet of that process, they had already developed a perspective on wage-earning that associated material survival with men. By the early nineteenth century, "embargo," "boycott," and "shortage" were conditions that sounded the alarm less for a recognition of women's economy in the household than for a stress on men's role in the marketplace. What had originated in the northeastern colonies as a gender *division* of labor was becoming, in the culture of the new republic, a gendered *definition* of labor.

Chapter III

"How Strangely Metamorphosed"

In the late seventeenth century, New Englanders had found in the culture of gender a way of mediating the economic stresses within their communities. When land shortages had prevented young men from claiming their places as heads of households, the Puritans had identified women as the source of the problem: women who had abandoned their proper place, women who resented their subordination, and, above all, women who had bargained with the devil to interpose themselves between males and property—literally, between men and manhood.

Albeit in more secular forms, eighteenth-century American society had also responded to the uncertainties of change through the idiom of gender. Amid the social, economic, and political upheavals of the Revolutionary era, Americans found reassurance in widely shared perceptions of manhood and womanhood. In the tenets of "manhood" were the promises of an orderly political life, of economic stability, and of the material welfare of the family. The precepts of "womanhood," on the other hand, promised private morality and sentiment and the coherent transmission of culture from parent to child. A dualism of appealing balance and comprehensiveness, this "republican" system of polarities was not merely an intellectual convention, but a deeply held and profoundly comforting way of conceiving secular society. Most important for the future, the "republican" gender system vitalized and extended the range of social experiences that might be organized through the culture of gender. This malleability helped insure the viability of gender as a primary category of experience through the industrial transformations of the next half century.

Those transformations were myriad. They touched virtually every aspect of daily life, from the patterns of city street sociability to the ways parents tried to raise their children. But at the core of the industrial transformation was a redefinition of labor—a reorganization of labor itself, a redistribution of its material rewards, and a restructuring of the relation of labor and social power. Historians have examined this phenomenon chiefly in terms of the impact of industrialization on paid labor—on the men who left their farms for the city, on the artisans who struggled against the demise of the craft system, and on the young women who entered America's first factories.

But the redefinition of labor attendant upon the coming of industrialization was equally, and simultaneously, a redefinition of *unpaid* labor. As paid labor was largely (although by no means exclusively) the province of men, so unpaid labor was largely (although by no means exclusively) the province of women, in the form of the unpaid household labor of wives and daughters. The gender system that had established that division had its origins far back in the European past. But the specific history of housework during the antebellum period reflected an interplay of that system with the ongoing redefinition of labor associated with early industrialization. An analysis of housework over the course of the first half of the nineteenth century, then, must be made in the context both of the regional economic changes of the period and of the impact of those changes in the largely male-defined realm of paid work.

Over the first half of the nineteenth century, the economic stirrings of the late eighteenth century assumed clearer shape and greater formative power in the northeastern United States. Several ancillary developments supported this process. Gradually the region evolved the more complex financial infrastructure required for industrial growth. As early as 1815, the banks and brokering facilities and insurance companies of the Northeast were sufficiently matured to encourage an initial redirection of investment capital from commerce to manufacturing. At the same time, state legislatures began to employ their powers of incorporation to promote improved internal transportation. Between 1800 and 1850, turnpikes, canals, and railroads began to crisscross the Northeast, opening up new markets, new patterns of commerce, and new regional economies. By 1812, Massachusetts alone had granted 105 charters for turnpikes, and New York, 57.[1] In 1817, the State of New

York authorized construction of the Erie Canal, which would quickly turn the upstate region into a shipping and receiving station for New York City's import commerce and manufacturing. Meanwhile, the steamboat had transformed the rivers into highways for the speedier and cheaper movement of raw materials and manufactured goods.

The extension of transportation networks reflected the internal migration of Americans through western New York and Pennsylvania to the states and territories beyond. Ohio grew from 45,000 to 231,000 in just the ten years between 1800 and 1810. Farther west, Indiana quadrupled its population from six to twenty-five thousand between 1800 and 1810. In the next decade it would shoot up to 147,000. Accounting for less than 1 percent of the total population in 1800, by 1830 the north–central region would hold 12.5 percent of the people of the United States, providing a growing market for the manufactured goods of the Northeast.[2]

The capitalized manufacturing that would exploit this new market did not develop evenly or suddenly in the Northeast. The large, power-driven factories that loom so large in American industrial mythology were not to become the norm until much later in the century, although they did appear early on in some parts of the region, most notably in Massachusetts. By 1836, the once-wooded banks of the Merrimack and Concord Rivers at Pawtucket Falls had spawned an industrial complex of eight textile companies, controlled by absentee owners in Boston and employing over 6,000 men and women altogether. The Hamilton Company alone employed over a thousand workers in Lowell, 316 of them (all women) in the single job category of weaver.[3]

But large factories and extensive mechanization were not the hallmarks of early industrialization for most northeasterners. Throughout much of the region, economic change proceeded more slowly and along different lines. In western Massachusetts, papermaking evolved from artisan labor toward mechanized factories through a prolonged intermediate period that combined considerable technological innovation with relatively small and locally owned mills. Shoemaking shops also remained small throughout most of the antebellum period. In the early 1830s, the largest shoemaking establishments in Rochester, New York, employed only fifteen to twenty workers and were not mechanized. Similarly, as late as 1850, fewer than one third of New York City's journeymen were employed either in factories or in unmechanized manufactories of twenty workers or more. Like Rochester shoemakers, most of New York City's craft workers remained in shops that were both small and unmechanized.[4]

The transformations extended beyond factories and mills. Early industrialization created an army of outworkers—needlewomen, tailors, hatmakers, shoe-stitchers and others who labored for piece rates away from the master's shop, often in their own homes or in the shops of subcontractors. In 1850, almost half of New York City's craft workers fell into this category, and the tentacles of outwork extended from the cities deep into the countryside. Men and women in "dozens of villages scattered throughout rural Massachusetts, New Hampshire, and Maine were doing work put out to them by Lynn and other cities," according to Alan Dawley. In 1850, a single general store in the small farming community of Fitzwilliam, New Hampshire, purchased palm-leaf hats, destined for Boston wholesalers, from over 800 outwork hatmakers residing in the area.[5]

Especially in the cities, outworkers were among the most vulnerable of early industrial wage-earners. Although workers in the countryside frequently had other resources to draw on, urban outworkers were more heavily dependent on their wages. It was not a secure position. Not only the vagaries of the market, but the character and temperament of job contractors determined when and whether outworkers would work, and how much and whether they would be paid for that labor. It was not uncommon to return work to employers only to be told that payment would be deferred or that the quality of the work merited only partial payment or no payment at all.[6]

The industrial transformation also required the power of uncounted manual laborers, largely native-born free blacks and immigrants who laid and maintained the canals and railroads, built the warehouses and docks, and moved raw materials and finished goods through the wharves and streets and across the roads of the Northeast. Like outwork, this was the wage work of the marginal in the antebellum Northeast. Excluded from the trades, black men found themselves largely restricted to these jobs; in addition to personal-service occupations, they worked most often as laborers, seamen, porters, and hod carriers. On rare occasions (but even then, only in the face of *de jure* as well as *de facto* discrimination) they worked as carters and draymen. German immigrants often took jobs as tailors in New York City's outwork garment industry. Especially after 1840, Irishmen (who also worked as watchmen and section hands on the completed railroads) began to replace black men as construction laborers and in various carrying occupations. When their husbands travelled with canal and railroad gangs, women sometimes went along as service workers.[7]

The new market networks that black and immigrant workers built with their labor steadily transformed antebellum agriculture. The growth of cities and improvements in transportation encouraged farming families to orient their production more fully to the city market and to depend on the cash they earned there for supplying many of their own needs—a dependence that was reinforced by the spread of cash-paying outwork. By the 1850s, general stores, acting as conduits between the countryside and the cash markets of the city, found it inconvenient to conduct exchanges on a barter basis. At the same time, the country custom of working for one's keep was quickly being replaced by the payment of wages. The interdependence of city and rural economies was felt in other ways as well. When the city market failed, now more than ever, agriculture felt the repercussions. During the panic of 1837, diarist Philip Hone took it as a sign of impending economic disaster that "[t]here is no money in circulation, and the farmer is compelled to '*dicker*' his wheat for molasses and tea and sugar," rather than sell it for cash.[8]

As they increased the infusion of cash relations into the countryside, the economic transformations of the antebellum period profoundly affected the human relations of daily working life. Probably most visible was the increased pace of work that attended the introduction of machinery. As Thomas Dublin has demonstrated, from the 1830s on, textile operatives were subjected to repeated speedups in production; between 1840 and 1854, the number of spindles per operative in the spinning department of the Hamilton Company more than doubled (from 129 to 294), as did the number of looms per weaver (from 1.3 to 2.9). But for many workers the pace of work accelerated even without mechanization. Declining piece-rates could, and often did, accomplish the same end, forcing workers to work faster and longer to maintain overall wage levels.[9]

The industrial speedup was accompanied by a slow erosion of the artisan system. Journeyman craftsmen—carpenters, coopers, millwrights, printers, bakers, and tailors, for example—found their labor increasingly divided into smaller and smaller components and their opportunities for upward mobility eroded. In the garment and shoemaking industries, the rise of the central shop signalled the coming of these changes. Often a combined retail and manufacturing establishment operated by a merchant entrepreneur, the central shop displaced the shops of master craftsmen, subdivided the work of journeymen into increasingly discrete units, and relied heavily on outworkers. By 1860, journeymen in the shoemaking industry in Lynn, where the central shop thrived, were no longer "shoemakers" at all, but pieceworkers on shoes—indeed, not even the makers of whole parts, like "heelers," but "nailers," "shavers," "blackers," or "polishers" working on parts of parts. The master craftsman disappeared, to be replaced by the shop foreman and, above him, the entrepreneur. Their labor reduced to small operations, workers could be quickly trained, and as quickly replaced. Correspondingly, they lost their ability to bargain for better wages on the basis of their mastery of the whole craft. Together they produced more shoes; individually they earned less money. In 1856, shoemaker Francis Rhodes retained enough of the old skills to make 792 pairs of women's shoes in fifty days "entirely by hand." It was a noteworthy accomplishment, but of an antiquarian sort; his competition was with the cheaper production costs of the factory, and he earned only 22 cents a pair.[10]

For black workers, these degradations of labor were compounded by the degradations of racism. A black mechanic had trouble getting paid work at all, for throughout the region white men refused to work alongside blacks. One visitor to Boston in the mid–1830s claimed that black men were entirely excluded from the craft shops employing whites in New York, and that in Boston, "with the exception of one or two employed as printers, one blacksmith, and one shoemaker, there [were] no colored mechanics in the city." Black journeymen who did find employment often had trouble collecting their wages from white employers, "and, as they know how strong the prejudice is against them, they dare not complain to a magistrate."[11]

Foreign visitors repeatedly warned workers in the "handicrafts and trades" against emigrating to the United States, arguing that their chances of success were "at best problematical."[12] Certainly working conditions and wages changed over the course of the antebellum years, but rarely did laboring men, black or white, earn more than $1.00 a day early in the period, or $1.75 a day toward its close. In Massachusetts, for example, both carpenters and foundry workers saw a rise from about $1.00 a day to about $1.25 a day between 1825 and 1845. Masons' helpers averaged only about 90 cents a day in 1825, however, and only about 97 cents a day by 1845. In 1860, their average daily wages stood at $1.00. (Over this period, masons' wages ranged from $1.25 a day to $1.60 a day.) Laborers could hope for 70 cents a day in the mid-twenties; by 1855 their daily wages had risen to just under $1.00. In the early 1860s, they sometimes exceeded that amount. On the eve of the Civil War, watchmen and section hands earned about $1.00 a day.[13]

Several caveats should be attached to these figures. Few men in this group had year-round employment; four days a week through three seasons of the year was good work for a laborer. At that rate, an apparent annual income of $313 for a laborer in 1860 (calculated at $1.00 a day, six days a week, year-round) was reduced to an actual income of closer to $156 a year. Even better-paid journeymen carpenters, bringing in $1.50 a day, would earn less than $250 a year on this basis.

These general speculations are supported by data from local studies. Norman Ware's early study of antebellum industrial workers concluded that mid–nineteenth-century New York shoemakers and journeyman printers had trouble exceeding $250 a year. In his more recent study of New York City workers, Sean Wilentz found that the average annual income of male workers in the trades in 1850 was $300—only half of the amount estimated by the *New York Times* to be the minimal subsistence income for a family of four. Even the highest paid of the trades, shipbuilding, averaged only $579.24, still below the *Times*' $600 floor. In Oneida County, New York, in March and April of 1827, textile worker Peter Billington averaged only 75 cents a day; on a full-time, year-round basis, that would have yielded an annual income of only $234. Over the period roughly from 1836 to 1850, the mean daily pay of male workers at the Hamilton Mills in Massachusetts declined from about $1.02 a day to 98 cents a day. For female operatives, the average daily pay remained unchanged at 59 cents, but that figure hid a significant restructuring of the labor force: a decline in average income at the upper end of the spectrum and a greater reliance on lower-paid workers. Between 1836 and 1860, the average daily pay of spinners at the Hamilton Company declined from 58 cents to 48 cents, of weavers from 66 cents to 60.5 cents. Alan Dawley has speculated that in 1850 the average male shoemaker in Lynn, Massachusetts, earned but $20 a month, or $240 a year.[14]

Urban life had always been characterized by the presence of large numbers of people working on the margins of the organized economy, earning small incomes in whatever ways offered. This remained true of the antebellum city. Indeed, as the structure of labor in general was degraded, the ranks of the laboring poor swelled. The poor sometimes trekked to the limits of the city, where they "eked out a precarious semirural existence" by keeping a few animals and working in quarries or as laborers, cinder-gatherers, or ragpickers. Others tried to make money as hired hands or street vendors, selling brooms, confections, chickens, eggs, milk, berries, coffee, and small merchandise. Often immortalized in children's books describing the busy street life of the antebellum city, the vendors' lot was in fact far from picturesque. Living from penny to penny and day to day, they gave the lie to the belief that in America there were no extremes of poverty and wealth.[15]

Antebellum reformers also provided evidence against that belief. In 1845, for example, Dr. John Griscom published a thin volume of observations entitled *The Sanitary Conditions of the Laboring Population of New York*. It was a subject he knew well. Former health inspector of the city, he had had a number of opportunities to examine firsthand the pestilent circumstances half of New York City's population lived in. He fortified his book with story after story of what he had seen: the white woman, wife of a laborer and mother of two children, who had been sick constantly since her family had been forced to move into a dank, dark cellar apartment; the two families ("consisting of ten persons, of all ages") who lived in a single ten-by-ten-foot cellar room with only one small window on Pike Street; the black couple on Sheriff Street who died within months of each other from fevers ultimately attributable to substandard housing.[16]

Griscom's was not the first or the only voice to be raised against the deteriorating living conditions of the laboring classes of New York City. Again and again, newspapers cited the dangers of fire and overcrowded conditions. In 1841, for example, the *New York Tribune* reported that a fire in a single house at 133 Canon Street had left forty black families without shelter. The following year, Charles Dickens published his *American Notes*, describing his visits to black families who lived in rooms without ventilation and relied for heat on charcoal fires whose "vapours issue forth [to] blind and suffocate." A decade later, D. W. Mitchell described "the extensive neighbourhood of excessively crowded tenement-houses; generally . . . three or four stories high, containing from ten to twenty rooms, badly lighted and ventilated; often a family—mostly foreigners—in each room. In the streets the air was foul, and, in the hot weather, sickening, with putrefying garbage. . . . In the Warm summer evenings all were out of doors or at the windows, men, women, and children. . . . [D]eath, langor, listlessness, and disease hovering around and over them."[17]

The problems of survival for the poor may have been magnified in New York, but New York was not the exception among antebellum northeastern cities. The industrial housing of Lawrence, Massachusetts, consisted largely of highly flammable "shacks" built from "slabs and unfinished lumber with over-lapping boards for roofs" and lined with sod for insulation. In New Haven in the 1820s and 1830s, some white workers were able to live in individual frame dwellings, but many poorer whites lived in "tenement houses" erected specifically for the working class, and blacks and the Irish occupied housing that reminded one observer most of all of "barracks."[18]

Not all of northeastern America's wageworkers and their families lived in such dire circumstances. Many did, though, and even those who were able to escape the worst of the cellar apartments and overcrowded conditions found decent housing harder and harder to come by and decent food harder and harder to afford. Overall, the antebellum period was characterized by rising prices. Although improvements in transportation and the growth of textile mills helped to reduce fabric costs, many "necessaries" grew more expensive over these years. In Massachusetts, the average cost of Indian corn rose from 70 cents a bushel in 1830, to 81 cents in 1840, to $1.17 in 1850; while pork showed a 50-percent rise between 1830 and the late 1850s. In 1834, $100 a year rented a city house large enough to accommodate a family of six; twenty-five years later, a cramped apartment in New York City cost as much. During the same period, the cost of wood for heating rose by about half in the Bay State. Coal, which was rapidly replacing wood as a household fuel, did not show a steady rise in price, but between 1833 and 1857 it was not uncommon for the cost per ton to spike as high as $9—a 30 percent increase over the more normal $7-per-ton price.[19]

Although improvements in transportation were increasing the variety of foods available to many people and lengthening the seasons during which those foods were available, tight budgets limited the extent to which working-class families could enjoy these improvements in the standard of living. Food historian Edgar Martin concluded that the working-class diet was confined largely to potatoes, corn, peas, beans, and cabbage. Whole milk was available from the surrounding countryside, but most urban working-class families probably drank a cheaper, watered-down variety or the swill milk from cows fed on the slop of city distilleries—if indeed they were able to afford milk at all. In the early antebellum period, city workers sometimes kept chickens or pigs, who were allowed to roam free in the streets. Much to the delight of the wealthier classes, that practice was gradually curtailed. Both meat and poultry were available in city markets, of course, but they were expensive, even when purchased for reduced prices at the end of the day. Both remained rare in the diets of working-class and poor families.[20]

The furnishings of working-class homes varied according to the ability of the family either to buy or to scavenge what it needed. In the second decade of the century, Ezra Stiles Ely complained of impoverished households in which "[o]ne bed, one chair, and the half of another, one table, one candlestick, one cup, an old pot, and a piece of a frying pan" made up "the complete inventory" of the furnishings. Other families had more: rag rugs to cover the floor, inexpensive factory-made tables and chairs, and perhaps a homemade mattress. A plain drinking tumbler could be bought for a dime and white granite plates and cups sold for about eight cents apiece.[21]

Cheaper furnishings, shoes, and clothing were now available for purchase by workers. On the other hand, their diet remained largely unaltered. Even at the close of the Civil War, when some forms of indoor plumbing were making their way into some American households, they remained unknown to working-class families; some did not even have outside privies. At a time when new forms of illumination were entering the homes of the more prosperous, the laboring classes still depended on candles for light. Their cooking was often in open-hearth fireplaces or over cheap (and dangerous) braziers. Ice, which allowed some families to preserve food against spoilage, was unaffordable among working-class families. Early industrialization was creating a distinctive working-class standard of living.

That ever-more-visible disparity was the focus of much of the organized labor protest of the antebellum period, as members of the working class questioned how they were to survive the steady erosion of their wages and standard of living. Speaking in Brooklyn in 1836, labor organizer Seth Luther charged that while "the *nominal* value of every article of necessity has been greatly increased, . . . the price of labor has not received a proportionate advance," and claimed that soon the working classes would be unable to afford even living space:

> It is much more difficult now, for a man to become possessed of a house to shelter his family than it was at that [the Revolutionary] period. The difficulty is constantly increasing in consequence of the rag money system, which is placing all the real estate, or nearly all, in the hands of unprincipled speculators and monopolizing aristocrats. . . . [T]hose who build houses in these days have none of their own and are dependent on a "combination" of landlords for shelter from the weather, and compelled to pay enormous rents or to be turned out of doors.

"[T]he producing classes" of America, he asserted, had been "most grossly, wickedly, and most abominably deceived."[22]

Clergyman William Henry Channing captured the same sense of betrayal as he surveyed the changes in American society over the course of the antebellum period:

> The victorious world, so confident and easy and jocular, so beautiful in its own right, so wrapped about in kingly purple—how strangely it is

> metamorphosed to the eyes of the child of God! Its factories change into brothels; its rents to distress warrants; . . . from under the showy robes of its success, flutter the unseemly rags of an ever-growing beggary; from garret and cellar of its luxurious habitations stare out the gaunt forms of haggard want. . . .

Channing may have exaggerated: early industrialization had not ground all segments of the working classes into poverty. But it was beginning to define sharper lines between the more and the less prosperous in Northeastern society.[23]

Concurrent with the demise of the old artisan culture was the gradual formation of a new middle stratum in northeastern society. The term *middle class*, as this group would come to be called, would begin to appear only toward the close of the period. Seth Luther generally envisioned the social order as consisting of "but two parties . . . the producers on the one part and the consumers and accumulators on the other."[24] In his *Address to the Working Men of New England* in the early 1830s, however, he acknowledged a more complex division: "the poor," "the middling classes," and "the rich."[25] Visiting the United States in the late 1830s, George Combe identified in Boston a "middle class of citizens" who owned enough real and personal property to pay city taxes but who were distinguished from the "rich," whose wealth allowed them to "live beyond the limits of the city. . . ."[26] By the 1840s, the anonymous "mechanic" who authored *Elements of Social Disorder* would drop the older distinction between "the rich" and "the workers" and draw the contrast instead between "the laboring classes," on the one hand, and "the rich and middling classes," on the other.[27] Other writers employed the term in a more positive sense, contrasting the middle class with the rich rather than with the workers. In 1850, George Foster defined "the great middle class" as the families "of the substantial tradesmen, mechanics and artisans . . . whose aspirations, reaching the full standard of well-to-do content, wisely fall short of that snobbish longing after social notoriety" associated with "aristocracy."[28] In the linguistic trail suggested by the appearance of this new term lay the dimensions of a sea change in the structure of society.

Central to the culture of late–eighteenth-century America had been concepts of "virtue," "equality," "industry," "independence," and a devotion to the "common weal." Taken together, these terms had described a system of values and aspirations based largely on the experience of manual work—both agriculture and the social relations of the craft shop. They expressed the belief that wealth properly resided in the act of production and belonged to the producer, and that men who worked steadily to perfect their skills—as yeomen or as artisans—deserved both economic independence and community stature. Especially from the model of the craft shop, this culture also revealed a strong strain of communalism, for personal ambition was to be tempered by the needs of the group. In the balance of the two—individual skill and devotion to the larger good—lay the essence of "virtue."

Deeply shared as these values were in colonial and early national America, they by no means described a culture of leveling. In the midst of the Revolution, the simple American craftsman or the honest American yeoman made an effective propaganda foil to the alleged decadence of the English, but some American craftsmen and some American farmers amassed considerable wealth. At the other extreme, this culture was in many ways a closed system: for blacks, native Americans, and women, neither artisanship nor industrious husbandry merited independence and community stature.

These ambiguities rendered the dual languages of artisan and yeoman virtue vulnerable to profound redefinition under pressure from the changing social and economic environment of the antebellum period. To be sure, the old meanings did not fade suddenly or completely. The vision of the independent American farmer retained its powerful grip on the American imagination throughout the antebellum period (and well after). At the same time, the memory of the social relations of the artisan shop underlay the theory of labor value that informed most labor dissent during the era. But even as labor activists called for a return to the "equality" that had presumedly characterized the pre–Revolutionary War period, and deplored the "dependent" condition "the *producer*" had fallen into, a new group of social observers had begun to associate that language with a very different set of social and work relations—and especially with entrepreneurship and economic individualism.[29]

This refocusing was evident in discussions of "industry," "economy," and the "common weal" in prescriptive antebellum literature. A case in point is a short piece that appeared in the August 1842 *Manual of Self-Education* titled "How to Get Rich." Like that of the artisan culture, the world described by the *Manual* remained profoundly male; yet two key changes had occurred. First, the republican association of "industry" with the craftsman or yeoman was replaced by a new association with "the man of business," who now became the embodiment of the virtue of "industriousness." Equally important, the concept of "industry" itself was altered. The purpose of industry was no longer conceived of as simple economic independence, but rather as profit and wealth.

Even the most diligent activity, if it did not yield a profit, was but an inferior and misguided effort:

> Be industrious. Every body knows that industry is a fundamental virtue in the man of business. But it is not every sort of industry which tends to wealth. Many men work hard to do a great deal of business, and after all make less money than they would if they did less.

At the same time, the profit-making relationships of the world of business replaced the old webs of mutual obligation as the networks through which the "common weal" was maintained: "Let your business be some one which is useful to the community," the editors of the *Manual* cautioned. "All such occupations possess the element of profit in themselves. . . . " In a sharp reversal of imagery from the earlier artisan/yeoman culture, individual profitability became the chief evidence of the value of an undertaking to the good of the community. The *Manual* did warn against an excessive love of money, but only, finally, because "the extravagant desire of accumulation" could lead to an imprudence that would defeat the goal of "getting rich."[30]

Other publications directed especially to boys and young men echoed this new formulation of the concept of the "community" as a creation of business and commerce. In his *Enterprise, Industry, and Art of Man*, popular children's author Samuel Goodrich was at great pains to explain that the important interdependencies and obligations among humans were those founded on national and international trade networks; concluding that "the true philosophy is to regard the whole human race, who hold commercial intercourse, as one family, and continually contributing to each other's happiness." "Virtue"—certainly for men—consisted in upholding one's specialized role in this complex economic community.[31]

The association of the old language of virtue and industry with the world of business and profit reflected an important restructuring of paid labor over the late eighteenth and early nineteenth centuries, and particularly the expansion of certain forms of paid work. As Stuart Blumin has observed, much of the growth occurred in occupations that were fully withdrawn from "direct participation in production" and existed exclusively "to organize and supervise the manual labor of others."[32] In combination with the professions—most notably teachers, physicians, lawyers, and ministers—these new positions would form the paid occupational basis for the emerging middle class.

This restructuring of paid labor had been underway as early as the late eighteenth century, when a new office work force had begun to emerge to provide the support services required by the financial institutions, exchanges, and insurance companies. In giving rise to a growing number of work-crew supervisors and to the subcontractors who operated between entrepreneurs and outworkers, the decline of the master's shop and the growth of the regional and national market had augmented the new middle ranks. Among these were lower-level management positions, supervisory jobs, jobs as shop clerks, distributors, agents, bank tellers, and nonproducing retailers and wholesalers. Over the course of the antebellum period, clerks, bookkeepers, and bank tellers constituted the fastest-growing sector of the paid labor force in many communities. In Utica, New York, the number of clerks increased by over 13,500 percent between 1817 and 1860. By 1855, there were almost 14,000 clerks employed in New York City, making that group the third-largest occupational category in the city, outstripped only by domestic servants and laborers. The 7,000 professionals comprised the eighth-largest category.[33]

Some of these positions were filled by failed farmers, some by former shop masters overwhelmed by the expansionism of the antebellum years, and some by former journeymen. But many of the holders of the new middle-level jobs were young men who no longer thought in terms of the old artisan/yeoman system at all. The sons of artisans, farmers, ministers, small merchants, or school teachers, they now turned their expectations of success and prosperity to business. Undoubtedly, many of them hoped one day to achieve the status of entrepreneur and employer.

As the reorganization of labor proceeded, drawing an ever-clearer line between manual and intellectual work, this group evolved an increasingly distinct identity, and its members began to claim for themselves and their occupations a special place and mission in the new republic. Even as they aspired to prosperity, they prided themselves on presumably remaining free from the corruptions of wealth and claimed for themselves the mantles of honesty and hard work. Contrasting their own bright expectations with the struggles of the emerging working classes, they perceived themselves as exemplars of eighteenth-century industry and independence. More than any other single value, they based their emerging identity on individualism and on the belief in self-culture and personal success.[34]

Clearly, this was a diverse group and included men who worked with their hands in a shop or factory or on the farm, as well as men who spent their days in offices and behind bank and retail counters. The income continuum did not necessarily move upward from manual to professional work, however. At the lower end, some forms of skilled labor (for example, some blacksmiths, confectioners, hatters, and printers) realized $700 annually, working six days a week for three quarters of the year. A shop foreman, risen from the ranks, might earn $800 or so, an income that equaled that of many teachers and ministers and surpassed the annual cash earnings of clerks and most farmers. Some professional men did much better than this, of course. Calvin Stowe, a college professor and the husband of Harriet Beecher Stowe, earned about $1,300 in 1850. As a young editor in the late 1830s, Thomas Nichols earned approximately $1,000, about what a successful small-town lawyer cleared annually during the same period. In 1857, Hunt's *Merchant's Magazine* suggested that the average businessman in New York City earned about $1,500 a year.[35]

Intellectual or not, some of the labor that underlay the new middle class was both rote and tedious, a point that Herman Melville made with particular force in his description of Bartleby the scrivener. A transcriber of legal documents, Bartleby copied "by sun-light and by candle-light," working ever on, "silently, palely, mechanically."[36]

Yet for much of the emerging middle class, as for much of the working class, the organization of paid labor remained decidedly nonindustrial. That is, the paid work of the new middle class was largely characterized by the absence of mechanization and even standardized procedures, by the importance of personal networks, and by a marked degree of flexibility in scheduling. The most common business form was still the partnership, usually based on family ties. The double-entry accounting system invented by the Italians five hundred years earlier remained common, and accounts focused on income and outgo rather than on capital expenditures. Most businesses were small. With perhaps as few as five or six employees, little management hierarchy was required, and both supervision and transactions were carried out largely on a personal and informal basis. Even Melville recognized the persistence of these conditions. Sharing the position of scrivener with Bartleby were two other men: Turkey, whose noontime tippling imparted to his afternoon's work "a strange, inflamed, flurried, flightly recklessness," and Nippers, a young man of "brandy-like disposition" who viewed his worktable as "a perverse voluntary agent, intent on thwarting and vexing him." Indeed, the lawyer who employed the two men counted himself fortunate to get a half day's work from each.[37]

There is no doubt that this emerging middle-level business and professional group was in a better, more prosperous economic position than were vendors, laborers, outworkers, or the bulk of craft workers during the antebellum period. This is perhaps most visible in the material circumstances of their households. While working-class families were forced into smaller and smaller dwellings, and often into cramped and overcrowded apartments, the emerging middle class expressed itself in terms of growing, separated, and increasingly elaborate residential space.

The ideal home of the emerging middle class was the "cottage"—a detached residence, often two-story, with a small yard. Designs for the structure varied, but typical was the one suggested by Catharine Beecher and Harriet Beecher Stowe in their 1869 *American Woman's Home*, which included a drawing room, a kitchen, a breakfast room (which might also serve as a sitting room and extra bedroom), and two second-floor bedrooms. Of these spaces, it was the drawing room, or main parlor, that most essentially defined the ideal middle-class home. Providing a separate "public" space where guests might be received, the parlor simultaneously protected family life from intrusion and provided a showcase in which the household could present the tangible evidence of its middle-class status: woven carpets, sofas, chairs, ottomans, tables, plant stands, vases of flowers, pillows, miniatures, statues, engravings, books. These were the objects whose possession stated the claim to industry, independence, and prosperity.[38]

Not all members of the emerging middle class lived in picturesque cottages, of course. Young men just entering the paid work force often took rooms with private families or in boardinghouses, as did some young married couples. Indeed, a number of observers were troubled that young urban married couples often chose boardinghouses or family hotels over the virtues of a private home, thus sacrificing privacy and domestic feeling to convenience. And although the practice was beginning to disappear, the families of grocers, small shopkeepers, and professionals still often lived above or adjacent to the husband's place of business.[39]

Middle-class household furnishings and diets depended on family budgets, but a few generalizations may be made. Most important, middle-class homes were fully furnished. Many articles were still homemade (pillows, bolsters, chair covers, and even some picture frames, for example) but prominent among the furnishings of the middle-class family was an array of tables, chairs, bed frames, and wardrobes that would have been unusual in the homes of even the moderately wealthy fifty years earlier. A growing number of middle-class homes also included both heating stoves and the new cast-iron cooking stoves—and some middle-class families were able to afford central furnaces and iceboxes.

Although illumination was from a mixture of sources (candles were still used in some more-rural homes), kerosene and oil were common in more-urban areas. And middle-class families had a far greater access to the foods that growing market networks could provide. Especially outside of the large cities, middle-class families often owned enough land to have their own gardens and to keep a few chickens and a pig or two. In the cities, bakers and country farmers supplied bread, vegetables, fruit, eggs, and milk to their doors—or these might be purchased in city open-air markets, where shoppers might also find poultry, pork, and beef, cakes, crackers, grain, and delicacies like strawberries.

Nevertheless, these were not the wealthy of antebellum society. In his study of wealth in antebellum cities, Edward Pessen suggests that one needed $20,000 in taxable property to qualify even for the lower ranks of the elite, and perhaps $6,000 or $7,000 of taxable property to place one among the "upper middle" levels of society. These levels of accumulation were beyond the reach of most members of the emerging middle class, or were achievable only over the course of a lifetime. As Pessen has demonstrated, regardless of the myth of "rags to riches," there was little dramatic social mobility in antebellum America. Only about 7 percent of those who *began* in the "upper middle group" were able to parlay their money, property, and family connections into real wealth. For the roughly 90 percent of the population that owned less than $4,500 in taxable property, such improvements in fortunes were rarer yet.[40] Even the ownership of a modest two-story house—a considerable expenditure for a clerk, schoolteacher, or shop foreman—represented taxable wealth of only about $700 to $1,500.[41]

For all of its exuberance and apparent self-confidence as the new arbiters of America's morals, moreover, the emerging middle class expressed a constant anxiety over its economic vulnerability. Ominously, Lydia Maria Child closed her 1828 advice manual, *The American Frugal Housewife*, with a section entitled "How to Endure Poverty." Visiting the new nation only two years later, Alexis de Tocqueville exaggerated the extremes of individual mobility, and yet he wrote as if to confirm Child's fears: "In no country in the world are private fortunes more precarious than in the United States. It is not uncommon for the same man in the course of his life to rise and sink again through all the grades that lead from opulence to poverty."[42]

The specter of economic disaster loomed large in the fears of middle-class men. In both their private and their published writings, they returned again and again to stories of friends wiped out "by the vicissitudes of commerce" and offered wisdom against "those seasons of pecuniary and commercial embarrassment, which have become of late so frequent and so distressing in our country." As diarist Philip Hone noted in the mid–1830s, the mood of speculation that fueled a constant rise in the cost of living in New York was "pretty hard" even upon the wealthy, but "harder still upon that large and respectable class consisting of the officers and clerks of public institutions, whose support is derived from fixed salaries." Pessen's study of wealth and power in antebellum America suggests that Hone may have been essentially accurate and that, among property-owners, the emerging middle class may have been in a particularly vulnerable position: examining Boston during the Panic of 1837, he discovered that "more than one-third [of the owners of the modest property assessed at $5,000 to $7,000] were badly hurt." This substantial portion of the upper-middle class was far larger than the roughly 2 percent of the wealthy harmed by the crisis.[43] Early industrialization had helped create the material base of the new middle class. At the same time, though, it had created conditions that made that material base difficult to maintain.

That precariousness was reflected in heightened anxieties about how even middle-class men would manage to fulfill the role of "breadwinner" that underlay their claims to familial and social dominance, that is, how even middle-class men would achieve manhood. It was a concern that informed much of the prescriptive literature on manhood published during the antebellum period. In his 1846 *Lectures to Young Men*, Henry Ward Beecher criticized (but also revealed the magnitude of) the pressure put on young men to choose lucrative careers, and to move up in them quickly:

> Shall the promising lad be apprenticed to his uncle, the blacksmith? . . . [T]he mother shrinks from the ungentility of his swarthy labor; the father . . . finds that a *whole life* had been spent in earning the uncle's property. These sagacious parents, wishing the tree to bear its fruit before it has ever blossomed, regard the long delay of industrious trades as a fatal objection to them. The son . . . must be a rich merchant, or a popular lawyer, or a broker. . . .

Writing in 1864, Thomas Nichols described the search for wealth that defined manhood in antebellum America: "[W]hy the universal and everlasting struggle for wealth? Because it is the one thing needful; the only secure power, the only real distinction. Americans speak of a man being *worth* so many thousands or millions. No where is money sought so eagerly; no where is it so much valued. . . . " He added that he suspected that "the American husband unconsciously values his wife in the Federal currency. . . . "[44]

Nichols may have been correct in his assessment: middle-class husbands may well have unconsciously looked to their wives as sources of prosperity. But moneymaking was not woman's chief role. Rather, her responsibilities were assumed to include, first and foremost, the unpaid labor of housework. Many women did participate in the paid labor force—as daughters before marriage and as wives with continuing (if small and periodic) obligations to add to the family income. But regardless of whatever else they might do, regardless of the ways and extent to which they crossed into the "male" realm of wage-earning, women bore the primary, virtually exclusive, responsibility for the day-to-day emotional and material arrangements of the family. An unmarried man, or a married man whose wife was temporarily incapacitated, might on an emergency basis be required to cook, clean, wash, or tend the children, of course. But no man with a healthy wife or adult daughter would expect for a moment to take on these duties. Housework was, above all, women's work.

Women's historians have long posed the following conundrum: is housework devalued because women do it, or are women assigned to housework because it is devalued labor? The history of housework during the antebellum era suggests that the puzzle cannot be solved—at least, not when it is framed this way. Gender and economic organization had never existed separately in the northeastern United States. Neither were they separable in the antebellum period. Men experienced early industrialization *simultaneously* through their economic lives *and* through their gender identities, with each of these shaping and being shaped by the other. In the same way, it was in both of these forms—as *work* and as distinctly *women's* work—that the history of housework unfolded through the antebellum period.

Chapter IV

"All the In-doors Work"

In January of 1845, Martha Coffin Wright was recovering from childbirth—and worrying about her housework. She had been doing the best she could, she reported to her sister Lucretia Mott: trying to keep an eye on the children, giving the house a perfunctory clean-up each day, wrestling with the growing pile of mending, and even managing some cooking. But most of the big jobs were going undone. "You advise me not to go and make myself sick, cleaning too early," she wrote; "it is a poor way, you say, and only has to be done again. You add that you and Maria [Mott's daughter] are going to do a little *temporary* cleaning, such as shaking carpets, washing windows, &c.[,] that '&c' being very comprehensive. Why bless you, that is all *I* mean to do." Perhaps she paused for a moment before adding: " 'Temporary' quotha. If I could find a kind that would be *permanent*, I would take out a patent."[1]

The gentle irony of the retort was characteristic of Wright's letters, but it was a gloomy joke she indulged in. As she put it elsewhere in the same letter, even in her period of recuperation she often felt that she was simply "too busy to live." Other women echoed the sentiment. In Brunswick, Maine, Harriet Beecher Stowe described her family responsibilities as a constant round of "hurry, hurry, hurry, and drive, drive, drive." Sarah Smith Browne of Salem, Massachusetts, prayed that her daughters "never will have to *drudge*" as she had. Susan B. Anthony, who remained single but had ample opportunity to observe the lives of married women, suggested that for a woman to marry was for her to accept "the position of maid of all work and baby-tender!" Growing up in the 1820s and 1830s, Caroline Clapp Briggs watched as her family's semirural life robbed her mother of "her health, her strength, and her life. . . . When old age came my mother was worn and weary. She felt none of my father's cheerfulness."[2]

Such characterizations of housework would have taken many antebellum northeasterners by surprise. Convinced that the economic and social "progress" of the early nineteenth century had ensured for women a life pleasantly devoid of all labor but the congenial duties of motherhood, commentators like the Reverend Hubbard Winslow could only imagine that women's occupations were delightfully "delicate and retired." When William Alcott, the author of a popular advice manual on the duties of married women, discovered that "many a young lady of mature years . . . honestly confessed that she should dread death far less than confinement to a single house, and to the cares of a household," he fully attributed the sentiment to an excess of coddling and a want of proper education. The problem, he assumed, was in the women, not in the work.[3]

Historians, too, have tended to discount the possibility that antebellum housework was either time-consuming or particularly taxing. On the one hand, most historical work on women in poor families has focused on their wage-earning labor, either inside or outside the household. In their benign neglect of the unpaid work poor women performed in their own households, historians of the working class have implied both that housework was of little importance to working-class family survival and that activities like cooking, cleaning, and mending occupied little time in the daily lives of working-class women. On the other hand, the secondary literature on antebellum America portrays a society in which middle-class wives were amply supplied with help and spent their own days entertaining guests and taking up the voluntary work of reform. As one scholar has rather succinctly put it, "[f]emale needleworkers and domestic servants fashioned the clothes, stitched the fancywork and tended the homes" that undergirded the lifestyles of women of the antebellum middle class.[4]

Such delightful freedom from labor may, indeed, have been the happy lot of that relatively small number of women whose families made up the elite of antebellum northeastern society. And certainly there were families among the laboring classes for whom the imperatives of wage-earning overrode any sort of unpaid labor a wife might perform in her own household. But for most women—women of the emerging middle class, like Wright and Stowe and Browne and Briggs, and the often more-anonymous women of the new working class—housework remained the personal responsibility and defining labor of women. It also remained hard work. The first step in understanding the economic and social significance of housework in the early industrial world of the antebellum Northeast is simply to reconstruct just what it was that wives were doing.

To contend that both middle-class and working-class wives were hard at work in the service of their families is not to say that they were all doing precisely the same things in precisely the same ways. The composition of a woman's domestic labor still depended on a number of variables, including the make-up and size of her family, the size of the family income, the extent of outside resources available to the household, the nature of her husband's work, and whether her household was located in the city or in the still-considerable farmlands of the Northeast.

Martha Coffin Wright's life was in many ways representative of the experiences of women in the emerging middle class. Her husband, David Wright, was a lawyer. They lived with their growing family in Auburn, New York—not an urban center (the Wrights themselves owned some farmland) but nevertheless a town enmeshed in the expanding market networks of the western regions of that state. While David attended to his practice (which often took him away from home) and earned most of the family income, Martha assumed responsibility for the day-to-day operation of the household.

Like many middle-class wives, Martha Coffin Wright had some paid domestic help. The household regularly included a hired cook, who also worked with Wright on the laundry. From time to time, Wright also hired women to iron, to sew, or to help with special cleaning projects. She was quite aware of what it meant to her own work life to be able to employ other women. Even when she was dissatisfied with a hired woman's work, Wright confided to her sister, "it was better to have her and be mad than to have to work hard, and be mad. . . ."[5] But this did not mean that having paid domestic help released Wright herself from labor. She may have worked a good deal *harder* when there was no help, but her letters and diaries from the 1840s suggest that, under the best of circumstances, she worked very hard indeed—making starch and starching the laundry, sorting clothes and hanging them out to dry, ironing, sweeping and dusting the parlor, dining room, entryway and bedrooms, cleaning carpets and windows, baking, preserving food, tending chickens, collecting eggs, selling berries to neighbors, making candles, and doing the family shopping—a list that does not include what were apparently Wright's most common, indeed ubiquitous, household duties: sewing and child care.[6]

Although the hired cook occasionally helped with the children, in the Wright household child-rearing was Martha's work, and she assumed it with both pleasure and good humor. Still, between 1830 and 1848, she gave birth to six children. For two decades, then, she had the constant care of at least one child under eight years of age (as well as numerous older children). Good-humored or not, Wright was not immune to the exhaustion that came with that responsibility. "[T]heir play makes me almost as nervous as their crying, they are so vociferous and boisterous," she wrote in 1844. "In desperation I have done as they do at the Rail Road 'changed the hour.' Fill them both up at ½ past 5, and at 6 stow them in their downy nests and they go quite as willingly as they did at 7 and I *breathe* an hour earlier. To think of your presuming to doubt my assertion that I should be glad to be 50." For Wright, even social visiting, which historians have sometimes taken as evidence of a leisured middle-class female life, did not signify freedom from household responsibilities. If nothing else interfered, there were always the children. After one especially trying visit, she wrote to her sister, "I came to the conclusion that I did not want to see anybody else till Willy was 21." On another occasion she remarked of an acquaintance, almost fifty years old, who was expecting her fifteenth child: "I should think she would commit suicide. . . . "[7]

For Wright, the supervision and rearing of children probably accounted for more time than any other single responsibility. In that, she was unremarkable among middle-class women of her period and region. But immediately behind (and often interspersed with) child care was that other haunting occupation of nineteenth-century women: sewing. "Considering there is only one day out of 7 that the baby sleeps long enough for me to take a needle in my fingers," she wrote her sister in January of 1845, "I ought to be differently employed than in writing now. . . . "[8] Wright's needlework was as various as it was ubiquitous. She mended old pantaloons and made new ones, made and remade dresses and baby clothes, fashioned purses, knit caps and socks, and made most of the household linens. She did sometimes hire a seamstress, but her diaries indicate that this was a rare expense. Usually, moreover, the seamstress was employed to work alongside Wright on a particularly difficult project, not to replace her.[9]

While no single woman can embody the diversity of household responsibilities borne by women across the broad middle ranges of antebellum society, Wright's experiences were not atypical. Like Wright, middle-class women frequently employed some hired help, but both the universality and the regularity of the practice can easily be overstated. Census records from the period indicate that less than 20 percent of northeastern households included live-in domestic servants—a figure that would exclude most of the middle class as defined by Pessen's calculations.[10] Visitors to the United States testified to the relative scarcity of servants, even in elite households. "We continue to hear many ladies complain of the labours of house-keeping in this country," George Combe remarked during his tour in the late 1830s. "When one makes a call in a forenoon, the lady of the house is rarely found sitting in her drawing-room, as is the custom in England, but appears to be engaged in some other part of the house." Touring the northeastern United States in the 1840s, Fredrika Bremer also commented on the absence of paid domestic help—in this case, among members of the professional class. She described the cottage home and garden of a physician and his wife in Worcester, Massachusetts, noting that ". . . here they lived without a servant, the wife herself performing all the in-doors work. This is very much the custom in the small homes of the New England States, partly from economic causes, and partly from the difficulty there is in getting good servants."[11]

Various observers commented on the comparative scarcity in the antebellum Northeast of women willing to take jobs as servants, but the decisive factor in whether or not a given woman had paid help appears to have been her own family's finances: the wealthier the household—and the more stable its income—the likelier the wife was to have paid domestic help some or all of the time. Among middle-class families, the most common arrangement was to hire a cook or washerwoman (the two jobs were sometimes combined) on a fairly regular basis, and to employ additional help as needed (and as able) for special projects, such as the much-dreaded spring cleaning (when women might be hired to whitewash as well as to clean) and during the wife's convalescence following childbirth.

As Wright's experiences demonstrate, the presence of paid domestic workers did not free the mistress of the household from labor. In the first place, servants often had to be schooled—not necessarily in the work per se, but in the particular routine, habits, and expectations of the individual household. Such training was time-consuming at best; at worst, it exposed all the class- and race-based pretensions to superiority that might characterize a mistress's attitude toward her employees. Elizabeth Cabot, a woman whose family income of $6,000 placed her among the elite, complained of the time and energy required to train hired domestic workers. "I have been scolding all my servants," she wrote to her sister in February of 1860,

> and endeavoring to make my mind content under the conviction that they will not learn to do things up to a satisfactory standard, but will always linger between the real excellence which is one's own ideal, and the barely tolerable which is theirs.

With patronizing generosity, she added: "At the same time they are an uncommonly respectable set of servants, and I don't wish to turn them away and know I shall do no better." Servants did not always share this resignation; one of the recurring (if often deserved) frustrations of household management was the departure of servants for more satisfactory or remunerative employment elsewhere, again setting in motion the cycle of searching out and training domestic help.[12]

But the presence of hired domestic workers seldom meant that the mistress's labor was limited to mere supervision and training. Although housework had changed over time (with some tasks completely disappearing in some households), women's letters and diaries evince that it had not been reduced to a one-woman job that could be entirely accomplished by a hired servant. Rather than freeing the mistress from labor, antebellum servants appear to have absorbed the work (either the tasks per se or the overall share of the household labor) that in an earlier time would have been taken on by other females in the household: adult female relatives, daughters, young girls hired from the neighborhood, or bound servants. Laundry, housecleaning, and some cooking were among the particular chores that had traditionally been performed by younger females in the family, but from which the emerging middle class was increasingly withdrawing its daughters in favor of education and the development of more refined social skills. In this context, the mistress was often simultaneously co-worker and supervisor. The experience of Caroline Clapp Briggs is instructive here. As a young couple, the Briggses boarded with a minister's family. Caroline and the servant split the laundry chores; the servant washing while Caroline ironed. Later, when she had two servants herself, Caroline continued to do part of the housework—although now not literally alongside her hired workers. While they cleaned, for example, she sewed and mended.[13]

Servants also enabled wives to assume the new and enlarged responsibilities industrialization gave rise to in middle-class families. Chief among these was the expanded attention to child care, which absorbed so much of Martha Coffin Wright's energy. Writers warned mothers to maintain constant vigilance against potential physical dangers to children. Lest their readers miss the point, descriptions of accidents involving children—burns, falls, injuries from runaway wagons and carriages—frequently stressed that the mishap had occurred when the mother was momentarily absent. The Providence-based *Ladies Museum* carried an especially grisly example of the genre, reporting on the injuries to a child who was attacked by a stray hog in the streets of Baltimore—an accident closer maternal supervision could presumably have prevented.[14] Meanwhile, prescriptive writers cautioned that children required more, and more deliberate, preparation for adulthood than had been necessary in an earlier, presumably simpler period. Lockean philosophy had suggested that children began life without a predisposition to either good or evil—a view that put great emphasis on the self-discipline and control of the parent shaping the child's character. Increasingly throughout the late eighteenth and early nineteenth centuries, this duty devolved upon mothers.[15]

Women took this responsibility to heart. In his 1856 advice manual for women, T. S. Arthur recommended that mothers should read ahead of their children in their studies, becoming proficient in history, geography, the classics, and modern literature. Harriet Beecher Stowe had anticipated the counsel: in 1850, in order that she might be better prepared to teach her children English history, she had launched on a reading of all of Sir Walter Scott's novels. Abigail Hyde, the wife of a Connecticut minister, judged herself "so far . . . from meeting the high responsibilities which devolve on me as a mother, that the conviction of my deficiency which sometimes forces itself on me is sometimes overwhelming." Lucy Stone devoted herself to the struggle for a more egalitarian conception of marriage; nevertheless, she made an abrupt hiatus in her career as lecturer to focus her attention on raising her first and only child. Like thousands of other women, Sarah Ayer joined a maternal society "soon after the birth of my little Sarah," and recorded in her diary her hope that "the meetings have been profitable." At stake, she considered, was the welfare, not only of little Sarah, but of "generations yet unborn."[16]

With the exception of nurses employed for a week or two immediately after childbirth, middle-class women appear, as a rule, *not* to have hired workers to help with child-rearing. To the contrary, the ability to attend personally to one's children was one of the marks of a good mother. Visiting the United States in the 1830s, Francis Grund observed the general ill-health of married women. "As the principal cause of this sudden decline, some allege the climate," he noted, "but I ascribe it more willingly to the great assiduity with which American ladies discharge their duties as mothers. No sooner are they married than they begin to lead a life of comparative seclusion; and once mothers, they are actually buried to the world." As it had for Martha Coffin Wright, the attempt to meet the standards of middle-class motherhood often left women with ambivalent feelings. The author of *Six Hundred Dollars a Year* (a description of the household economy of a prosperous mechanic's family in the early 1860s) purchased "a little coach" that allowed her to keep her new baby with her at all times. It was what she should have wished as a mother, but as an individual, she recognized in the baby coach a symbol of the loss of her own freedom: "[I]ndeed, after this I was seldom able to go out in the daytime without taking him with me."[17]

If child care was the central and most time-consuming family labor for most middle-class women, needlework appears to have often ranked a close second, as it did for Martha Coffin Wright. The amount of sewing and mending a woman did varied both with the size of her family and with the season: the crisp winds of autumn sent wives racing to make caps and repair winter coats; in the spring, they set to work on light dresses and shirts for the summer. But the litany of entries in letters and diaries—"Mended all day to day," "I sewed all the afternoon," "Finished my dress and did my week[']s mending"—reminds us that, with children or without and throughout the year, sewing and mending were always with middle-class wives. Needlework could sometimes be a shared enterprise, as women either worked on a common project or simply enjoyed the "cosiness in being together & sewing uninterruptedly." But it could also be isolating work. After thoroughly scouring the house in May of 1858, Sarah Smith Browne looked forward to company and a more relaxed schedule; but it was time to begin on "the Spring wardrobes," and although she had several callers over the next few days, she found herself forced to "leave them & sew away."[18] Indeed, so commonplace a fixture was the sewing basket in a woman's life that its absence was often marked as a special triumph: " . . . commenced cleaning the children[']s room and Willis's room also finished them both and got them in order before 4 o'clock . . . *did not sew a stitch today* . . . "![19]

The clothing that middle-class women made for their families was one of the most visible products of their household labor in the antebellum era, but it did not encompass the full extent either of their sewing or of their more general household manufacturing. Certainly, over the antebellum years a greater selection of goods became available for purchase in shops and city markets. Yet this variety did not spell an immediate end to household production. In 1864, Lydia Maria Child recorded in her diary the manufacture of seventeen articles of furnishing for her household, including an afghan, a case for glasses, a door mat, towels, curtains, and pillowcases. In addition to her family's clothing, Sarah Browne sewed "[pot] Holders, Dish towels &," as she put it, "all kinds of paraphernalia" for her household. At forty-one years of age and married to a successful merchant, Lucy Stone "dried all the herbs and put up all the fruits in their season. She made her own yeast, her own bread, her own dried beef, even her own soap." Martha Coffin Wright made her own soap and manufactured the candles her family used for lighting, as did Sarah Campbell in Schodack, New York, who recorded that she had made "three hundred candles and boiled twelve pailes [of] soap." Indeed, domestic manufacture was taken for granted as an aspect of even "genteel" housewives' work. In *The American Woman's Home*, Catharine Beecher and Harriet Beecher Stowe assumed that wives might be called upon to manufacture mattresses, pillows, and curtains, to repair furniture and make picture frames, to bake bread, to produce much of the family's clothing and bed linens, as well as to make candles.[20]

The items that women manufactured for their families' use were often made from materials purchased on the market. But, even in comparatively urban areas, some middle-class wives still themselves produced a portion of the raw materials that their families consumed. Both Lucy Stone (just outside of Boston) and Martha Coffin Wright (in Auburn, New York) kept chickens and worked a family garden; Stone also tended a horse and a cow. Sarah Preston Hale hired someone to prepare the ground for her garden plot, but she planted and tended beans, peas, and strawberries for her family's table. Harriet Robinson grew lettuce, tomatoes, rhubarb, and grapes. In New York City, artisans' wives raised hogs, setting them free to scavenge what food they could on the streets to compensate for not having enough space to keep the animals on their own property. The anonymous author of *Six Hundred Dollars a Year* shared the care of the garden with her husband. They planted the patch together. He then hoed and weeded it each morning before leaving for his work, while she picked the produce as it came ready, selecting some for immediate consumption and preserving the remainder for later use.[21]

Even as they continued to produce directly for their family tables, however, middle-class wives, especially in urban areas, found more and more of their time taken up with shopping. In many ways, there was little that was new for women about this work. As we have seen, colonial households had rarely approached self-sufficiency. Goodwives had traded with neighbors, local merchants, and itinerant peddlers for goods not produced in their own households. To be sure, by the nineteenth century most of this trade was cash rather than barter-based. But the basic patterns of women's trade had changed remarkably little over the course of a century and a half. All of the older networks—including the reliance on peddlers—persisted into the antebellum period, as women bought such items as fish, apples, eggs, and yarn from vendors at the kitchen door.[22]

Also dating from an earlier period was the practice of calling on the aid of out-of-town friends, in the hope that they might be able to find some item not locally available. Living in New York City, John Pintard had been particularly proud of his wife's readiness to perform this service for "her country friends," noting that " . . . she is an excellent judge of goods . . . [and] always takes a bill & receipt for every article she purchases, w[hic]h she incloses with the parcel." In the 1820s, Mary Kinsley and her aunt, who resided in Boston, pursued the custom, trying to find a leghorn hat for Mary's friend Eliza, who lived in New Haven. Even the trips to retail stores to purchase combs, ribbons, fabrics, hats, and other family necessities were hardly new to women's work schedules.[23]

As the considerable amount of manufacturing still occurring even in middle-class homes suggests, these shopping trips seldom signified a household entirely dependent on the marketplace for supplying its needs. They did indicate a decline both in the overall amount of household production and in the overall number of household producers.[24] But much of the increased purchasing corresponded simply to the growing importance of possessions in middle-class households, where the ability to display variety—in foods and furnishings, in clothing and table settings—was a sign of class security. Rather than replacing women's household manufacturing, trips to the shops and markets of the urban centers supplemented it.

Along with the sewing and mending, the soap-making and quilting, the gardening and shopping, there remained to middle-class women those most quotidian of household labors: cooking, cleaning, and doing the laundry. Few events disrupted the smooth operation of family life—or the best-laid plans of a wife and mother—like laundry day. "I have been trying to catch time enough together ever since the reception of your letter to answer it," Luella Case explained in a letter to Sarah Edgarton:

> but of all flying things, these hours and days are the most alert—at least I would sooner undertake to put salt on the tail of the wildest rover of the woods, than to stop one of them when its wings are spread long enough to say "how dye do". . . . Shall I tell you what prevented? Well, it was washing-day. . . .

In fact, even with hired help, "washing-day" was often several days, and sometimes threatened to take over the entire week. "[W]hen we first came," Louisa Meigs of Rouse's Point, New York, wrote to her mother, "washing and ironing lasted from Monday—till the ensuing week—I have now reduced it within three days—and hope to bring it down *to two*. . . . " Soap was made in advance, but the clothes had to be sorted, presoaked, washed, hung to dry, starched, ironed, and put away. Catharine Beecher recommended that a wife plan on spending two full days and part of a third getting it all done: Tuesday to wash, Wednesday to iron, and Thursday to finish ironing and fold and put away the clothes. (The remainder of Thursday was to be reserved for mending.)[25]

With luck and help, laundry was a weekly undertaking. Cooking and cleaning, however, recurred with dreary, daily regularity, a point that Lydia Maria Child underscored grimly in her summary of activities for 1864:

> Cooked 360 dinners.
> Cooked 362 breakfasts.
> Swept and dusted sitting-room & kitchen 350 times.
> Filled lamps 362 times.
> Swept and dusted chamber & stairs 40 times.

There is no doubt that women sometimes enjoyed aspects of this work. Cooking especially could be the source of both great pride and great pleasure—particularly on holidays and during celebrations, when a woman might display her special skills at making a pudding, bread, or pastries. But those occasions were comparatively few and far between, and they were often times of such hard labor for women that the feelings of satisfaction were lost in a fog of weariness. For the most part, cooking was simply the business of preparing the family's daily food—if anything, the least flexible of the responsibilities that a woman had to fit into her regular routine. William Alcott had been distressed to discover how many wives "regard home—the kitchen, especially—as the grave of all true freedom. . . . " Perhaps he had talked with women like Sarah Smith Browne: "On my soul," she confided to her diary, "I hate the drudgery of a kitchen."[26]

Equally demoralizing were the annual and semiannual house cleanings that represented middle-class women's efforts to cope with the dirt of daily life in the antebellum period—the grime created by open-flame lighting, the soot of wood- and coal-burning stoves, and the mud carried into the house from unpaved streets and walking paths. Sarah Smith Browne described the time-consuming and laborious process with heavy irony in her diary for 1858:

> [April 19] . . . I . . . begin to turn my thoughts towards the "*spring cleaning*". . . .
>
> [April 21] . . . I have commenced operations in regard to Spring Cleaning. In the upper chamber I overhaul all bags, boxes & bundles, in pursuit of Moths. I find a few & am answerable for their extermination. . . .
>
> [April 22] . . . Mrs Cody, my pillar in the Spring overturn comes. We take up six carpets in one day. . . .
>
> [April 23] The Panorama of the Spring Cleaning reaches the Closet scene. Amid Crockery & Glass the tangible overpowers. At night the shining inmates give a grand triumph to the tableau of table furniture.
>
> [April 24] Chilly, discouraging! the marble ornaments & engravings accompanied by multitudinous books are to shake off the soil of the past year. . . .
>
> [April 25] I am tired & sick with headache. . . .
>
> [April 26] . . . I am too feeble to arrange the prodigious quantity of disarrangement. . . .
>
> [April 27] . . . Today I am better & the panorama will move on to the Furniture cleaning! Chairs [,] Tables, Desks, bureaus &c to be varnished & waxed. . . .
>
> [April 30] . . . I set up my pictures. Napoleon's face is well washed, but there are stains on his character. Walter Scott's ideality stands out gloriously free from dust. . . .
>
> [May 3] . . . Mrs Cody cleaning tins. They shine like the Pleides. You see my thoughts *can* soar, even in the midst of kitchen closets. . . .

Even with Mrs. Cody's help, the work took two full weeks. Harriet Robinson, who also hired women to help her with the spring cleaning, devoted two or three days to the scrubbing of each room and used the annual event as the occasion for repairing and remaking carpets worn down over the course of the year. For Robinson, the entire process often took up to a month to complete.[27]

One final point should be made about the work of middle-class wives: for many women of this group, "domesticity" included at least some direct cash-earning responsibilities. In the second year of her marriage, the author of *Six Hundred Dollars a Year* earned over $100 manufacturing and selling artificial flowers. During the subsequent years she earned an additional $350 from the flowers and from sewing. Other women made money by saving bottles, rags, and paper for resale; by selling kitchen fat, eggs, and berries; by sewing or doing copying work for pay; and by taking in boarders.[28]

For many middle-class women, some form of income earning was an ongoing aspect of their household responsibilities. Lydia Maria Child listed among her employments for 1864 the articles she wrote and the time she spent correcting page proofs and keeping up with published material, activities necessary to her career as an editor and author of advice literature and children's stories. In a letter to her husband in the winter of 1850, Harriet Beecher Stowe described the hardship created for wives who were required to perform both paid and unpaid labor for the household economy:

> There is no doubt in my mind that our expenses this year will come to two hundred dollars, if not three, beyond our salary. We shall be able to come through notwithstanding; but I don't want to feel obliged to work as hard every year as I have this. I can earn four hundred dollars a year by writing, but I don't want to feel that I must, when weary with teaching the children, and tending the baby, and buying provisions, and mending dresses, and darning stockings, sit down and write a piece for some paper.

At this period of their lives, the Stowes were earning "seventeen hundred dollars in all."[29]

Middle-class women contributed to their families' finances in other, less visible ways. Common among these was their work in providing services as a part of the wages of workers hired by their husbands. Visiting in Stockbridge, Massachusetts, in the 1830s, E. S. Abdy noted that in some places journeymen still received "board, lodging, washing, and mending" as part of their pay. He did not mention whose labor supplied these compensations, but it was certainly that of either the wife or a daughter. When Sarah and Samuel Campbell, who operated a store in Schodack, New York, expanded their business, the four carpenters they hired received their meals as part of their pay, "which," Sarah noted in her diary, "makes my family quite large[.] I do not visit at all."

As they had in earlier periods, middle-class women also often spent time working in the businesses their husbands owned, saving the business the profits that would otherwise had been paid out in wages to a clerk. "Attend[ing] the store" was a common, if somewhat erratic, intrusion into Sarah Campbell's other responsibilities, which included the care of six children. Similarly, her husband's absence often required that Anna Jackson Lowell, who had children, housework, and a school to attend to, *also* mind the family store.[30]

The cash-earning responsibilities that often remained periodic and unseen among middle-class wives were frequently the most visible aspect of working-class women's labor responsibilities to their families. Any woman might well be called on in an emergency to set aside her other household duties in favor of assuming part of the burden of wage-earning, and for some middle-class women this was a continuing responsibility. For many more working-class women, however, in whose families the cash requirements of survival could rarely be stabilized in the efforts of one person, cash-earning was the domestic work around which all other tasks constantly had to be organized.

Poor and working-class mothers and wives were ever-present and resourceful agents in the petty commerce of the streets. From the early hours of dawn, they could be seen going about their labors. First came the ragpickers—women in the most destitute of families—armed with their hooks and baskets, "poking into the gutters after rags before the stars go to bed." Close behind them came the swelling ranks of street vendors, some of them country women carrying their farm produce to town, but many of them city women hawking roots and herbs they had dug themselves, or berries and apples bought from a country woman on the edge of town, acquired from a wholesaler, or purchased cheap at the end of the previous day's market, breaking the morning peace with the cries of their wares:

> Fine matches! good Matches!
> Will you please to have any,
> In pity do take some,—
> Three bunches a penny.

When they were able to afford the fee, women rented their own stalls in the city markets, but many hucksters roamed among the markets' customers, offering candy, baked goods, and coffee for refreshment. Still other women ran taverns and groceries in their own dwellings.[31]

The hucksters' wares were often products traditionally associated with women's work, now being vended on the cash market. Many working-class women—married as well as unmarried—found even more direct ways of converting their household skills into money. Long before the transition to early industrial capitalism, married women had plied their domestic skills for the benefit of other people's families—either in work-swapping arrangements with other wives or as paid household workers. Poor women, both immigrant and native-born, now drew on this tradition as one of their most likely means of earning money for their families. In an attempt to avoid "live-in" work in an employer's house, married women concentrated on strategies of selling their domestic labor within their own homes—working at home as outwork needlewomen, for example; or, like one street vendor's wife, "occasionally perform[ing] house-labor" on a per diem basis. Relying on another long-standing and widespread "domestic" tradition, other working-class women took in boarders, articulating the cash value of their housework entirely within the membership, physical confines, and daily patterns of their own homes. For many married women, marketing domestic skills necessarily meant leaving home. The immigrant women who worked as cooks and laundresses for railroad construction crews often travelled a considerable distance to get paid for their housework. Married black women, who were excluded from most forms of employment, sometimes had little choice but to accept positions as live-in maids and cooks, jobs that kept them from their families and often required that they place their children with relatives or friends for much of the week. Equally important, even when done entirely within a woman's own home, the exchange of domestic labor for cash created a double shift that was debilitating to the woman and disruptive to family life. When he visited New York, Englishman E. S. Abdy met Susannah Peterson, a black woman whose husband was temporarily unemployed because of illness. Susannah's strategy of taking in washing permitted her to earn money while staying home, where she could care for her six children and nurse her husband, but only at a considerable cost: "her business sometimes keeping her up nearly all night."[32]

Like some middle-class wives, many working-class women appear to have bolstered their families' incomes by working in shops that their husbands presumedly owned and operated. William Bell, a police officer in New York City in the 1850s whose duties included citing small businesses for operating without a license, discovered that the economically marginal junk and secondhand shops he visited were often in fact staffed by women. When he "Called at Wm. P. Bennett['s] Second Hand Clothing Store" on James Street, for example, Bell found Bennett's wife running the shop—and apparently functioning as its full proprietor, since she claimed that she had stocked the store, buying "her goods exclusively at Auction."[33]

At the same time, working-class wives remained responsible for performing most of the *unpaid* labor that went into the household economy—and for organizing other family members' contributions. Like wives in more prosperous households, they provided the bulk of the work that transformed the goods brought into the household into family consumables: they washed and sewed and mended clothing; they chopped and boiled and roasted food; they laid fires; they carried water and fuel into the house and lugged it back out—or (far more convenient if one was living in a second- or third-floor apartment) simply dumped it out the window into the streets.[34]

As it had in earlier periods, in some respects poverty simplified these most mundane household labors. Most working-class households lacked the cash to buy food ahead or in large quantities, with the result that (especially in poor urban families) there was less need for wives to spend time preserving food. In any event, the crowded apartments of the urban working poor afforded little space for the maintenance of extensive larders—or, for that matter, for complex cooking and baking operations (assuming the household could afford more than a skeletal selection of cooking utensils). Food was from the street or the market to the table, with minimal intermediate processing. Since working-class families had less money to spend on clothing, washloads were smaller. Similarly, households with fewer possessions did not need the extensive cleaning required by multiple rooms and a more elaborate array of furnishings. In poor families, moreover, immediate issues of providing warmth, food, and clothing took precedence over providing a cleansed and polished environment.

But poverty also increased the core labor of housework, particularly in urban areas. In New York City, where the poor lived largely in tenements, water for laundry (or for drinking or cooking—indeed, the food itself) had to be carried up as many as three or four flights of stairs—that, or the laundry must be carried down. From Lynn, Massachusetts, Mary Paul Guild, a former mill operative whose household was on the margin between the working and the middle class, complained to her father of the difficulties of living on an upper floor: "We live *up stairs* as usual. I wish we could afford to live in a lower tenement, it is so hard for me to do my work up stairs though I manage not to go over the stairs more than once or twice a day. . . . " She was five months pregnant at the time, and needed, as she recognized, "to be saving of my strength."[35] Even where the laboring classes lived in separate "cottages" or hastily constructed "barracks," housing conditions exacerbated the problems of domestic labor. Quarters were often cramped—filled, not only with people, but also perhaps with the tools and materials of outworkers. The oily soot of cheap coal stoves and charcoal burners collected on floors and walls, their fumes lingering in the air. Wives living with their families in the sod-insulated shacks of Lawrence constantly fought silt and sludge. In the cellar apartments of larger cities, rainwater and sewage seeped in with every downpour. However simplified the domestic routine, under these conditions even the most basic of household labors—scrubbing a floor, arranging bedding, or preparing a meal—required a herculean effort.

Finally, the constant and pressing need for money meant that fewer household members other than the wife were present to help with the domestic labor of working-class families. Only under unusual circumstances did working-class households contain hired domestic workers—although they sometimes did when the household was also a boardinghouse or in the event of the wife's being seriously ill. Mary Paul Guild was in poor health during the autumn of 1861 and anticipated that she might "have to keep a girl all winter." But Guild's husband was out of work and she worried how "we can manage to pay her."[36]

Central to working-class housework were the wife's efforts in organizing, overseeing, and leading an intricate battery of activities aimed at avoiding cash expenditures. Among the most common forms of purchase-substitution labor in poorer families was scavenging: for food, for discarded clothing, for household implements, and for fuel. The line between finding and stealing was necessarily a fine one—and one often most honored in the breach. As urbanization diminished the possibilities for providing one's own raw materials and implements and poverty precluded their purchase, wives in poor families appear to have crossed that line more and more frequently. When Mary Brennan stole a $3 pair of shoes in 1841, for example, "[s]he assigned her great destitution as the sole cause of the theft." Brennan was not unusual. Throughout the antebellum period, women appeared in published crime reports on charges of the theft of common and basic household implements: washtubs, frying pans, dish kettles, clothing, and other items that seemed destined, not for resale, but for immediate use.[37]

Equally important to the laboring-class household was the wife's skill and diligence in maintaining friendly contacts with her neighbors. Social relations with a strong economic base, these female networks provided families with additional avenues of access to goods and services necessary to survival. New to a building, neighborhood, or community, a woman depended on her peers for information on the cheapest places to buy, the best places to scavenge, and the most favorable times to evade the police, should the requirements of her household conflict with the requirements of the law. Amicable relations with one's neighbors could yield someone to sit with a sick child or a friend from whom to borrow a pot or a few pieces of coal. One woman "went herself to *Whitehall* after a load [of wood from municipal authorities], and came up to see it delivered" when her neighbor was in danger of going without heat. In the event of fire, women often found that it was female neighbors who "exerted themselves in removing goods and furniture, and also in passing water" through the bucket brigade. In the direst of emergencies, a friendly neighbor could become a temporary mother for a child whose family could no longer support it.[38]

On the other hand, conflict with one's neighbors could create material hardship. Mary Pepper, of Boston, complained that a neighbor had had her arrested as a drunkard for no other reason than to get her evicted: "An its all along of your wanting my little place becaise ye cant pay the rent for your own . . . ," she charged. Stronger neighborly ties might have shielded Pepper from the authorities, protecting her apartment, her freedom, and her family.[39]

In the midst of all this, in the laboring poor and working classes, as in the middle class, women were primarily responsible for child care. Rarely were they able to accomplish this to the satisfaction of middle-class reformers—or perhaps to their own satisfaction. Many working-class families simply did not have the option of withdrawing their children from the paid work force or of providing them with the education that might have prepared them for an economically secure future. Sending their children into the streets to scavenge or sell newspapers or roasted corn or potatoes, working-class mothers knew that they were teaching skills that might well lead to injury or arrest. Particularly given the circumstances they faced, what is striking about antebellum working-class mothers is not their failure, but their remarkable success in finding ways to care for their children. A group of Italian immigrant women in New York left their children together to take care of each other while the mothers went out to beg. Other women took their children with them as they wandered through the streets looking for bits of food or clothing. One woman, a vendor who lived with her shoemaker husband in a cellar apartment, took in an orphan "and fed him gratis" for weeks.[40]

Rural women performed virtually all of the core labor of housework undertaken by women in more urban areas: they swept and washed floors, did laundry, hung clothes to dry, ironed, cooked, baked, bound up cuts and scrapes, made and mended clothing, and took responsibility for virtually all of the child care—at least until sons were old enough to be helpful to their fathers in the barn and the fields. But country women, far more often than women in urban areas, also produced the raw materials necessary to their household labors.

Farm life had not remained unchanged in the midst of the economic revolution of the antebellum period. Families bought and sold regularly in local stores, carried their products to city markets, and supplied hundreds of outworkers for the new industries of the Northeast. Nevertheless, particularly for wives, day-to-day life on the farm continued to look much as it had in the colonial period. Women did sometimes buy commodities that they might have manufactured in an earlier period. One woman included among her purchases such items as soap, thread, pins, dishes, tea, and several types of cloth. The soap, thread, and cloth she might, in another time, have made herself.[41]

And yet a vast amount of household manufacturing remained common on farms. More prosperous country women not only sewed, but also frequently manufactured the fabric that they used. They "carded, spun, and wove the wool and flax, making the blankets, fulled cloth, and linen of the family," purchasing only the fabrics they could not provide for themselves. Living outside of Burlington, Vermont, in the 1820s, Hannah Matthews Stone, who was the mother of seven children, "wove all the cloth for the family's wearing." In February of 1845, Sarah Smith added a quick note to her husband's letter to his family, explaining that she was then busy with "spinning weaving sewing and so on to prepare for our anticipated journey" to Michigan. Spending the winter of 1851 with her family in Albion, New York, Philena Thorp, a former hired housekeeper, soon found herself re-immersed in the traditional work of cloth-making: "Sarah and Myself have finished spinning last week and mother has got one peece of mine half out[.] Sarah is going to weave the next peas next week. . . . " The considerable extent of this labor in the antebellum period was suggested in censuses of home manufactures; although the amounts were falling, as late as 1855, New York State *households* produced almost a million yards of textile goods.[42]

Spinning and weaving were only the prelude to knitting and sewing, of course; once produced, yarns and fabric still required hours of labor before they became usable in the form of clothing or household linens.

Recovering from illness in 1822, Mary Ann Archbald suggested the full scope of the household textile manufacturing system: "I was able to sew & knit which is a good thing as there was much of both kinds to do—first 14 woolen check shirts for winter & then 12 of coarse linning [linen?] for summer[. T]he girles has all the spinning to do & were very busy. . . ."[43]

Farm wives were also far more likely to produce the food they cooked than were city women. Women from more urban areas, where meats and produce could be more readily purchased in the market, often found themselves utterly unprepared for this work, should necessity require that they undertake it. Recently married and moved to the country, one young wife wrote home to her friend, ". . . we *butchered* [S]aturday, and yesterday, we tried out the lard and made some *sausages*; wouldn't you like to see me diving into all these sorts of things[?] I imagine you would laugh heartily."[44]

Butchering animals and preserving meats were only a few of the ways country women directly provided the food for their families' tables. Sally Brown, of Plymouth Notch, Vermont, dried fruit and made her own cheese, cider, applesauce, and molasses; she put her daughters to work catching partridges, gathering berries, making turkey cages, and milking the cows. Living on a farm in northern New York, Phebe Eastman grew her own vegetables, foraged for wild berries, salted down her own pork, and boiled her own lard. Journalist Thomas Nichols remembered farm wives hard at work making "plenty of butter and cheese" for their families.[45]

Not all of the household manufacturing of farm wives was for their own families' consumption. Like their counterparts of an earlier era, they also produced a variety of goods for sale: yarn and cloth from their spinning wheels; eggs and milk products from their barnyards; fruits and vegetables from their gardens and orchards. The father of the family sometimes transported these goods to market. Thomas Nichols recalled wagons loaded not only with "hogs, frozen stiff," but also with "tallow, butter, cheese, dried apples, apple-sauce, honey, home-made cloth, woollen socks and mittens. . . ." Sometimes women and children carried the produce to town themselves, paying the fee to sell it in the market; New York City's Washington Market, for example, was frequently crowded with farm women who "came in great numbers with their butter, pot-cheese, curds and buttermilk." Other women left their goods on the doorsteps of regular customers. Still others sold their produce to local vendors for resale to households; one mechanic's wife, lacking either the inclination, the time, or the means to raise chickens herself, complained that she had to deal with a woman "who bought eggs at two shillings a dozen and supplied them to me at double that price."[46]

In urban and suburban areas, the character of housework was sharply circumscribed by class—and so it was, as well, in the countryside of the rural Northeast. Indeed, class definition may well have overridden rural-or-urban distinctions. Like poor urban households, poor farming households were unlikely to have the equipment for elaborate food processing and preservation, or the space for extensive kitchen gardens. If, in the poorest of city families, food often went directly from the street to the table, in poor rural households it went from the woods to the table. Rural foraging replicated urban scavenging. Also like women of the urban working classes, the poor women of the countryside were more likely than their more prosperous neighbors to engage in wage work—either hiring themselves out as field workers or becoming outworkers in regional manufacturing enterprises.[47]

Because their husbands' place of business coincided so closely with their own, farm wives assumed hidden responsibilities for the general operation of the farm. As a matter of course, for example, they were expected to cook for hired workers and to provide medical aid when anyone in the household, relative or hired worker, fell sick. Although women appear not to have worked in the fields (as distinct from the kitchen garden, the chicken coop, and the dairy) on a regular basis, when need arose they plowed, planted, and harvested, and raked and stacked the crop side-by-side with the men—leaving that work only long enough to prepare the meals for the full work crew.

Commonly, wives in more prosperous farming households were aided by the presence of both hired women and daughters. Caroline Clapp Briggs, who observed the price in happiness and health that farm life exacted from her mother, often helped with the household labor. In addition, she recalled, her family employed two women, whose regular household duties were sometimes supplemented with work in the fields. Mary Ann Archbald and Sally Brown both put their daughters to work spinning. When Brown's daughters could not keep up with the load, she hired Mary Thompson to help out. Phebe Eastman hired a succession of girls and young women to spin the yarn she wove. Occasionally, she also hired workers to help with her cleaning and child care.[48]

Hired domestic servants and unpaid daughters only supplemented the labor of rural wives, however. A woman who identified herself as "Aniss" wrote to newspaper columnist Jane Swisshelm complaining about "rich" farmers who expected their wives to "cook, milk and churn" even during those times when the men "lounge around and rest." Caroline Clapp Briggs remembered of the 1820s and 1830s that "[m]erriment was an unusual gift in women of those days, who were generally overworked and anxious." Echoing that sentiment, woman's rights advocate Lucy Stone recalled, as among the sharpest memories of her childhood, watching her "mother's health give way under the hard work" of the family farm.[49]

Indeed, their remoteness from the bustle and "progress" of the city was a mixed blessing for farm women. If their farms prospered, they saw their families comparatively well fed and well clothed and their children protected from the health and safety dangers of more urban areas. But they also worked with tools and under conditions that had changed very little since the late eighteenth century. At a time when some city families were discovering gas lighting, farm women still spun and sewed by candles they had made themselves. Although the spinning jenny had originally been intended for domestic use, most rural household spinning was still done at single-spindle hand wheels. Apparently with rural women chiefly in mind, Caroline Gilman suggested in 1838 that what wives needed most in the way of new technology was an improved churn: "The churn is an unwieldy article," she observed, "and something should be devised to save the labor which is called into requisition to 'making butter come.' " In 1838, unfortunately for farm women, most of the energy of American inventiveness was being channeled toward capitalized manufacturing.[50]

Ironically, the snail's pace at which the industrial revolution came to the farmhouse reflected in part the growing commercial orientation of agriculture. By the mid–nineteenth century, farming was a business in the Northeast—albeit often a precarious one, with stiff competition from the West. Focused on profit and loss, farm families were far more likely to invest hard-earned dollars in the clearly commercial enterprises of the farm—the cash crops and stock—than in the family labor that did not lead to a cash nexus. Much of their labor unremunerated, farm women's work appeared to have little to do with the world of agricultural profit and loss and was able to make but a weak claim to the deployment of cash resources.[51] George S. Boutwell, later to become governor of Massachusetts, congressman, senator, and Secretary of the United States Treasury, remembered that in his own parents' household this pattern of decision-making reigned. The family lived in a house of unpainted white pine; cooking was done at an open-hearth fireplace; and the rooms were "destitute of furniture, except of the plainest sort." Boutwell's father, however, was the first farmer in the neighborhood to own a cast-iron plow.[52]

But it was in Mary Wilkins Freeman's "The Revolt of 'Mother' " (a story based on Freeman's own memories of farm life in pre–Civil War Randolph, Massachusetts) that the simmering resentments of such family dynamics found their classic expression. For years, Mrs. Penn had worked on in silent resignation—washing the family's clothes, cleaning the family's house, making the family's meals, raising the children—while all of the family's earnings had been poured into her husband's work. When Mr. Penn decided once again to improve *his* workplace (by building a new barn), rather than *hers* (by spending money on the house), the accumulated anger of decades exploded: "You see this room, here, father, you look at it well. You see there ain't no carpet on the floor an' you see the paper is all dirty, an' droppin' off the walls. . . . You see this room, father; it's all the one I've had to work in an' eat in and sit in sence we was married."[53]

Freeman gave her story a happy turn: Mrs. Penn simply moved the family into the barn. Few wives would have dared such rebellion. Perhaps few would even have considered it. In her study of household service, Faye E. Dudden has speculated that wives may have shared their husbands' tendency to denigrate the importance of their unpaid labor. Dudden argues that rural women were far more reluctant to hire workers to help them with cooking, cleaning, and child care than to assist in the labor they performed for the market: keeping chickens for an egg business, making cloth to be sold, milking, and the like. Apparently they felt they could justify the expenditure only when the labor could be immediately reconverted into cash.[54]

Few wives in antebellum America enjoyed a life free from labor. Family life depended on the smooth performance of an extensive array of unpaid occupations in the household, and on the presence in the household of someone to provide that work—to supervise the children through the vicissitudes of a changing social and economic order; to make and mend clothes, quilts, pillows, and other household furnishings; to shop for items the household could afford to buy, and scavenge or forage for those it could not; to clean, cook, and bake; and, whenever necessary, to move from unpaid to paid labor to bolster the household income. The growth of manufacturing and of the cash markets of the Northeast had not rendered this labor superfluous. Nor had it reduced housework to unskilled labor. Whether a family lived in a cottage in a town in western New York State or a tenement in Boston, housekeeping remained a vocation of, as Catharine Beecher put it in 1841, "almost incalculable anxieties, vexations, perplexities, and even hard labor."[55]

It was also a vocation that was changing. As the antebellum period wore on, housewives discovered what historians have sometimes failed to see: that, in many ways, women's "traditional" domestic labor was no longer traditional.

Chapter V

"The True Economy of Housekeeping"

Although much divided the laboring classes from the new middle class in antebellum America, the two groups shared a growing alarm about the impact of early industrialization on family life. Working-class men decried an economy in which their wives and children were forced into wage-work. Cherishing a vision of homes fully sanctified against the incursions of the marketplace, they demanded a "family" wage large enough to provide the entire support of the household. Only then, as William English claimed in 1835, would "our wives, no longer doomed to servile labor, . . . be the companions of our fireside and the instructors of our children." It was an ideal shared by members of the new middle class, who confidently celebrated what they supposed to be the complete and successful withdrawal of wives and daughters to "that paradise . . . that bright and central orb," the middle-class home, where neither "strife" nor "selfishness" could enter.[1]

Working-class households had comparatively little power to effect what they so ardently desired; the uncertainty of wages and the climbing costs of housing, food, and clothing all limited their options for shaping the home as a refuge from industrialization. But middle-class families went to great lengths to attempt to make their homes refuges from the rest of society: they divided their residences from their places of business, expelled journeymen and apprentices from their families, and fled farther and farther from the mercantile centers of cities, founding new neighborhoods where prosperity and poverty, family and factory, home and work need never meet.[2]

It was a futile effort, even by the middle class. At almost every point, lived experience bore down hard on the rhetoric. Unless a women was literally to confine herself within doors—scarcely a feasible alternative, given her various responsibilities to her family—she simply could not avoid contact with the larger society she was presumably to be protected from. The layout of antebellum communities, in which widely disparate economic groups still resided on adjacent streets and alleys and mingled in the open-air markets and commercial districts, made such isolation virtually impossible. Living in New York City in the early 1840s, Lydia Maria Child vowed not to allow the "bloated disease, and black gutters" of the city to "constitute the foreground of my picture," but to focus instead on "the pretty parks, dotted about here and there; with the shaded alcoves of the various public gardens, with blooming nooks, and 'sunny spots of greenery.' " Yet her best efforts soon crumbled under the oppressive reality she constantly encountered, a world where "[l]ife is a reckless game, and death is a business transaction," and where even the most optimistic observer was overwhelmed with "an appalling night-mare sensation of vanishing identity; as if I were but an unknown, unnoticed, and unseparated drop in the great ocean of human existence. . . . " Women of the laboring poor and working classes, meanwhile, lived their lives almost as much on the streets as in their homes.[3]

But industrialization, in all of its social, cultural, and economic manifestations, was not merely a specter that waited around the corner for women and men who ventured from their homes. Equally, it was a process *of* the family. As much as in Samuel Slater's mill, American industrialization had been born in American homes—in the material aspirations of European colonists, in the poor soil of New England farms, in family fertility patterns and inheritance strategies, and in countless individual household decisions to purchase rather than produce goods and services. And as it had in part originated in families, so industrialization continued to be a process of family (as well as community) life in the antebellum years—a process that was reshaping how much money households had and how they spent it, how men understood their family roles, and how children perceived their futures.

The industrialization of the household involved much more than changes in family purchasing habits and interpersonal dynamics, however. At its core, industrialization was a reorganization of labor, and that was its chief characteristic in the household as well as in the paid workplace. Over the first half of the nineteenth century, as new technologies replaced older ones and new household needs dictated new labor priorities, both the content and the structure of women's daily work was steadily transformed. As we shall see, the historic relations of gender would give that transformation a distinctive cultural spin, leading contemporary observers to conclude that the central effect of industrialization on housework was to isolate it from the changes in the paid labor market. A century and a half later, that conclusion has been deeply inscribed in our own cultural assumptions. But if we set those assumptions aside for a moment, what is most striking about the early industrial period is, not how different housework was becoming from paid labor, but rather how closely the reorganization of the two forms of work were replicating each other.[4]

To some extent, the changes taking place in households were the direct result of changes occurring outside of them. The reorganization of paid labor and the precariousness of family incomes as a result of that reorganization inevitably sent shock waves reverberating through family life and often necessitated major adjustments in the labor of wives. In the mid–1840s, following the worst financial collapse in the history of the young nation, Lydia Maria Child (whose own marriage suffered from recurrent financial difficulties) cautioned middle-class mothers to raise their children with an eye to the possibility that they would one day be poor, since even "[t]hose who have wealth, have recently had many and bitter lessons to prove how suddenly riches may take to themselves wings. . . ."[5]

The most dramatic illustration of the way changes in the larger community reshaped individual households was the impact of early industrialization and urbanization on the homes of the urban laboring classes, and therefore particularly on the work environment of urban laboring-class women. In *The Sanitary Condition of the Laboring Population*, John Griscom vividly rendered the settings in which many laboring-class wives spent much of each day. "A short time ago," he wrote in one passage,

> I met with the case of a woman, the wife of a tailor living in a noted court in Walker-street, and occupying partly a basement, in which she was compelled to pass much of her time. She has lived there six months, four of which she has been sick with rheumatism, and, on that account, unable to work. Otherwise, she would be able to earn considerable by assisting her husband. They have four children depending upon them, and are

> obliged to seek assistance from the public, in consequence of this sickness. She attributes her disease to the water in the cellar, which runs in, and obliges her to bale out, and wipe up, at every storm.

Griscom was keenly aware of the additional work created for women by "[t]he almost entire absence of household conveniences. . . ." Only a page earlier he had commented on "[t]he deficiency of water, and the want of a convenient place for washing, with no other place for drying clothes than the common sitting and bed room. . . ." But he was more particularly concerned about the health conditions surrounding that labor. Noting the lack of ventilation in most tenement housing, Griscom observed that husbands and sons at least escaped during the hours of their paid employment; while women, who bore a greater responsibility for labor within the home, "*both night and day*, inhale the polluted atmosphere of the dwellings, and are more continually under all the other bad influences of their unfortunate situations."[6]

Many husbands left the conditions of their dwellings only to encounter the equally pernicious conditions of the paid workplace, of course. If their absence from the household did not allow them to avoid the dangers of early industrialization, however, it did significantly affect the organization and scope of their wives' labor. As husbands spent more of their time working away from the household, their ability (and perhaps their willingness) to perform unpaid labor within their families diminished. Certainly, family members other than adult women continued to do part of the household work. Poor men often built the shanties that their families lived in to avoid rents. Husbands sometimes laid morning fires and prepared their own breakfasts. Especially during periods of unemployment, adult males may have participated more regularly in household chores, freeing their wives to earn cash. Depending on the economic status of their families, children ran errands, scavenged, looked after younger siblings, and helped in other ways as their ages permitted. For varying reasons, however, the family's unpaid labor force was shrinking. Middle-class children spent more time in school. Working-class and poor children spent more time at paying jobs. Fewer and fewer husbands earned their incomes where they lived. Increasingly over the antebellum years, the household labor of these various family members gradually devolved upon married women.

This appears to be the explanation for women's growing responsibility for shopping. As we have noted, the mere presence of purchasing activities among a wife's responsibilities was not new. But the extent and frequency of those activities, as recorded in the running entries in antebellum women's letters and diaries, was. "In the afternoon out shopping . . . ," "went out and bought materials for another comfort[er] . . . ," "went down street this morning bought some muslin . . . ," "Went out in the afternoon.—bought a pair of flat irons for which I paid 75 cts . . . ," "went out a little after dinner to see about Some purchases that I made at Tufts which in all amounted to $11 96 cts. . . . " In the seventeenth and eighteenth centuries, the husband often had done at least a part of the family's purchasing, taking a portion of the payment for his work in goods, or (a pattern that persisted among some country people) buying various needed items when he took the farm produce to market. Even at the beginning of the nineteenth century, middle-class husbands frequently purchased the family food, perhaps because the open-air markets seemed too rowdy and unclean for their wives. At mid-century, however, as men came to think of wage-earning as their primary contribution to family maintenance—and as they found shopping less and less compatible with their own work routines outside of the household—shopping seems to have fallen mainly to women. In the 1850s, according to one observer, shopping was men's work only in urban families that took in boarders, and even in those cases the shopping in question was apparently confined to the purchase of groceries.[7]

At the same time, shopping had become a more complicated task. Particularly in the cities, a woman was less likely to know the person she made her purchases from than her mother would have been, and she was less likely to know the quality of the goods she purchased. In warning homemakers against the perils of bargain hunting, Elizabeth Ellet suggested some of the pitfalls that awaited every woman who went to the market: "Cheap tea, coffee, sugar, &c., are all adulterated; cheap vegetables and fruits are generally stale; cheap meat is that which has been sent ready killed to the market, and therefore is by no means as fresh as might be wished; cheap poultry and fish are to be regarded with very great suspicion." Indeed, wives did well to regard the whole market "with very great suspicion."[8]

This devolution onto women of labor that had been either wholly men's or shared by the husband and wife, a process fostered by the growth of wage labor during early industrialization, was also one of the dynamics involved in the growing special association of women with child-rearing. In the colonial period, the responsibility for forming a child's character had been understood to belong primarily to the father in his role as the moral instructor of the family. But, as T. S. Arthur pointed out in his advice to young mothers, many fathers in the pre–Civil War era found it impossible to become deeply involved in the rearing of their children. When called on to share in the burdens of child care, they simply shrugged and asked rhetorically, "Am I not at my work all day?"—a response that not only underscored their assumption that the raising of children to adulthood was properly women's work, but also illuminated the growing ideological separation of cash-earning labor from the household.[9]

Other writers also noticed that husbands were contributing less to the general household labor. Acknowledging that cleaning up yards and unclogging drains was really "man's" work, William Alcott nevertheless was forced to concede that husbands seemed to take a less active role in the physical upkeep of family dwellings than they should have. Consequently, he included that subject in his advice to the young wife, concluding that "it can do no harm to remind the housewife of it, that she may remind him."[10] We can only speculate on whether an occasional reminder was enough to take care of the problem.

Husbands who spent their days in detached work settings—whether they worked in shops or offices in a separate neighborhood, or were lawyers whose business took them out of town, or laborers on travelling construction teams—surely had trouble finding the time to clean yards and clear drains. But at least some women saw the problem of men's withdrawal from household labor as a question of attitude rather than time. "Cleo Dora" addressed this subject in a letter to the editor of the *Anti-Slavery Bugle* in 1846. What husbands needed to be reminded of, she thought, was that the meaning of the female "helpmeet" was to *help*, not to perform *all* of the family labor, and certainly not to be kept hard at work long after her husband had come home to relax: "I pray you," she concluded, "be more just and now and then exhort husbands to do their parts."[11]

The organization of the "outer" world impinged upon the work of the household in other ways as well. As husbands and children increasingly answered the call of factory bells and office schedules, wives necessarily found their own work reorganized to conform to the timetables of early industrialization. Women's work had always been influenced by the comings and goings of the rest of the household, of course, but the prescriptive literature of the antebellum period suggests a new time consciousness, one directly tied to the discipline of the paid workplace. Reflecting this change, William Alcott complained that in some families, "instead of having breakfast upon the table at eight, it does not arrive until three, five, ten, and sometimes nearly fifteen minutes afterward." Alcott was a man who did not believe that wives should see themselves as participants in the economics of family accumulation. Nevertheless, his own comments betrayed just how inseparable the two worlds of "work" and "home" remained, for he used the example of women's cooking for their husbands' employees to make his point: "Do you know how much is the value of the time of ten men, who are compelled by your tardiness to wait ten minutes for their dinner?" he demanded of his readers. "Here are a hundred minutes of valuable time lost to them; how much is that a month?—how much a year? I say nothing of the vexation, but only the pecuniary loss."[12]

As we shall see, working at an open fireplace or on an early nineteenth-century cast-iron stove, wives themselves had a good deal to say "of the vexation." Yet they appear to have taken the admonitions to heart, and they certainly felt the pressure of the new time-discipline in their work. Racing to meet her husband's precise schedule was one of the complaints "Cleo Dora" included in her description of the burdens of the latter-day "helpmeet." In her 1839 *Lady's Annual Register*, Caroline Gilman emphasized the role of the clock in a wife's daily life, recommending that any woman who felt inclined to idleness should "[c]ount the tickings of a clock; do this for an hour. . . . " Harriet Beecher Stowe also recognized the new pace of women's work, declaring that in the nineteenth century the wife had become the very embodiment of time in the family.[13]

All of these changes affected housework—increasing its labor, decreasing its work force, and altering its rhythms. But the antebellum reorganization of housework was not merely reactive, not merely a response to external conditions. In a very real sense, housework itself was being industrialized—and industrialized in ways that often bore strong resemblances to the transformations in paid work.

Over the course of the antebellum period, and particularly in the emerging middle classes, new household technologies continuously reshaped the work of wives. As historian Faye E. Dudden has pointed out, an 1871 list of essential equipment for every woman's kitchen—which included "a raisin-seeder, egg beater, syllabub churn, apple-corer, potato-peeler, and farina kettle"—would appear to bespeak "the limitations rather than . . . the power of mechanical aids" in the performance of a woman's daily work.[14] If the comparison is with Lowell's clamorous mills, the observation is probably accurate enough. Antebellum households contained nothing to compare with the power spindles and looms of the New England textile industry. But Lowell was not the standard of early American industrialization. The shop of the shoemaker or the garment worker offered far more representative examples. Compared with the needle, last, and awl of the shoemaker or the needle and thread of the tailor, the implements of the kitchen look neither meager nor particularly primitive. On the contrary, they look rather like the basic tools of early industrialization.[15]

To focus only on the hand tools of antebellum housework, however, is to miss the considerable extent to which new technologies of the antebellum period reorganized the labor process itself. From *outside* the household, of course, several new technologies had already significantly affected housework: the development of the power spindle and loom had removed most textile production from urban homes. Making cloth more easily accessible, they had raised expectations about the amount of clothing that a family should have and, in so doing, had acted as catalysts to increase the time and labor women spent in sewing. Similarly, the canal boats, steamships, and railroads that brought new goods to city markets had contributed to the increased time women spent shopping. But technological changes occurred *within* the household, as well as outside it. Central furnaces, new heating stoves, indoor pumps, iceboxes, oil lamps, and, perhaps most important, cast-iron cooking stoves and sewing machines were permanently and fundamentally reshaping the conditions and nature of wives' work.

Like those of the paid workplace, the new technologies of the middle-class household were promoted chiefly for their low cost and "labor-saving" capacities. This view was propounded in an 1821 article in the *Ladies' Literary Cabinet*, which claimed that "[t]he female sex" had been among the great beneficiaries of the "labour-saving machines" of modern civilization; and it was echoed in the comments of various observers of antebellum American society. James Dawson Burn commended the virtues of the cast-iron cooking stove, which would, he was confident, "enable the housewife to wash, stew, boil, bake and heat her irons at the same time, and, if necessary, she may cook for a dozen of people without inconvenience."[16]

Women did not find the new stoves so entirely satisfactory. Whether one used wood or coal, the cast-iron stove had to be filled, lighted, and fed; the draft had to be regulated, and the ashes removed. To prevent unpleasant odors from accumulated grease and spillage, the stove had to be cleaned daily. To prevent rusting, it had to be blackened periodically. The blackening and the regulating of the fire meant that the woman who tried both to cook a meal and to present herself in a reasonable condition to eat it was doomed to failure. As often as not, she appeared at the table covered with smudges of soot and ash. More unpleasant, cast-iron stoves burned hot; often, as one woman put it, producing "roasted lady" along with the roasted meat.[17] It is perhaps no wonder that middle-class wives shared a special dread of kitchen work, or that, if they could afford it, they so often hired a cook.

The introduction of the cooking stove had several other important ramifications for middle-class housework. As cooking and eating utensils had become more plentiful and varieties of food more available, eighteenth-century "middling" households had gradually abandoned single-dish meals in favor of more complex preparations. By the end of the century, the transition to multiple-dish dinners had been enshrined in cookbooks, which included directions for dressing meats and making both dinner and dessert pies.[18] With its specialized compartments for baking and its multiple cooking forms, the cast-iron cookstove, which became increasingly common in middle-class homes after about 1830, reinforced the new standards. Far from "labor-saving," the new stove may well have served precisely the end that Burn suggested: to increase productivity, both by increasing the number of people a woman might be expected to cook for and by diversifying the products of cooking.

The new sewing machines that began to appear in middle-class homes near the end of the antebellum period had a similar effect on women's work. Sarah Smith Browne, who once noted that "[t]he sewing machine monopolizes our time," was less than sanguine about the common assumption that the new technology would relieve wives of one of their most constant burdens: "I was once told, if I owned a sewing machine I should have 'nothing to do,' for a great part of the time," Browne observed. "Had I been poetical enough to have imagined such a reality, I should have been wofully disappointed. But I am too much of a diver down to the base of assertions, to cr[e]dit, without being convinced—so I am not discomposed. . . ."[19]

The intrepid Martha Coffin Wright discovered, much to her annoyance, that heating stoves, too, were a mixed blessing to the housewife, providing a warmer working environment only at the price of a string of problems: "As I was looking over my letter," Wright wrote to her sister in November of 1841,

> whack! went the stove equal to a cannon and now both windows are open to let out the smoke. . . . Bang! goes the *blamed* stove again. I had got all the smoke out and closed the windows, and then raised the door to get the stove hot again—before it was too hot I shut it nearly down and it *chosed* to *puff*. . . .

As Harriet Beecher Stowe put it at the conclusion of the Civil War, it was still "intelligent women, who are brought up to do the work of their own families" who were the real "labor-saving institutions" of the household.[20]

Equally important, if perhaps less immediately apparent, was the impact of the changes in housework in severing women from their traditional knowledge of housewifery. In her study of poor and working-class women in antebellum New York City, *City of Women*, Christine Stansell has pointed to the ways the new poverty of the industrialized metropolis made anything like eighteenth-century "notable" housewifery impossible for laboring-class women. In the context of the wage dependency of the urban poor, Stansell observes, the skills of gardening, of manufacturing their own household goods, and of keeping the family's pigs and chickens were virtually irrelevant, since poor families lacked both the raw materials and the space for these activities. Under these conditions, housekeeping became a "makeshift" enterprise—as Stansell puts it, "the catch-as-catch-can" routine of the destitute.[21]

One might want to qualify Stansell's characterization slightly. Many of the skills of the new "makeshift" housekeeping of the urban laboring classes were, in fact, traditional skills of the poor: as we have seen, for example, scavenging (whether in the form of foraging in the forests or swiping the fruit of unguarded trees) was an old and honored domestic art among the poor. Moreover, throughout the colonial period, few households among the urban poor had been able to acquire and keep pigs, chickens, and gardens. In a sense, then, the housekeeping of the antebellum poor was less a "makeshift" variant of a middle-class theme than a separate and distinct tradition.

Yet Stansell is correct that that tradition was changing. In part, the changes were simply quantitative, as more and more of the rural dispossessed (both native-born and immigrant) made their way to antebellum cities. Women brought up in the countryside—whether it be the countryside of New England or old England or Ireland—could not immediately transfer their skills as rural foragers to the city. In Boston or Hartford or New York, it was of little use to a woman to know how to cut pine knots for lighting or where to find the best berry patch or peat bog. Far more telling for the survival of her family would be her cleverness in knowing where to find odd bags of coffee or flour or how to blend into a crowd during a fire as she "profit[ted] by stealing goods during the conflagration."[22]

In part, the transformation of working-class housewifery was directly related to the new wage-dependency and to the problems of maneuvering, with very little cash, through an increasingly cash-defined market. Women in all but the wealthiest families had to apportion their cash budgets carefully, but among the urban poor this conserving was a particularly developed skill. A woman must know, for example, when the market vendors slashed their prices at the end of a day's trade, so that more could be purchased with less; and what pawnbroker was likely to give the most on account for clothing, to be held over until the next payday; and how long a bill, along with a landlord's or grocer's patience, could be stretched before the credit was exhausted and the family thrown out on the street or reduced to scavenging for food. These were the fine calculations of cost the welfare of the family depended on—the art forms as well as the survival strategies of the housewives of the new urban poor.

While it was the new urban poverty that most fundamentally reshaped the labor of urban laboring-class wives, it was the new prosperity of industrialization that precipitated the severest disruptions in the work of middle-class women—in particular, the new domestic technologies that gradually interrupted the practical transmission of traditional bodies of knowledge from one generation of women to the next. Coal- and wood-burning stoves burned differently and required different tending than had the old open-hearth wood fireplaces. The new cast-iron construction affected cooking temperatures and heat intensity, and the design of the stoves—their new baking compartments and the new arrangement of pans over the fire—required new techniques for controlling cooking speed and temperatures. Some designs were so difficult to operate that households reverted to earlier versions in search of the tastes and textures they had become accustomed to. In 1840, Samuel Rodman of New Bedford, Massachusetts, noted in his diary: "Had a new grate put into our kitchen stove this m[ornin]g, probably the last as the verdict of the family is decidedly against a continuance of the 'Rotary', the defect or failure in baking being the most important objection." Catharine Beecher agreed that making decent baked goods was one of the great challenges of the new stoves. "We cannot but regret," she lamented in her 1869 *American Woman's Home*, "for the sake of bread, that our old steady brick ovens have been almost universally superceded by those of ranges and cooking-stoves, which are infinite in their caprices. . . ."[23]

Sewing machines had a comparable impact on the traditional crafts of women's domestic labor. Although women could and did still use hand-stitching for much of their sewing, the increased speed of the new machines made it desirable that any woman who could get access to one should use it as much as possible. Alas, sewing at a machine was not a skill that was latent in the female chromosome: it had to be learned—virtually from scratch. While some earlier domestic employments (spinning, for example) might have honed some of the same motor skills as operating the treadle of a sewing machine, from the turn of the century onward, fewer and fewer American women had had cause to practice those older crafts. In any event, developing the even rhythm of an expert spinner would not have prepared a woman for the mysteries of the actual sewing mechanism, which seemed to have a malicious will of its own: "The machine behaves like an imp sometimes," Elizabeth Cabot complained to her sister in 1860, "will break the needle and then the thread, and do all manner of odious things with no apparent cause. . . . " Cabot nevertheless concluded that all women should learn to operate the unruly contraptions. Her reasons for that decision demonstrate the capacity of the gender ideology to absorb and embody even the sharpest contradictions: sewing at a machine, Cabot believed, "would be excellent training . . . because it so insists on having everything perfectly adjusted, your mind calm, and your foot and hand steady and quiet and regular in their motions."[24] The new work discipline of early industrialization, it seems, was the perfect regime for developing the placid and demure qualities required by the domestic female ideal.

Understanding domestic labor as a collection of technological systems, each of which was based on a shared body of knowledge and skills and many of which were undergoing profound change, may help to explain a widely discussed phenomenon of the antebellum era: the apparent failure of many mothers to pass along domestic skills to their daughters. The problem was recognized widely enough to provide one of the central themes for the most popular novel of the antebellum period, Susan Warner's *The Wide, Wide World*. First published in 1850, *The Wide, Wide World* is something of a female-centered *Pilgrim's Progress*, recounting the long and arduous journey of little Ellen Montgomery toward Christian womanhood. Much of that journey is chronicled through the symbols of women's domestic labor, as Ellen undergoes a slow and painful education in the mysteries of housewifery.

Ellen is raised in the city. We learn little of her mother other than that she is ill and unable to adequately prepare her daughter for adulthood—a point that is underscored by Mrs. Montgomery's inability to accompany the child on her harrowing expeditions to the city's stores. When her parents travel abroad in a vain attempt to restore her mother's health, Ellen is sent to the country, where she will receive at the hands of her Aunt Fortune the domestic education her mother could not provide.

Housework is not the only aspect of Ellen's education that must be completed in the countryside, and Aunt Fortune is not her only mentor. Sympathetic though her situation is, Ellen is an annoyingly self-centered child, painfully deficient in self-discipline and benevolence, qualities she eventually learns through the model of her beloved Alice Humphreys. But in the course of the story, it is often in her ignorance of, and disrespect for, housework that the abysmal state of Ellen's soul is most concretely rendered, particularly in contrast with the domestic expertise of her aunt. Dividing her attention between skillet, pan, and coffeepot, dashing now to the pantry for cream, and now again for flour, turning the pork, stirring the potatoes, bubbling the hot fat "as if by magic, to a thick, stiff, white froth,"[25] Aunt Fortune—while not the emblem of ideal womanhood in the novel—is the very embodiment of accomplished housewifery. It is a tradition Ellen must come to value and must acknowledge a bond with if she is to continue toward her goal: a necessary reunion with a female domestic experience disrupted by the process of urbanization. Casting Ellen as Everywoman, Warner transforms her domestic education into a parable of the condition of young women in general in the antebellum era.[26]

It was an allegory Warner could count on her readers to understand. Indeed, the problem of educating daughters in the skills of housewifery was noted by a variety of observers, both men and women, and was generally diagnosed as acutest among middle-class and wealthy urban women. Englishman James Dawson Burn (always a jaundiced observer of women's work) complained bitterly about the problem, claiming that while "[i]n the country, young women are instructed in all the household duties . . . in the towns it is difficult to find a girl who can . . . do the duties of a domestic establishment." To Burn's mind, access to markets and to the new "labor-saving" technologies had so simplified the labor of housework that urban mothers no longer practiced the skills of housewifery themselves. Much less could they teach their daughters.[27]

Females who published advice on the proper running of a household seldom assumed that urban women of even fairly prosperous households lacked work to do. But some of them *did* agree with Burn that the lack of domestic training in the daughter spoke primarily of the misguided values of the mother. Novelist Louisa Tuthill suggested that many women were too involved in voluntary charitable work to pay proper attention to their domestic responsibilities, especially to the rearing of their children. Caroline Gilman contended that mothers preferred to see their daughters spend their time in "intellectual" pursuits. Elizabeth Ellet thought that "Americans in general have little attachment to home" and that daughters in particular were encouraged to learn "to shine in society" rather than "to perform the homely duties. . . ."[28]

Catharine Beecher, who returned to this theme again and again in her writings, agreed with many of her contemporaries that Americans in general, and specifically mothers in prosperous families, tended to denigrate the manual labor of housework. But in tandem with this interpretation, Beecher suggested another: that unpaid housewives were experiencing an abrupt reorganization of their labor, one that rendered some aspects of their traditional knowledge obsolete while requiring new skills as yet imperfectly learned. Housework was especially difficult in the United States, Beecher contended, since in America the volatility of a democratic society constantly conspired with the fluctuations of an expanding economy to disrupt the old, known routines. In this state of constant transition, mothers themselves had never been adequately trained for their domestic responsibilities, and therefore made poor teachers for their daughters. Devoting page after page of *The American Woman's Home* to the new technologies of the household—chimneys, ranges and cooking stoves, illuminants, furnaces, earth-closets—Beecher provided her reader with a step-by-step education in the new arts of housewifery. As she acknowledged, developing the new skills could be difficult and frustrating. In some areas, like baking in the ovens of the new cast-iron stoves, even she could offer only a few general suggestions and a wish of good luck. "The problem in baking, then," she concluded, "is the quick application of heat rather below than above the loaf, and its steady continuance. . . . Every housewife must watch her own oven to know how this can best be accomplished." The anonymous author of *Women's Influence and Woman's Mission* agreed with Beecher's diagnosis of the general problem. Taking to task the nineteenth-century housewives who "smile with condescending piety at the blinded state of our respected grandmothers," she observed caustically that at least eighteenth-century women had been educated to their work.[29]

Women sought to adapt to the new skills of housework in a variety of ways. As Elizabeth Cabot's experience using her mother-in-law's sewing machine suggests, women readily pooled information and skills with their relatives and neighbors. Sarah Smith Browne, too, recorded this form of skill- and equipment-sharing, noting in her diary that "M. A. [?] P. comes and practices on the sewing machine. . . ." But they also avidly consumed the flood of women's journals, treatises, and household manuals that promised to disclose the new mysteries of shopping, recipes for foods that had not been widely available in the eighteenth century, new cooking methods and kitchen designs, and information on the most efficient overall organization of household labor. Furthermore, as the antebellum period wore on, these reference works grew more and more detailed—a process which may be seen as culminating in Beecher and Stowe's 1869 *American Woman's Home*.[30]

As well as adding work and raising standards of performance, the domestic inventions of the first half of the nineteenth century frequently created their own health and safety hazards in the home, especially for the women who cared for them. Lamp fuels were highly flammable. Cleaning and lighting the lamps was skilled and painstaking work, labor that the mistress of a household usually reserved for herself even when help was available. In 1869, Harriet Beecher Stowe echoed Martha Coffin Wright's frustrations with the heating stove, adding a warning that, in a closed room, a stove

> burns away the vital portion of the air quite as fast as the occupants breathe it away. The sealing-up of fireplaces and introduction of air-tight stoves may, doubtless, be a saving of fuel: it saves, too, more than that; in thousands and thousands of cases it has saved people from all further human wants, and put an end forever to any needs short of the six feet of narrow earth which are man's only inalienable property.

Visiting in the northeastern United States, Fredrika Bremer complained of the "dry, close, unwholesome heat" of furnaces, "which always gives me a sensation of pain as well as drowsiness in the head," and of the "heat of the gas-lights." She thought that such conditions helped explain "why women [in the United States] . . . should be delicate and out of health. . . ."[31]

Although the work performed there by wives was largely unpaid, the transformations going on in middle-class homes did not differ as dramatically from the paid work of their husbands as sentimental contemporary descriptions of the "home" generally implied. There are two points to be made here. First, as we have seen, the transformations of paid work in the antebellum period were both slow and uneven. Most artisans still worked in small-scale shops where their labor, if increasingly specialized, was far from fully mechanized. Similarly, business methods remained distinctly "pre-modern," and office procedures were far from either routinized or fully rationalized. If much of women's work remained comparatively casualized, this did not, in and of itself, distinguish its organization from that of paid work in the antebellum period.

At the same time, many women expressed the feeling that the traditional rhythms of housekeeping were being supplanted by a new time- and task-discipline, one they associated with the world of paid business. The parallel was most clearly developed in the various household advice manuals that achieved such great popularity among middle-class women in the antebellum years—another characteristic that may help explain precisely *why* these manuals were bought and read so widely. In her 1841 *Treatise on Domestic Economy*, Catharine Beecher argued that the economy of housework required the "wisdom, firmness, tact, discrimination, prudence, and versatility" of a politician, an economy of time and expenses "bound by the same rules as relate to the use of property," characterized by the "system and order" of a business, and, like an office routine, intended "to promote systematic and habitual industry." Beecher qualified the comparison only to the extent of noting that, where accounting procedures were concerned, businessmen seemed rather too "desultory." She may not have been far wrong on this point. Less than a decade earlier, when Secretary of the Treasury McLane had attempted to survey the manufactures of the United States, his field reporters complained that entrepreneurs were unable "to state, with accuracy," the capital investments and operating costs of their businesses.[32]

Women acknowledged the similarities between housework and paid work in the very way they went about their daily lives. It was not unusual, for example, for a woman to refer to her domestic responsibilities as her "business." "Linus says I must wright a few lines," Sarah Smith began her letter. "I commence with giveing you some account of my business which is spinning[,] weaving[,] sewing and so on. . . . " She meant, of course, not work done at home and destined for the market, but work done within the family and entirely for the family's use.[33]

In her study of domestic service in nineteenth-century America, Faye E. Dudden has commented perceptively on the changing relationships of servants and mistresses over the course of the early nineteenth century, noting that the work of supervising servants offered growing "parallels to the work of entrepreneurial or managerial men."[34] But it was not only in this paid work relationship that wives saw housework as similar to business. Their understanding of the household and its resources as an ongoing economic enterprise was reflected also in the assiduity with which middle-class wives kept household records, reducing even that most hallowed of woman's missions, child-rearing, to an exact rendering of accounts. When Ann Garfield sent her son Nathaniel to a wet nurse for weaning, she kept a detailed list of the clothing and supplies she sent with him: "5 diapers[,] night gown[,] night Cap[,] 2 check aprons[,] white jane apron . . . , 7 plain squares[,] day Cap[,] Yellow blanket [for] cradle[,] small Pillow, pillow case[,] small rose blanket . . . ," and on and on. She expected every item to be accounted for upon his return.[35]

Although wives often complained that their husbands did not adequately inform them of the full range of family finances and debts, women apparently often kept the household accounts. Sarah Smith Browne spent large parts of at least three days in January of 1858 engaged in this activity, which was routine enough in her experience to warrant the simple entry: "[S]et down as usual, accounts."[36]

Women also established economic networks that resembled the family networks that supported their husbands' businesses. As we have seen, through these networks, women were able to stretch the family resources—to obtain items unavailable in their own communities, or to get better prices, or both. The exchanges of service were based on friendship, but they retained a degree of formality that recognized the time and work involved. "[T]he lady for whom I wished the hat purchased has changed her mind," one New Haven woman wrote her friend in Boston: "I am very sorry to have put your Aunt to so much trouble . . . in shoping. . . . I hope I shall never trouble you again in this way."[37] Here, too, however, women were careful to keep exact accounts. "[T]here was a little defficiency in your purse," a New Haven woman wrote her Guilford friend. "[Y]ou said there was 7$ and a half[.] I counted it . . . and found there was but $7.32[.] Were you aware of it . . . ?"[38] Sometimes, the woman requesting the service indicated the value she attached to it by suggesting that her correspondent keep the "money that was left, to compensate in part for your trouble, time, &c."[39]

Individually in their private correspondence and journals, and perhaps in response to the swelling tide of expert household advice manuals, women articulated their own understanding of the role of housework in the economy. Not infrequently, wives expressed an awareness that husbands' wages did not fully cover the cash needs of the family. They assumed that some income-producing responsibilities might well be included in a woman's "housework." In *The American Frugal Housewife*, Lydia Maria Child discussed a variety of ways wives could add to the cash resources of the family, including selling vials and bottles ("Apothacaries and grocers will give something for them"), rags ("the white ones . . . bring a higher price"), ashes, and grease. Growing up in Northampton, Massachusetts, Caroline Clapp Briggs described her household work in a way that defied easy division into paid and unpaid labor:

"We were a very busy family," she remembered, "having only one servant [and three boarders]; a good deal of housework was done by my sister and myself, and after that there was always sewing and sometimes copying,—anything we could find to do to eke out a living." Clapp did not distinguish between the work she did for her family's three boarders (which brought necessary cash into the family) and the unpaid work she did for her own family: both were "housework." At the same time, both forms of labor, as well as the sewing and copying that she did for pay, were included in the general category of "ek[ing] out a living."[40]

Women recognized the economic value of housework in a second way. Implicitly or explicitly, many wives in the antebellum period defined housework as the labor required to bridge the gap between a cash income and the actual labor value of household maintenance, and thus as labor of essential economic worth, necessary to the structure and prosperity of industrial society. Women frequently noted the importance of their work in avoiding cash outlays. As prices rose in Massachusetts in 1836, Lydia D. Pierce recorded the efforts of wives to stretch out their family budgets:

> Flour is very high[.] [P]eople begin to use potatoes with their flour. . . . I put six boiled potatoes into a batch of nutcakes today and they were certainly very good[.] [T]ry it if you please[.] [T]hey put potatoes into bread, pie crust, biscuit[,] nutcakes and I don[']t know what else[.]

She closed with evident self-satisfaction: "[N]ecessity is the mother of invention you know."[41]

"The true economy of housekeeping," Lydia Maria Child explained, "is simply the art of gathering up all the fragments, so that nothing be lost. . . . Nothing should be thrown away so long as it is possible to make use of it. . . . " Harriet Beecher Stowe considered that it was the function of wives to be "the care-taking and saving part of creation—the authors and conservators of economy." Caroline Gilman was even more pointed in her contention that families "owed their prosperity full as much to the propriety of female management as to the knowledge and activity of the father."[42]

At issue here were two competing conceptions of how the nineteenth-century economy operated. Against the notion that early industrialization had created a fully cash-based economy to which both women and women's work were peripheral, women posed their own experience: that antebellum life continued to rely upon a combination of labors, some paid and some unpaid, and that "economy" was still a process that required the saving and conserving, as well as the getting, of resources. In this, housewives of the antebellum period reflected the continuing importance of the colonial concept of stewardship to material life. As Stowe noted, "as a general rule, man earns and woman saves and applies." That the economic value of saving and applying went largely unrecognized sometimes elicited a sharp response from women. When Martha Coffin Wright's husband, David, claimed that women's chief economic contribution to their families was to drive their husbands into bankruptcy through extravagance, Martha responded:

> Women are very apt to look on with apprehension and endeavor to avert by such arguments as they can use, the mania of speculation, the reckless endorsing for others and the thousand unprofitable schemes that are hurrying [men] to ruin, but those arguments are not spoken through a trumpet, nor on the house top. . . .

Her conclusion was particularly telling, however: "[T]he innumerable acts of self denial that [women] practice with the hope of keeping back the crisis," she observed, "are untold. . . . "[43]

Occasionally, women formulated their understanding of the economic value of housework in more concrete terms. In 1836, in her *Recollections of a Housekeeper*, Caroline Gilman noted that *some* aspects of household labor had already achieved a wage form and wondered why the wife's housework should not be similarly de-privatized: "We have a partial system, which it appears to me might easily be carried through the whole order of social life. We have our chimney-sweeps, our wood-sawyers, our bakeries; why not have our grand cooking establishments, our scourers, our window-cleaners, &c?" From this proposed wholesale commercialization of housework Gilman excepted only child-rearing, which she believed should remain in the hands of individual mothers.[44]

In 1848, Jane Sophia Appleton published a story entitled, "Sequel to the 'Vision of Bangor in the Twentieth Century.' " A response to a utopian sketch that denigrated women's abilities to function outside of the home, the "Sequel" describes the experiences of a man who dreams he has been transported forward to the year 1978. Among the advances of the twentieth century, according to Appleton—and the single change most essential to the promotion of women's civil and political rights—is the de-privatization of housework and the conversion of cooking, child care, laundry, sewing, and cleaning into collective and socially valued labor "command[ing] as high remuneration as any."[45]

Appleton's sketch drew deliberately on the ideas of Charles Fourier, whose utopian model of a collectivized community aroused considerable interest among antebellum social reformers. Indeed, the reorganization of domestic labor was an aspect of several of the utopian and religious movements of the period. Of particular interest among these was Shakerism, which had actually been founded much earlier in Europe but thrived in America during these years. By the mid–nineteenth century, a majority of the Shakers were women—a fact at least some observers, Mary Antoinette Doolittle among them, attributed to the visible importance that Shaker communities attached to women's domestic labor. Doolittle, an elderess in the Shaker community at Mount Lebanon, New York, contended that this was because the Shakers recognized "woman's rights, and her capabilities as a counselor and co-worker with man in all that pertains to physical and spiritual life."[46]

The Shaker community preserved the division of labor by sex, and domestic labor remained the work of women. Indeed, individual women continued to perform domestic labor for individual men, with a particular woman assigned to do the mending and sewing of a particular man. Yet several principles distinguished the Shaker community from the wider society. First, Shakers believed in celibacy. Women's work was not performed in the relation of marriage. Indeed, women, like men, did much of their labor in same-sex groups. Equally important, the Shakers disavowed the private ownership of property; wealth was shared in the community. Finally, not only labor, but decision-making, was divided by sex; Shaker women maintained their own hierarchy of authority through a council of elderesses parallel in structure to the council of elders. While the elders may well have had greater decision-making power in the overall affairs of the community, the elderesses oversaw the organization of women's separate lives.

Doolittle argued that these principles were of decisive importance to the organization and quality of life among the Shakers. With the founding of the Shaker church, she argued:

> Woman was no longer a slave in bonds, forced as it were to bear down the name of some man to posterity and bend over the cradle and sing lullaby as her only right, and the highest aim of her existence; but she became a co-worker with her brother man in every department of life. Hence they stood shoulder to shoulder, each occupying their own sphere, yet working in harmonious relations together.

This structuring of labor, property ownership, and social relations may well have served to underscore the equal importance of women's domestic work. Unable to subsume individual women's labor under their own, Shaker men evidently attributed a greater value to housework than was the case in antebellum society generally. "Brethren and sisters [are] mutually interested in each other's labor and prosperity," Doolittle noted. The historical record indicates that Shaker men demonstrated this interest concretely, through the invention and/or improvement of various mechanisms to simplify household labor: a washing machine, a stove-cover lifter, a pea-sheller, a butter-worker, a self-acting cheese press, the common clothes pin, an apple parer, and the flat broom.[47]

Although women occasionally objected in private to attempts to discount the value of their household contribution, in their published writings they more often counseled each other to silence and forebearance. Catharine Beecher advised women to *expect* to have their schedules disrupted by "a heedless husband, and young children. . . . " At such times, a woman did well to check her frustration: "In many cases . . . it is impossible not to feel some irritation. But it *is* always possible to refrain from angry tones." Elizabeth Ellet agreed, adding that a wife should not anticipate recognition of either the difficulties or the accomplishments of her labor:

> Neither would we have domestic economy and home duties vaunted, or made the constant theme of conversation; they are the private employments of a woman. . . . When a man returns to his home . . . , fatigued and perhaps disappointed by the business of the day, he does not want to be annoyed by the details of domestic accidents. . . .

Ellet was candid about the basis for her advice: "Men," she reminded her readers, "are free to come and go as they list, they have so much liberty of action, so many out-door resources if wearied with in-doors, that it is good policy, if nothing else, to make home attractive as well as comfortable."[48]

Ellet's less-than-subtle reminder that women were economically dependent on marriage for their survival probably did not need proof for her female readers. Most women knew all too well that, for them, the presumably free contract of marriage was often the only contract available. Although some women (for example, Catharine Sedgwick in *Married or Single?*) tried to make the argument than an unmarried life could be satisfying both materially and emotionally, contemporary studies of the low wages and unhealthful working conditions of wage-earning women demonstrated all too clearly that survival was tenuous for the woman alone. The political economy of antebellum life offered few vocations other than housework for most women.

Chapter VI

The Political Economy of Housework

Health reformer John Griscom was a man of nineteenth-century sensibilities. When he appealed for improvement in the housing conditions of the laboring classes of New York City, he sought reform, not only as "a measure of humanity, of justice to the poor, [and] of safety to the whole people," but also, and most earnestly, in the interest of "economy to the public treasury." That interest was affected in several ways, the most obvious of which was the direct cost of charity. What Griscom was more concerned with, however, in invoking "the public treasury," was the lost economic potential of people who lived—and died—in the miserable conditions of the antebellum urban working classes: " 'Labor is wealth,' " he reminded his readers, not only a commodity to be bought and sold, but also a resource to be "protected, improved, and facilitated . . . ." To the extent that the productive potential of labor was dissipated, the wealth of the society was diminished.[1]

Living in a period of substantial (though uneven) economic expansion, Griscom could assume that his readers would grasp this last point quickly, and would share his sense of its gravity. His goal was a more specific one: to underscore the connection between the productive capacity of labor and the living conditions of the laboring classes. In doing so, he hoped to prompt among the more prosperous classes a conviction that it was in their own interest to raise the living standards of the poor. "Sound vigorous health is an essential pre-requisite to the proper performance of all labor," he insisted—and that was a function of the home.[2] The "private" sphere of laboring-class life redounded directly upon the profit-and-loss ledgers of the employing classes. The mechanic, manufacturer, or construction boss who thought to multiply his gain by pushing laboring-class families into an ever-worsening material environment was simply losing value on his investment.

In attempting to delineate this linkage between the profits of the paid workplace and the conditions of the household, John Griscom came as close as anyone in the antebellum period to developing a theory of the economic value of unpaid domestic work. He did not finally offer such a theory. Rather, he ended his analysis as he had begun it, with the bleak prediction that the laboring classes—their "whitened and cadaverous countenance[s]" peering out from the "dark and damp" caves that passed for homes—must inevitably die out altogether if employers did not ensure some improvement in the material conditions of working-class homes.[3]

Although Griscom himself did not develop all the implications of his argument, his analysis does provide a window through which to begin to explore the general economic functions of antebellum housework, especially the role of household labor systems in structuring and supporting the emergence of industrial capitalism in the Northeast. This is a question that goes beyond the simple matter of whether or not housewives were "working." It also goes beyond the matter of whether changes in the organization of domestic labor were similar to the changes historians have associated with the advent of industrialization in paid work. At issue is whether the labor that women were performing within and for their families was in some way integral to the process of industrialization itself—not only to the fact that industrialization occurred, but to the particular shape it assumed in the antebellum Northeast.

By and large, historians of the economic transition of late eighteenth- and nineteenth-century America have assumed that "industrialization" was, by definition, a phenomenon of the paid workplace, exterior to family life. The comparatively few studies that have looked beyond the shops and factories to the households of the Northeast have done so primarily by way of examining the *effect* of industrialization on the presumably distinct systems of the family; focusing, for example, on paid outwork and other cash relations in the household.[4] According to this model, households were altered by industrialization, but the purposes, structures, and labor patterns of family life were not themselves instrumental in the transition.

This is a model with a number of limitations. Perhaps most glaringly, identifying the process of industrialization with the reorganization of paid work severely circumscribes our ability to observe and understand the role of gender in the structuring of an emerging industrial economy. Although women have been involved in cash-based labor throughout the history of the United States, much of that work has been comparatively unorganized and erratic, interwoven with their unpaid labor. Consequently, the history of paid work, especially when "paid work" is analyzed as an experience separable from other aspects of social life, is most visibly a history of men's experiences. The result is a construction of industrialization as a largely genderless process—genderless both because men are treated as un-gendered creatures, and because the transformation is assumed to have raised gender issues only peripherally. Only women have gender, in this analysis, and women appear in the story only when they, too, enter regular wage work. Any possible larger role of gender in the transformation is reduced to the matter of discrimination against women in hiring, firing, promotion, and on-the-job treatment.

But this is surely too narrow a formulation of the reach and depth of gender as a central category of experience in American society, particularly given the preeminence of gender as the organizing principle of both labor and authority in the preindustrial era. Left unexamined is the larger importance of gender, not only in the disposition of paid labor in industrial society (that is, in who takes what paid job and how they are treated there), but in defining the very concept of labor on which industrial capitalism was based. The ways *unpaid* labor within the family may have contributed to the transition to an industrial society, and particularly the specific ways the very unpaid character of housework may have played a constitutive economic role in the larger processes of industrialization, remain at best ancillary to the discussion. The questions, then, are two: What was the material relation between unpaid housework and the emergence of an industrial economy; and was it significant to this relation that unpaid housework was almost exclusively the province of women?

In the colonial period, family survival had been based on two types of resources: the skills of the wife in housewifery, and the skills and property of the husband in agriculture. Both sets of skills involved the production of tangible goods for the family—such items as furnishings, food, and fabrics. Both were likely to involve some market exchange, as husbands sold grain and wives sold eggs or cheese, for example. And both involved services given directly to the household. By the early nineteenth century, however, husbands' contributions to their households were focused disproportionately on market exchange—on the cash they brought into the family—while their direct activities in producing both goods and services for the family had vastly decreased.

The meaning of this shift has often been misread, interpreted as an indication that households were no longer dependent on goods and services provided from within but had instead become reliant upon the market for their survival. As we have seen, there is certainly some basis for such a conclusion: by the antebellum period, many families did not have access to the raw materials and resources necessary to produce the array of goods once characteristic of households throughout the Northeast. At the same time, the "market dependency" of antebellum households can be overstated. Outside of the elite, few antebellum families had access to enough cash to be literally market-dependent, even had the market been fully and plentifully enough developed to provide all of the goods and services required for family survival, which it was not. One could certainly purchase a variety of clothes, for example; but, as we have seen, even urban women were often unable to find the particular items they sought in local stores. Similarly, in the cities one could purchase an array of prepared foods: bread, pies, coffee, roasted corn, meals to be eaten on the premises, and even hot meals to go. But most Americans would have found themselves going hungry had they tried to depend upon these services, which were largely limited to urban areas and restricted even there.

More important, few families could afford to purchase all of the goods and services they required for "maintenance." This lesson is perhaps most graphically drawn in the cycles of pawning and redeeming that underlay the household economies of the laboring poor. There just was not enough cash to cover even the most fundamental of needs: food, clothing, and shelter. But even in less-marginal households, consumerism was sharply curtailed by the amount of available cash. Choices constantly had to be made: to purchase a new cloak or try to refurbish the old one for another season, to hire a woman to help with the wash or lay aside some money to buy a house. In these patterns of mundane decisions lay the essential economic character of antebellum households: they were in fact "mixed economies"—economic systems that functioned on the bases of both paid and unpaid labor and were dependent on both. They required paid labor for the cash to purchase some goods and services. Equally, they depended on unpaid labor in the household to process those commodities into consumable form and to produce other goods and services directly, without recourse to the cash market.

On the simplest level, housework was the labor of the second sort—the labor provided directly to the family. In that sense, domestic work retained its "traditional" character and seemed to belong to a world in which household maintenance had depended largely on labor exchanges within the family. But the growing complexity of household economies in the early nineteenth century—that is, their increasingly "mixed" character—had imparted to domestic labor a second, more "modern" function: that of mediating between the demands of the cash market and the often-quite-different imperatives of family survival.

Women's expanded labor as shoppers, discussed above, exemplifies the new economic function of housework. In the context of her family's increased dependence on the market for both raw materials and finished goods, a woman's proficiency as a shopper could have direct and grave implications for her household's ability to survive and prosper. A knowledge of both prices and materials was essential, with the best bargain being struck, often, only by purchasing in bulk and adding one's own (unpaid) labor to the product once it was carried home. The wife of a machinist explained with pride the strategies through which she attempted to manipulate the market to her family's greatest advantage: "I know I saved at least a quarter pound of soap each week by my plan of always cutting up a large quantity of it into pieces of conventional size, and spreading them out in the attic to harden well. A piece of soap thus hardened will not melt away as rapidly as a fresh one. . . . " She also found that a knowledge of fabrics enabled her to stretch the household clothing budget: "I have always found it the cheapest way to buy good material, even if at first the cost is greater, than to get a coarse or thin article," she advised.[5] Perhaps with the model of shopping in mind, Harriet Beecher Stowe defined housework as "the science of *comparative values*." It was a science she had studied carefully. Her own purchasing activities included buying furnishings, clothing, fabrics, and food, as well as the constant array of little items (ribbons, combs, etc.) that constantly intrude upon the graver matters of daily life.[6]

Housewives found that the new "comparative" function of housework (its importance in mediating between the cash market and family survival) effectively redefined the entire domestic system, reshaping the economic relations of even women's most traditional labors. This was clearly the case with household manufacturing and women's horticultural work. As we have seen, both persisted at surprisingly high levels in many families, and both supplied essential products. But they persisted less as independently valuable forms of labor than as expressions of—and in exquisite tension with—the extent of the family's cash resources. As Catharine Beecher observed, "[E]very woman must accommodate herself to the peculiarities of her situation. If she has a large family, and a small income, she must devote far more time to the simple duty of providing food and raiment, than would be right were she in affluence, and with a small family." As Beecher suggested, these decisions were based largely on market factors: first and foremost, the size of the household income, but also the size of the family and its access to markets. Most middle-class women abandoned spinning and weaving simply because they could obtain fabric cheaply enough on the market to make it not worth their labor time to manufacture the cloth themselves; they did *not* give up sewing, both because ready-made goods were *not* widely available and because their cost was *not* low enough to prompt a redirection of household labor. In 1847, Martha Coffin Wright decided to quit keeping her own chickens for essentially the same set of reasons: "they are so troublesome in the gardens and it costs as much to feed them as to buy eggs."[7] In the overall consideration of the value of her labor, it made sense simply to purchase the eggs and to spend her time elsewhere in the family economy. In few households, however, was the family so small, the market so abundant and cheap, or cash so plentiful, as to permit wives to give up household production altogether.

Indeed, as we have seen, in a number of households the family-to-cash relationship was sufficiently out of balance to require wives to produce, not only for their families, but also directly for the market itself. Sometimes this labor was quite visible—for example, when a wife took in wash, sold strawberries, or did outwork in the needle industry. But when a woman's labor supplied a part of the wage contract between her husband and a hired worker, or when her presence in the family store obviated the need to hire an additional clerk, her contribution was likely to remain largely invisible, since no separate accounts indicated the money she saved her husband by doing so. Seldom was the cash that these women supplied to their families inessential, even in the emerging middle class. The author of *Six Hundred Dollars a Year*, for example, recorded that the first $100 of her earnings from sewing and making artificial flowers bought the clothing, blankets, and furnishings necessary for her first child. Her second $100 of earnings purchased the family a government bond. That bond and the additional $250 that she earned over the course of the following several years were the basis of a family savings program.[8]

In an important sense, then, the product of the labor of housework was the household itself, conceived as an evolving array of requirements, some stable and long-term, some arising from the contingencies of the moment, founded on the material and psychosocial needs of its members. The departure of men from the household to sell their labor power as a commodity on the market had made this the specialized work of women; industrialization had made it essential.

Much of the work of producing the household was indirect and focused on creating the general conditions necessary for individual members to go about their daily work. In both working-class and middle-class households, food had to be cooked,[9] clothes had to be laundered, and floors had to be scrubbed. Mattresses and pallets had to be aired, dishes had to be washed, candles and lamps had to be tended, and fires had to be built and regulated.

But much of the labor of housework involved the direct maintenance of family members—for example, by nursing them back to health when they were ill. While some households had recourse to a physician or a midwife, most of the daily health care of children, husbands, and servants was provided by wives. When Sarah Munro's son Josiah fell ill with the measles, the family called in a doctor, but it was Sarah who tended him through the crisis. In March of 1826, Sarah Connell Ayer recorded in her diary that it had been a particularly difficult month for her: " . . . I have had a very sick family. Our hired girl, boy, and the children have all been confined at once with the meazles. I have had no time to write, my time being fully occupied in attending the sick." The illness of household members could pose problems beyond simply augmenting women's regular work. It could also create gaps in the family labor system—gaps the wife usually had to fill. Hattie Bardwell's illness in November of 1858 meant not only that her mother had responsibility for her care, but that Hattie's share of the housework devolved upon her mother. The author of *Six Hundred Dollars a Year* described the difficulties of a neighbor whose husband was in poor health. The woman not only nursed her husband herself, but also took over operation of the family store and "toiled constantly with her needle to supply the deficiency" of income created by the medical bills.[10]

Child-rearing also illustrated the complicated ways housework "produced" the household, both in the present and into the future. As we have seen, particularly in nineteenth-century cities, where the dangers to children were legion, a mother's ability to supervise her children could literally mean the difference between life and death. Especially in laboring-class households, moreover, child-rearing also involved producing new contributors to the family economy. Although children in poor families sometimes left the household early to participate in paid work, they could also be taught skills within the household to benefit the family. As Lydia Maria Child pointed out, there were many ways, both directly remunerative and not, even "[a] child of six years old can be made useful":

> Children can very early be taught to take all the care of their own clothes.
>
> They can knit garters, suspenders, and stockings; they can make patchwork and braid straw; they can make mats for the table, and mats for the floor; they can weed the garden, and pick cranberries from the meadow, to be carried to market. . . .
>
> I once visited a family where the most exact economy was observed. . . . In this family, when the father brought home a package, the older children would, of their own accord, put away the paper and twine neatly, instead of throwing them in the fire, or tearing them to pieces. . . .

Child concluded with a story intended to underscore the ultimate economic value of this training:

> The other day I heard a mechanic say, "I have a wife and two little children; we live in a very small house; but, to save my life, I cannot spend less than twelve hundred a year." Another replied, "You are not economical; I spent but eight hundred." . . . A third one, who was present, was silent; but after they were gone, he said, "I keep house, and comfortably, too, with a wife and children, for six hundred a year; but I suppose they would have thought me mean, if I had told them so." I did not think him mean; it merely occurred to me that his wife and children were in the habit of picking up paper and twine.[11]

Child's story may have been pure fiction and her style sentimental, but her point was well taken: the working-class household remained a system of economic interdependencies in which even children played key roles. Training children for those roles was primarily the responsibility of the wife.

The aims of education for middle-class children were often contradictory. On the one hand, many moderate households needed children to assume roles of economic usefulness; for example, working in the family garden or shop. As a child, Caroline Clapp Briggs earned a penny for each bushel basket of wood chips she collected. Equally important, it was clear that children *would*, in the future, have to make their way in a world characterized by an increasingly complex market structure—a reality that made it mandatory that they begin to learn early about money. At the same time, middle-class mothers were expected to protect children from the corruptions of the marketplace—from greed, overriding ambition, and selfishness—and to imbue them instead with the values of charity and benevolence. Perhaps nowhere was the resulting paradox more evident than in Child's *American Frugal Housewife*, which instructed mothers to teach children simultaneously *to care* and *not to care* about individual accumulation: "In early childhood, you lay the foundation of poverty or riches, in the habits you give your children," she cautioned. "Teach them to save everything. . . . " In the next breath she added, "not for their *own* use, for that would make them selfish—but for *some* use."[12]

Much of the work performed by wives in their own households had roots in the distant past. As we have seen, however, the conditions of urbanization and early industrialization had reorganized those services, rendering them more complex to perform or shifting a greater proportion of responsibility to the wife. The general management of the household—a responsibility women had borne since the original European settlement of North America—had also grown more difficult over the course of the early nineteenth century. Laboring-class women oversaw families whose viability depended on a complex balance of purchasing, wage-earning, borrowing, scavenging, and stealing—and whose intricate labor systems involved children as well as adults. Women of most economic strata expressed dismay at what Catharine Beecher called the "multiplied cares and perplexities" of housework.[13]

Against the backdrop of uncertainty that was the constant companion of much working-class life in the antebellum years, the economic value of the work that poor women did—whether paid or unpaid—is plain enough. The issue may be less clear in the case of middle-class wives, however, since much of their work was overlaid with a class significance that easily obscures its character as labor. The full meaning of this labor for women can be understood, then, only by distinguishing the wife's role as a member and symbol of the middle-class family (in itself an icon of enormous social power) from her position as unpaid laborer in the household. Baking, an important aspect of a woman's traditional responsibility to supply her family with good, substantial meals, offers a case in point. By the antebellum period, home baking had assumed powerful class-trappings. On the one hand, poor women often lacked the facilities to bake at all for their own families. On the other hand, as Ruth Schwartz Cowan has pointed out, the availability of fine wheat flour had installed white bread as "one of the first symbols of status in the industrial period" in urban middle-class homes—with the effect of adding to (not diminishing) the work of women there. Not only was white bread more energy- and time-consuming to prepare than the quick-breads it replaced, but the presence of fine flour on the market (for those who could afford it) created an expectation that genteel wives should produce elaborate pastries, cakes, and confections as a part of caring for their families.[14]

Perhaps the most ambiguous of women's new "status" work was cleaning, however. Indeed, one can easily come away from the primary sources convinced that, for middle-class women at least, house-cleaning had become an obsession rather than a necessity. Much of the evidence for this conclusion comes to us indirectly, in the form of criticism of "the blessed followers of Saint Martha"[15] (who was too preoccupied with the cares of her household to listen to the teachings of Jesus). In the prescriptive literature of the antebellum period, these were women whose fastidiousness as housekeepers drove all congeniality from their homes—women like Miss Ophelia in Harriet Beecher Stowe's *Uncle Tom's Cabin*. Setting it down as a rule that "there is a medium . . . in all things," popular household-advice writer Elizabeth Ellet declared:

> A woman who worries all within her reach by her ultra-housewifery, who damps one down with soap and water, poisons one with furniture polish, takes away one's appetite by the trouble there is about cooking the simplest thing, and fidgets one by over-done tidiness and cleanliness, is almost as much to be avoided as a downright slut . . . ; she exercises a pernicious influence on all, and is a misery to herself and others.[16]

Here was tidiness with a vengeance—and, indeed, a vengeful appraisal of over-tidiness!

No doubt Ellet had known such women and seen such households. And yet this image of the middle-class wife, hell-bent on "ultra-housewifery," requires both modification and comment. In the first place, as the frequency of epidemic diseases suggests, antebellum cities were not very healthful places. Concerns about cleanliness, while they may have functioned as class shibboleths, were also quite reasonable. Moreover, although over the course of the antebellum years cities began to provide some basic municipal services, erecting safeguards against the environment was still assumed to be the business of the individual household—and particularly of the individual wife. For poorer women, this was an almost impossible task—a failure middle-class and elite reformers relentlessly noted.[17] But protecting their families from the dangers of the environment challenged the best efforts of middle-class women as well. And lest wives relax their vigilance, health reformers like William Alcott stood ever ready to remind them of the hazards yet unseen: "I have seen families accounted perfectly neat . . . ," he warned his readers, "but were they truly so? Look at the cellars, the kitchens, the drains, and the yards! See the putrefied vegetables and the fluids, the half spoiled meat, the offal matter, the heaps of manure, the vaults!"[18] Female prescriptive writers reinforced the point. In books like *The American Woman's Home*, in which thirteen of the thirty-eight chapters were devoted to matters of family health, housewives learned that only an aggressive assault on the domestic sources of disease would ensure their families' safety.

Whatever they might have wished, none of the women whose letters or diaries form the basis of this study even approached the model suggested by Ellet. Quite simply, they did not have enough time—or enough energy. Like most contemporary housewives, they were too busy racing to keep up with the small catastrophes wreaked by small children, or the larger catastrophes wreaked by stoves and furnaces. The perfectly ordered household was, for most middle-class women, simply beyond the realm of the possible.

The most troublesome difficulty in conceptualizing the economic value of antebellum housework lies less in accounting for any individual activity, however, than in finding some way to measure the whole. In a society that calibrates economic activity almost exclusively in cash terms (whether we mean the society of the antebellum Northeast or that of the late twentieth century), the very unwaged character of housework seems to set it outside of the realm of the economy. How do we measure something that is largely defined by its alienation from the standard measures? The difficulties are compounded by the fact that antebellum housework created no single item in which the value of the wife's labor power was embodied and through which that value could be converted into cash or new capital—in short, no single item to count. Looking for widgets and ratchets, we find instead unspoiled food, swept floors, and mended vests—a frustratingly amorphous foundation to build an economic evaluation on. Indeed, we cannot easily even standardize the food, floors, or vests, since women's unpaid labor differed from household to household, place to place, and season to season. Although certain allotments of time appear to have been fairly standard (especially among middle-class wives), there was no single routine.

But the problems that plague attempts to calculate a concrete value for housework are not unique to that work, certainly not for the antebellum period and, arguably, not for the years since. Most paid work in the early nineteenth century—as now—was imperfectly standardized at best. Even in the most routinized occupations (in the new central shops of the shoemaking industry, for example, and in the textile mills), workers found ways to leave the imprints of their own rhythms, preferences, and work customs on the patterns of their labor. Moreover, seldom, if ever, does a wage packet represent the full market value of the labor embedded in it. If it did, there would be no profits to be converted into new capital. Wages, as Marx observed long ago, reflect the social relations of workers and bosses, and the cash constraints on the worker for survival. It is a continuum of economic interdependencies that defies easy distinctions between paid and unpaid work.

Equally important in terms of attempting to fix a concrete economic value for women's unpaid domestic labor, under some conditions antebellum housework did achieve a cash value—a market-based calculation of what it would have cost women's families in cash to replace their labor. This occurred in two types of circumstances: when women's domestic work was transferred outside of their own household and performed for pay, and when it was performed at home but for someone to whom that were not bound by ties of kinship. As we have seen, in women's own lives, this movement back and forth between cash-earning and non–cash-earning identities was extremely casual. Not only did many women produce items directly for sale, but, during the antebellum years, many women also did (or had in their lifetimes) offer their skills at cleaning, cooking, child care, and sewing on the market. Indeed, the antebellum era was the last period during which most adult women shared the experience of having been at some point in their lives *paid* household workers. To an extent never later repeated, even middle-class wives were likely to have worked as "hired help" in their youth. Moreover, the work that women performed as paid household workers closely corresponded in kind and organization to the work that they performed for their own families. In both personal and material terms, the two experiences were far more comparable than they would be later, when the market forms of household labor would themselves often be highly capitalized industries. In the half century before the Civil War, then, there still existed a correspondence between paid and unpaid domestic labor that can provide at least one measure of the market worth of housework: the cost to a family to replace the unpaid labor of the wife by purchasing it on the market.[19]

Such a calculation is necessarily rough and somewhat arbitrary. The contingency-based character of housework meant that no two women divided their time among various tasks in exactly the same way. Unobserved by efficiency experts, moreover, women did not leave minute-by-minute records of their workdays. In attempting to convert the wage levels of paid domestic servants into a wage value for housework, then, one can only estimate a "typical" allocation of tasks.

As was the case with other wage-earners, the wages of domestic servants varied somewhat from place to place. In northeastern cities in 1860, a woman hired both to cook and to do the laundry earned between three and four dollars a week. Seamstresses and maids averaged two-and-a-half dollars a week. On the market, caring for children was at the lower end of the pay scale, seldom commanding more than $2.00 a week. If we assume that a woman did the full work of a hired cook and child's nurse, and also spent even an hour a day each sewing and cleaning (valued at about three cents an hour apiece), the weekly price of her basic housework would approximate $4.70. Even if we reduce this almost by half to $3.00 a week (to allow for variations in her work schedule and for the presence of assistance of some sort), taken at an average, this puts the price of a wife's basic housework at about $150 a year—over and above the value of her own maintenance (which would have been figured into the wages of a live-in cook or maid).[20]

To this should be added the value of goods a wife might make available to the family for free or at a reduced cost. Among poorer households, this was the labor of scavenging. A rag rug found among the refuse was worth half a dollar in money saved; an old coat, several dollars. Flour for a week, scooped from a broken barrel on the docks, could save the household almost a dollar in cash outlay.[21] In these ways, a wife with a good eye and a quick hand might easily save her family a dollar a week—or fifty dollars or so over the course of the year. In households with more cash, wives found other ways to avoid expenditures. By shopping carefully, buying in bulk, and drying or salting extra food, a wife could save ten to fifty percent of the family food budget. Calculated on the basis of the weekly family budget published in the *New York Tribune* in 1851 (in which $4.26 was allowed for food), this could mean a savings of from 40 cents to over $2.00 a week. Wives who kept kitchen gardens or chickens or made their own cheese could (again, judging from the *Tribune* budget) produce food worth a quarter a week (the price of one fourth of a bushel of potatoes in New York in 1851).[22]

But there was also the cash that working-class wives added to the household, by their needlework or vending, or by taking in boarders, running a grocery or a tavern from their kitchen, or working unpaid in their husbands' trade. A boarder might pay $4.00 a week. Subtracting a dollar and a half for food and rent, the wife's labor-time represented $2.50 of that amount, or $130 a year.[23] Outwork needlewomen averaged about $2.00 a week, or a hundred dollars a year.[24] Calculated on the basis of the pay for a "helper" in a trade, the wife's time working in her husband's occupation for the equivalent of a day a week was worth some $20 a year.[25]

The particular labor performed by a given woman depended on the size and resources of her household. In this way, housework remained entirely embedded in the family. Yet we can estimate a general market price of housework by combining the values of the individual activities that made it up: perhaps $150 for cooking, cleaning, laundry, and childrearing; another $50 or so saved through scavenging or careful shopping; another $50 or so in cash brought directly into the household. This would set the price of a wife's labor-time among the laboring poor at roughly $250 a year beyond maintenance, or in the neighborhood of $400 a year when the price of a single woman's maintenance purchased on the market (about $170 a year) is included. In working-class households with more income, where the wife could focus her labor on money-saving and on taking in a full-time boarder, that price might reach over $500 annually, or between $600 and $700 including maintenance. These shifts in the nature of a wife's work, and in the value of that work, as a husband's income increased seem not to have been entirely lost on males, who advised young men that if they meant to get ahead, they should "get married."[26]

Calculated at the replacement cost, the work of middle-class wives supplied comparable value to the economies of their households. Their diaries suggest that most middle-class women spent, conservatively, several hours a day in sewing and mending, including the periods during which they devoted whole days and weeks to these activities. Most were involved in almost constant child care. Even with hired servants, middle-class wives also spent hours each week cooking, baking, working with hired help on the laundry, and doing the housecleaning required by their families. If we estimate this work at two hours a day each for cleaning and sewing, or about seventy cents a week, another two dollars a week for cooking, washing, ironing, sorting, and putting away the clothing, and two dollars a week for child care, we get a figure of roughly $250 a year for just these portions of the cash value of middle-class housework. If the wife engaged in the extensive household manufacturing described by such women as Harriet Beecher Stowe and Lydia Maria Child, then the value of her labor—in direct purchase avoidance—might easily increase by $50 to $100 a year. The purchase of a single feather bed could cost $25 to $30, and pillows and bolsters could cost several dollars apiece.[27] If, like the author of *Six Hundred Dollars a Year* or

Martha Coffin Wright, the wife added some cash earnings to her family's economy, then the value of her labor rose commensurately. If the family took in a boarder, the value of the wife's labor might increase the family budget by $156 a year. By her careful shopping, she might save the family another $60 to $70 a year on groceries alone.[28] The exact value varied from woman to woman, but it would seem judicious to conclude that the labor of a middle-class wife might easily be worth upwards of $700 a year to her household.

Few women, either working-class or middle-class, could realize the cash value of their household contribution outside of marriage. The Harriet Beecher Stowes were the exceptions. Even middle-class women who became teachers seldom earned more than $1.50 a week plus board, and were paid only during the school term.[29] The full-time seamstress who earned $2.50 a week would make only $130 annually—assuming she was employed year-round. Many needlewomen earned far less. A full-time cook and washerwoman would do better, since she would customarily receive meals and lodging with her wages, but she seldom earned more than $156 a year. Thus, the maintenance value of wives' housework was *not* directly transferable into paid labor. It existed only within, and was inseparable from, the institution of the family.

There is a second sense in which the cash value of housework was embedded in the collectivity of the family. In large part, the wife's labor could not be extracted from the ongoing processes of household life or indeed from the labor of other household members. Even the child who earned a few pennies a week selling roasted corn could point to those coins as evidence of his or her work. The mother who retrieved meat scraps to make a broth to feed that same child could claim part of the value of those pennies only indirectly and after the fact. This gave housework a peculiarly diffuse character, even in the context of the household.

Because of her need for access to cash, the wife's dependence on a wage-earner in the family was particularly acute. She was not the only member benefiting from the amalgamation of labors that the household represented, however. A single adult male, living in New York City in 1860, could scarcely hope to get by on less than $250 a year: $4.00 a week for room and board ($208 a year) and perhaps $15 a year for minimal clothing meant an outlay of almost $225 before laundry, medicines, and other occasional expenses.[30] Many working-class men did not earn $225 a year, and for them access to the domestic labor of a wife might be the critical variable in achieving a maintenance. Even men who did earn this amount might find a clear advantage in marrying, for a wife saved money considerably over and above the cost she added for her own maintenance. By supplying for free the cooking, cleaning, and laundry services that must otherwise have been purchased with cash, a wife stretched a man's income and improved his security against the market.

The marital exchange was not an even one. A single adult female paid two thirds to three quarters of the price paid by men for room and board.[31] Since she made much of it herself, her clothing was likely to cost half of what a man's cost. Most women did their own laundry. On this basis, the cost of an adult female's maintenance ran well under $200 a year—probably in the neighborhood of $170, even if she bought all of her clothing. By these rough estimates, in exchange for access to cash, a working-class wife contributed to the family a cash value worth twice her maintenance. It was this surplus that combined with her husband's income to raise the *household* resources to the level of a maintenance. In short, this surplus allowed families to survive on $300 or $400 annually at a time when observers calculated $600 as the minimal threshold of subsistence.[32]

Historians have frequently analyzed the working-class family as a collectivity, run according to a communal ethic. But by law and custom the family was not an egalitarian society. The husband owned, not only the value of his own labor time, but the value of his wife's as well. And this was a prerogative of manhood that working-class males were ill-prepared to give up. Indeed, the rhetoric of the family wage suggests that working-class males were engaged in a historical process of strengthening their claims to those prerogatives.[33]

Perhaps it would seem absurd to quibble over who owned the poverty or near poverty that so often characterized working-class households. There were things to be owned, however, and ownership could make the difference between subsistence or destitution if the household broke up. First, the husband possessed his own maintenance, and any improvements in it that became possible as a result of the labor of his wife and children. He also owned whatever furnishings the family had accumulated. Although a table, a chair, clothing, bedding, and a few dishes seem (and were) scant enough property, they were the stuff life-and-death transactions were made of in the laboring classes; pawned overnight, for example, clothes were important "currency" to cover the rent until payday. The husband also owned the children his wife raised, whose wages (when they reached their mid-teens) might amount to several hundred dollars a year—almost as much as his own.

To be sure, wives commonly benefited from some or all of these sources of value, and both personal and community norms tended to restrain husbands from taking full advantage of their position. Not only the affectional bonds of the family, but the expanding cultural emphasis on the husband as the "protector" and "provider" may have helped emotionally mediate the structural inequities of the household.

At the same time, community norms did not prevent the expression of individual self-interest in marriage, and the stresses of material hardship were as likely to rend as to create mutual concern. The frequency of incidents in which a wife had her husband arrested for battery and then "discharged at her request" suggest a complex and less-than-romantic dynamic of dependence in antebellum families. The continuing development of cash-exchange networks throughout the antebellum period and the relegation of barter largely to domestic transactions heightened that dynamic. A man could look for cheaper accommodations or eat less to reduce his cash outlay, even if these choices might prove destructive in the long run. But wives remained dependent—both structurally and, in most cases, in actual fact. Ezra Stiles Ely recorded an episode that underscored the inequity of the relation. An Irishwoman, the deserted wife of a mariner, had fallen ill and been sent with her children to the New York Almshouse. When she recovered, she was determined "to obtain of [her husband] half his pay, that she might leave the almshouse, and support her children." Her power to accomplish this was severely limited, however. When Ely last saw her, she had taken her children to the Battery, where the ship her husband served on was anchored. "[S]he had sent a request to see him," Ely noted, and waited "in expectation." But her husband preferred to stay on board ship—with his wages. "In this situation,"Ely concluded, "she remained for nearly half the day. . . . "[34]

The unpaid labor of middle-class wives also produced value necessary to the middle-class household economy. Unlike laboring-class men, middle-class husbands enjoyed high enough incomes to have purchased a comfortable maintenance on the cash market. Many earned enough money to purchase room, board, clothing, and medical care for an entire family. Averaging perhaps $1,000 a year, however, middle-class husbands' incomes were seldom sufficient *both* to cover the costs of present maintenance *and* to provide the kinds of savings and investments that might hedge against future markets. Here was the value of the labor of the wife. Overseeing patterns of both purchase and consumption, substituting her own labor in home manufacturing for the labor value contained in the prices of commodities, allowing the household to avoid altogether or to decrease payment for cooking, laundry, child care, and cleaning, and often also adding outright to the family's cash income, the wife's labor created the surplus that could be translated into home ownership, an expanded business operation, savings, or investment. Indeed, this was precisely the fate of $350 of the $450 earned by the author of *Six Hundred Dollars a Year*, whose income provided the basis of a savings plan that eventually enabled the family to purchase its home.

The "status" work of middle-class wives also added to this value. The labor that women expended in cleaning and decorating homes ultimately accrued in the market value of the property. Both the status value and the market value created by the wife's labor redounded to her only indirectly, however, for nineteenth-century observers tended to assess the degree of a household's "gentility" as a measure of the husband's income—as Child's anecdote of the three mechanics suggested; it would have been the *mechanic* who would have been deemed "mean" if his companions had known the size of his household budget. That his wife was a skilled housekeeper would not have occurred to them. Indeed, as households became involved in market purchases, their material environment was assumed to reflect the husband's earning power, rather than the wife's labor. Because of this way of seeing, status production—a responsibility that wives assumed not instead of, but in addition to their other work—became an invisible component of most of the unpaid domestic labor that women performed.

The right of married women to hold and negotiate property in their own names was not clearly established in law until the third quarter of the nineteenth century. Prior to that time, the value created by middle-class wives (and made tangible in cash earned or saved and in property) belonged to their husbands. Even after the passage of married women's property acts, moreover, wives' rights extended only to property held in their names. Unless they were specifically conveyed to the wife, investments, savings, and properties acquired during marriage and representing, in part or in whole, the labor of the wife, were the possession of the husband.[35]

But husbands were not the sole beneficiaries of the economic value of housework, or of its unique invisibility. Employers were enabled by the presence of this sizeable but uncounted labor in the home to pay both men and women wages that were, in fact, below the level of subsistence. The difference was critical to the development of industrialization in the antebellum Northeast.[36]

The growth of capitalized manufacturing in the antebellum era was in many ways stunning. For example, as early as 1826, the Boston

Manufacturing Company was showing profits of almost 20 percent, and some mills were doing even better than that.[37] To remain competitive with imports and still maintain these profit levels, however, manufacturers constantly had to reduce the costs of production, either directly through wage cuts or indirectly through further mechanization. The latter required massive capital investment. But capital accumulation remained low in the Northeast. In each of the crises of 1815 to 1820, 1837 to 1840, and the late 1850s, currency contracted, slowing investment overall and creating erratic, short-term fluctuations. There was little stability for shop and factory owners in the antebellum economy. In New York City's "metropolitan industrialization," where a tenth of all manufacturers controlled roughly 30 percent of all capital, small shopkeepers found access to capital increasingly constricted. As late as 1860, most mills in the region did not last ten years.[38]

At a time when the level of capital accumulation in the Northeast remained precariously low, then, the margin of profit available from "sub-subsistence" wages was crucial. Occasionally mill owners acknowledged that the wages they paid did not cover maintenance. One agent admitted: "So long as they can do my work *for what I choose to pay them*, I keep them, getting out of them all I can. . . . [H]ow they fare outside my walls I don't know, nor do I consider it my business to know. They must look out for themselves. . . ."[39]

More often, however, both capitalists and the political economists who rose to their defense maintained that they did indeed care about their workers, and that the wages they paid represented the true value of the labor they received, including the value of producing that labor. John McVickar thought well enough of the *Encyclopædia Britannica*'s discussion of political economy to have it reprinted in the United States. It asserted coolly that "the cost of producing artificers, or labourers, regulates the wages they obtain. . . ."[40] In *Public and Private Economy*, Theodore Sedgwick carried this optimism about the relationship of wages to subsistence one step further—at the same time revealing the dangerous uses the belief that wages represented subsistence could be put to. Since "a little, a very little only" was required to maintain laborers, Sedgwick argued, even at current levels of payment "in the factories of New England, very large numbers [of workers] may annually lay up half their wages; many much more. . . ."[41] Presumably, then, wages not only covered, but exceeded, the value of maintenance. The other shoe would fall, again and again, as employers used the fact of working-class survival to justify further cuts in wages. The value of unpaid housework in mediating those cuts would remain invisible.

The value created by middle-class housework also accrued both to individual employers and to the expanding regional and national economies. Even when employers paid high enough salaries to provide present security for a family, they seldom provided either the income or the job security to ensure a household's well-being against the erratic boom-and-bust cycles of business and the unemployment consequent upon those cycles. To have done so would have been to restrict vastly the growth and flexibility of their own operations. Women's unremunerated labor in the household provided the needed "safety net," enabling middle-class families to maintain some degree of both material stability and healthiness in a volatile economic environment and in an often deteriorating physical environment. In addition to its direct financial implications for business, middle-class housework provided a second, more amorphous, but nonetheless important value for the developing industrial economy. It supported the continued existence of a comparatively prosperous sector of society—one that, because of its comparative well-being, understood the expansion of financial institutions and capitalized manufacturing to be generally congenial to its interests. In this sense, wives' unpaid domestic labor played a key role in the emergence of the middle class, both as a coherent economic group and as a symbol of the security presumably available to all families in the new republic.

Finally, like laboring-class wives, middle-class wives found themselves at a growing disadvantage as workers. Regardless of the value they created for their homes and for the larger economy, by and large they owned neither property nor cash, and they were specialized for a type of labor that could be exchanged for maintenance only in a single context: marriage.

In putting the history of housework in the context of early industrialization, it is important to underscore the role of unpaid domestic labor in the creation, definition, and workings of class in antebellum America. "Class" is both a useful and a slippery term in American history—useful in delineating real distinctions of material well-being and opportunity as well as of world-view, aspirations, and identity among different social groups, but slippery, because it is so amorphous, and because defining class clearly involves more than simple calculations of cash income. The newly minted physician may have an enormous debt burden and a very low income, but compared to most Americans his or her prospects for the future are bright indeed. Thus, present income levels offer a poor way to comprehend the long-term meaning of class in American society.

The history of housework in the antebellum years offers further caution against narrow, cash-based formulations of class. Households may have been increasingly likely to define themselves against the cash marketplace, in terms of wages and salaries, but their actual position in the economic order of early industrialization was a function of a combination of cash and *other* types of resources. Critical among these additional resources was the unpaid labor of the wife.

Housework affected the class position of families in several ways. Some of these were dramatically visible and symbolically quite powerful. In her ability to furnish and maintain a comfortable dwelling, for example, a woman represented her family to the world as "respectable" and prosperous. But housework also supported and helped define the class position of households in other, often less apparent, respects. By clever buying or scavenging, a wife could save cash that might cover emergency medical expenses or accumulate toward investment. By skimping, she might keep her family out of the almshouse, or, as Martha Coffin Wright contended, enable the family to survive bad financial decisions by the husband. Through her networks of friends and family, she might build barriers against periods of need. A family's ability to rise to middle-class prosperity—or its inability to forestall decline into economic marginality—might well depend first and foremost on the skills and resourcefulness of the wife.

In turn, the class position of a household—understood as its composite relationship to the vagaries of the cash marketplace—also defined the nature and function of housework. This was not merely a case of the precise tasks undertaken by a given woman, although, as we have seen, this varied to some extent depending on whether her household was more or less precariously situated. But the overall economic condition of the household also determined the form in which the material value of housework would accrue to family members—especially to the husband. For working-class men, the value of women's unpaid domestic labor registered primarily in the present, in enabling the household (and the husband himself) to realize a maintenance from day to day. Housework had the same function in middle-class households, but there it provided the additional bonus of enabling capital accumulation into the future. Put simply, a wife *was* a good investment for a man who wanted to get ahead.

Much had changed—and little had changed—in the household labor of women over the course of the antebellum years. Like their colonial counterparts, antebellum women worked hard in their families, maintaining the basic operations of the household, seeing to it that children survived to adulthood, that adults survived from one day of work to the next, producing many of the goods required by their families, and maneuvering in the marketplace to obtain what could not be produced internally. In the midst of all this, they grappled with the clever and cantankerous new machines and the heart-sinking dangers, the new prosperity and the new poverty of an increasingly industrial society.

As we have seen, twice during the first two hundred years of European settlement—first during the early years of colonization and then again during the Revolutionary War—Americans had publicly recognized and valued the economic importance of that labor. But those were periods of exceptional circumstances, circumstances that ran against the overall grain of economic development in the United States. Over the course of the second quarter of the nineteenth century, and as an aspect of the process of industrialization, antebellum Americans would embrace a growing conviction that housework was not really labor at all, but rather merely a new form of leisure reserved to married women as the last preserve of a way of life antecedent to and apart from industrialization. Occasionally, to be sure, a husband would acknowledge the value of his wife's labor. In his autobiography, Thurlow Weed attributed largely to his marriage "whatever of personal success and pecuniary prosperity I have since enjoyed." His wife, he wrote, "*more* than divided our labors, cares, and responsibilities. But for her industry, frugality, and good management, I must have been shipwrecked during the first fifteen years of trial."[42] In at least one court case, moreover, a judge went so far as to award a husband damages for the value of services lost when his wife's arm was injured.[43] These recognitions were dwarfed, however, by the growing cultural perception that housework, and perhaps particularly middle-class housework, stood outside of the economy and was not a part of it. The "ideology of spheres," as historians have identified that way of seeing social life, would represent the final phase in the industrialization of housework—the denial that it produced any economic value at all.

Chapter VII

The Pastoralization of Housework

The culture of the antebellum Northeast recognized the role of wives in the making of contented and healthy families. Indeed, the years between the War of 1812 and the Civil War were a period of almost unabated celebration of women's special and saving domestic mission. "Grant that others besides woman have responsibilities at home . . . ," wrote the Reverend Jesse Peck in 1857, "[s]till we fully accord the supremacy of domestic bliss to the wife and mother. . . . "[1]

As recent historians have recognized, this glorification of wife- and motherhood was at the heart of one of the most compelling and widely shared belief systems of the early nineteenth century: the ideology of gender spheres. An elaborate set of intellectual and behavioral conventions, the doctrine of gender spheres expressed a worldview in which both the orderliness of daily social relations and the larger organization of society derived from and depended on the preservation of an all-encompassing gender division of labor. Consequently, in the conceptual and emotional universe of the doctrine of spheres, males and females existed as creatures of naturally and essentially different capacities. As the Providence-based *Ladies Museum* explained in 1825:

> Man is strong—woman is beautiful. Man is daring and confident—woman is diffident and unassuming. Man is great in action—woman i[n] suffering. Man shines abroad—woman at home. Man talks to convince—woman to

> persuade and please. Man has a rugged heart—woman a soft and tender one. Man prevents misery—woman relieves it. Man has science—woman taste. Man has judgment—woman sensibility. Man is a being of justice—woman of mercy.

These "natural" differences of temperament and ability were presumed to translate into different social roles and responsibilities for men and women. Clearly intended by the order of nature to "shine at home," Woman was deemed especially ill-equipped to venture into the world of nineteenth-century business, where "cunning, intrigue, falsehood, slander, [and] vituperative violence" reigned and where "mercy, pity, and sympathy, are vagrant fowls."[2]

Particularly in the antebellum Northeast, the ideology of gender spheres was partly a response to the chaos of a changing society—an intellectually and emotionally comforting way of setting limits to the uncertainties of early industrialization. Historian Ann Douglas, who has been among the chief proponents of this view, has argued that the sentimentalization of the home and of womanhood allowed the white, Protestant, upper middle class to resolve profound contradictions in its own behavior—to seem to cherish the very values its own activities so clearly denied. "Sentimentalism," Douglas asserts, "provides a way to protest a power to which one has already in part capitulated"—in this case, "economic expansion, urbanization, and industrialization."[3]

While it helps to illuminate the complex patterns of internal stress that characterized the culture of the emerging middle class in the antebellum Northeast, this view of the functioning of the ideology of gender spheres poses a number of conceptual difficulties. Most problematic is its tendency to divorce the genesis of belief from action and to frame ideology almost as an afterthought to behavior—a rationalization for choices already made and actions already taken in the arena of social experience. As a number of historians have demonstrated, however, the ideology of gender spheres was far more integrally joined to social behavior in the antebellum Northeast than this would suggest—not merely describing conduct, but shaping it; not only justifying behavior, but infusing it. The ideology of spheres was an evolving reservoir of meaning through which antebellum Americans conceived both their choices and the significance of those choices. It is this far more dynamic view of antebellum culture, and of the role of gender within it, that allows us to understand the importance of the ideology of gender spheres for the history of women's unpaid domestic labor in the period of early industrialization.

The traits that presumably rendered Woman so defenseless against the guile and machinations of the business world not only served to confine her to the home as her proper sphere, but made her presence there crucial for her family, especially for her husband. Even the most enthusiastic boosters of economic expansion agreed that the explosive opportunism of antebellum society created an atmosphere too heady with competition and greed to foster either social or personal stability. However great his wisdom or strong his determination, to each man must come a time

> [w]hen body, mind, and heart are overtaxed with exhausting labor; when the heavens are overcast, and the angry clouds portend the fearful storm; when business schemes are antagonized, thwarted by stubborn matter, capricious man, or an inauspicious providence; when coldness, jealousy, or slander chills his heart, misrepresents his motives, or attacks his reputation; when he looks with suspicion on all he sees, and shrinks from the frauds and corruptions of men with instinctive dread. . . .

It was what Melville called the "damp, drizzly November" of the soul, and he recommended that at such times men take to the whaling ship. Most writers sought a different solution, however. What was needed was not a voyage, but an anchor, a balance both social and psychological, a refuge: "one place of sweet repose . . . of calm and sunshine amid the lowering storm . . . ; one heart which is true. . . . " In the standard rhetoric of the ideology of the spheres, that place was Home, and that one true heart, the heart of Woman.[4]

Whatever the proclivities or ambitions of individual women, the presumed contrasts between the sexes permitted Woman-in-the-abstract to be defined as the embodiment of all that was contrary to the values and behaviors of men in the marketplace, and thus, to the marketplace itself. Against its callousness, she offered nurturance. Against its ambition, she pitted her self-effacement and the modesty of her needs. Against its materialism, she held up the twin shields of morality and spiritual solace. If business was a world into which only men traveled and where they daily risked losing their souls, then wherever Woman was, was sanctuary. And Woman was in the Home.

The contrast between Man and Woman melted easily into a contrast between "workplace" and "home" and between "work" as Man engaged in it and the "occupations" of Woman in the home. Most writers of prescriptive literature did acknowledge that women were involved in activities of some sort in their households. For example, T. S. Arthur worried that a woman would be unable to keep the constant vigilance required to be a good mother if she also had to attend to " 'the operations of the needle, the mysteries of culinary science, and all the complicated duties of housekeeping.' " His language is revealing, however: housework consisted of "mysteries" and "duties"; it was a different order of activity from the labor that men performed. Indeed, some observers cautioned that the wife and mother should deliberately stay clear of employments that might involve her in the economy. As we have observed, William Alcott was among this group. Noting that a woman " . . . has duties to perform to the sick and to the well—to the young and to the aged; duties even to domestic animals," Alcott nevertheless cautioned that "[v]ery few of these duties are favorable to the laying up of much property, and some are opposed to it. So that while we commend industry—of the most untiring kind, too—we would neither commend nor recommend strong efforts to lay up property." The advice was not only consistent with, but reflected a critical aspect of, the ideology of spheres: to the extent that workers in the household identified themselves with the labor of the marketplace, the function of the home as a place of psychological refuge would be undermined.[5]

Thus, the responsibilities of wives in their households were generally described in the prescriptive literature less as purposeful activities required and ordered by the welfare of their individual families than as emanations of an abstract but shared Womanhood. As Daniel C. Eddy explained:

> Home is woman's throne, where she maintains her royal court, and sways her queenly authority. It is there that man learns to appreciate her worth, and to realize the sweet and tender influences which she casts around her; there she exhibits the excellences of character which God had in view in her creation.

Underscoring the essentially passive nature of Woman's functions, Eddy concluded: "Her life should be a calm, holy, beautiful walk. . . ."[6]

Men sometimes recognized exceptions to this definition of women's work as a way of being rather than as a conscious form of labor. In his concern that women should be freed from other demands in order to have time to spend with their children, for example, T. S. Arthur indicated a general understanding that attending to children was an onerous responsibility. William Alcott went somewhat farther, admitting that not all women took easily to motherhood and that some women might well have to cultivate the art of loving and rearing children. But most writers simply assumed that skilled mothering came to women as a part of their very femaleness.[7]

Deeply embedded in the gender culture of antebellum Americans, the images and language of the ideology of spheres did not remain distant and distinct from daily life. To the contrary, the imperatives of the ideology—most notably the conviction that Woman resided in a universe utterly separated from the turbulence of commerce and industry—inexorably provided the framework within which the experiences of individual women were comprehended. Indeed, especially in the prescriptive literature, idealized images of Woman and of the Home were evoked with a directness that in effect offered them up, not as constructs in a system of intellectual conventions, but as simulations of living people and tangible locations in the geography of daily social intercourse. Thus, for example, Jesse Peck couched his exposition of domestic ideals in the rather mundane setting of a husband's return home from his day's work:

> With what fond longings does he turn toward that bright paradise, his home, and gaze upon that bright and central orb, whose genial light kindles with soft and heavenly radiance upon the scene of loveliness which invites him to rest. With what refreshing gladness does he retire from the noise, and strife, and selfishness of the gentile court, into this *sanctum sanctorum* of the world's vast temple. As he settles into his easy chair, and hears sweet voices call him father, feels the soft press of affection's hand upon his fevered brow, and love's charming kiss upon his lips, and his heart receives the endearing caresses of her who calls him husband, what delicious, holy pleasure melts and fills his soul!

The metaphors of ideology were transformed into the data of behavior. With no loss of prescriptive power—indeed, with the enhancement that arises from the immediacy of lived experience—the symbolic assumed the garb of daily experience.[8]

The consequence of this conflation of ideology and behavior was to obscure both the nature and the economic importance of women's domestic labor. It was not only Woman-in-the-abstract who did not labor in the economy, but also, by extension, individual women. It was not only Woman-in-the-abstract, but presumably, real women who guided the ongoing functions of the home through the effortless emanations of their very being, providing for the needs of their families without labor, through their simple presence in the household. As romantic narrative played against lived experience, the labor and economic value of housework ceased to exist in the culture of the antebellum Northeast. It became work's opposite: a new form of leisure.

The heart of this dialectic of selection and symbolic reconstruction was a cultural process Raymond Williams has identified with the structure of feeling characteristic of pastoral literature—a rendering of the present in the image of a nostalgically conceived past "in which all things come naturally to man, for his use and enjoyment and without his effort. . . ."[9] In seventeenth-century English literature, Williams found, the pastoral myth functioned to obscure the ravages to the rural peasantry attendant upon the formation of a landed gentry. By conceiving of the land as an Eden, the pastoral poets, many of whom depended on the munificence of the new gentry, were able to celebrate the enclosure of the countryside into a series of elaborate private estates without acknowledging the social cost of that transformation. Williams points out that what is missing in the pastoral poems is any evidence of the labor required to create and maintain these latter-day Edens:

> What is really happening [in the poetry] . . . is . . . a magical recreation of what can be seen as a natural bounty and then a willing charity: both serving to ratify and bless the country landowner. . . . Yet this magical extraction of the curse of labour is in fact achieved by a simple extraction of the existence of labourers. The actual men and women who rear the animals and drive them to the house and kill them and prepare them for meat; who trap the pheasants and partridges and catch the fish; who plant and manure and prune and harvest the fruit trees: these are not present; their work is all done for them by a natural order. When they do at last appear, it is merely as the "rout of rurall folks" or, more simply, as "much poore," and what we are then shown is the charity and lack of condescension with which they are given what, now and somehow, not they but the natural order has given for food, into the lord's hands.[10]

Williams' interest centered on the significance of pastoralization as a process through which the emerging rural bourgeoisie justified dislocating the peasantry from their customary lands and rights and appropriating the value of their labor as a wage-dependent class. But the history of housework suggests that pastoralization was also a gendered process. The counterparts to the seventeenth-century English pastoral poets in antebellum America were the writers of prescriptive domestic literature. Under their pens was gradually fashioned a powerful evocation of the Home as a new Eden—a paradise delivered up to husband and children from a benevolent and bountiful nature, without the curse of labor.

William Alcott's description of the wife's labors in *The Young Wife* provides a striking illustration of the pastoralization of housework in descriptions of the antebellum home:

> Where is it that the eye brightens, the smile lights up, the tongue becomes flippant, the form erect, and every motion cheerful and graceful? Is it at home? Is it in doing the work of the kitchen? Is it at the wash-tub—at the oven—darning a stocking—mending a coat—making a pudding? Is it in preparing a neat table and table cloth, with a few plain but neat dishes? Is it in covering it with some of nature's simple but choice viands? Is it in preparing the room for the reception of an absent companion? Is it in warming and lighting the apartments at evening, and waiting, with female patience, for his return from his appointed labor? Is it in greeting him with all her heart on his arrival?[11]

Clearly, Alcott was quite familiar with the types of work performed by women in their own families, and his description is all the more interesting on this account: cooking, baking, washing clothes, mending and darning, serving meals, building fires, attending to lamps—it is a surprisingly accurate catalogue. It is also incomplete, of course. Missing from this picture is the making of the soap that the wash might be done, the lugging and heating of the water, the tiresome process of heating and lifting cast-iron irons, the dusting and sweeping of rooms, the cleaning of the stove, and the making of the stocking and the coat now in need of repair.

Even the domestic tasks Alcott acknowledges, however, are not to be contemplated as true work, a point made explicit in his identification of only the husband's employments as "labor." With "labor," indeed, the wife's activities have no truck, for there is no "labor" here to perform. A little washing, a touch of the needle, and a moment's stop in the kitchen are all that are required; the food appears virtually as a gift of nature, and the compliant fires and lamps seem to light and tend themselves. In Alcott's ideal home, children do not knock over the solar lamp (as they did in Sarah Munro's parlor) and stray sheep do not require emergency resuscitation (as one did in Mary Ann Archbald's kitchen).[12] On the contrary, all is ordered, and the ordering of it is not only *not* burdensome or tiring, but the certain vehicle of good health and a cheerful disposition. Far from laborious, housework is positively regenerating.

As Alcott's depiction of the home suggested, prescriptive writers sometimes undercut the existence of household labor even as they seemed to acknowledge it. In an article entitled "Woman's Offices and Influence," J. H. Agnew granted that women might find themselves caught up in "the busy drudgery of hard housekeeping," but that one comment was his only mention of women's domestic labor in a four-page article devoted to women's role in the family. The chief functions of the wife and mother, according to Agnew, were: "*To make home happy*," "*to check the utilitarianism, the money-loving spirit of the day*," "*to soften political asperities in the other sex, and themselves to shun publicity*," "*to regulate the forms and control the habits of social life*," and "*the exemplification and diffusion of Christianity*"—all of which was to be accomplished in "the quiet retirement of the home."[13]

The pastoralization of housework, with its emphasis on the sanctified home as an emanation of Woman's nature, required the articulation of a new way of seeing (or, more exactly, of *not* seeing) women as actors, capable of physical exertion. Most specifically, this applied to women as laborers; but the "magical extraction" of physical activity from the concept of Womanhood in fact proceeded in much larger terms and was most apparent in the recurring celebrations of female "influence." Typically invoked as the female counterpart to the presumably *male* formal political power,[14] the concept of indirect womanly "influence" supplanted notions of women as direct agents, and thus as laborers. As Agnew's discussion of women illustrated, the contrast between presumably male "power" (physical as well as moral) and female "influence" could be drawn quite explicitly:

> We may stand in awe, indeed, before the exhibition of *power*, whether physical or moral, but we are not won by them to the love of truth and goodness, while *influence* steals in upon our hearts, gets hold of the springs of action, and leads us into its own ways. It is the *inflowing* upon others from the nameless traits of character which constitute woman's idiosyncracy. Her heart is a great reservoir of love, the water-works of moral influence, from which go out ten thousand tubes, conveying the ethereal essences of her nature, and diffusing them quietly over the secret chambers of man's inner being.

Woman does not herself *act*. Rather, she "gets hold of the springs of action." An idiosyncracy in the human order, she is not so much a physical as an ethereal being. Agnew concluded: "Let man, then, exercise power; woman exercise influence. By this she will best perform her offices, discharge her duties." It is the crowning touch of the pastoralization of housework: the home is the setting not of labor, but of "offices" and "duties." Therefore, what is required for the happy home is not a worker but rather "a great reservoir of love."[15]

The pastoralization of household labor became a common feature of antebellum literature, both private and published. It was a pastoral perspective that framed Horace Bushnell's memory of his childhood. His mother, he recalled, bore a heavy load of responsibilities, "training her six children, clothing her whole family in linens and woolens, spun every thread, and made up in the house also to a great extent by herself. She had a farm-and-dairy charge to administer, also the farm workmen to board, and for five or six months in a year the workers, besides, of a homespun cloth-dressing shop. All this routine she kept moving in exact order and time, steady and clear as the astronomic year. . . . " Bushnell wondered, "What mortal endurance could bear such a stress of burden!" But the question was rhetorical, for he already had his answer: the mortal endurance of Woman. His mother, he testified, managed all of this work with "scarcely . . . a look of damage." Under the spell of true womanhood, it seemed, even the most exhausting labor lost its power to debilitate.[16]

The pastoralization of housework also shaped much of the fiction of the period. In a piece entitled "The Wife" (published in the *Ladies' Literary Cabinet* in July of 1819 and included in *The Sketch Book* the following year), Washington Irving described the plight of a young couple forced by the husband's disastrous speculations to give up their fashionable life in the city and move to a modest country cottage. One might anticipate that such a move would entail numerous headaches and a good deal of hard work, especially for the woman. But such was not the case for Irving's "Wife." Mary goes out to the cottage to spend the day "superintending its arrangement," but the substance of that process remains a mystery; for the packing and unpacking, cleaning, hanging of curtains, arranging of furniture, putting away of dishes, sorting of clothes, and adjusting of new domestic equipment one might expect to be required under such circumstances remain undisclosed in the text. Indeed, all we learn is that when next encountered by the narrator, Mary " 'seems in better spirits than I have ever known.' " Transformed into a creature who is far more sylvan nymph than human female, Mary greets her husband and the narrator "singing, in a style of the most touching simplicity. . . . Mary came tripping forth to meet us; she was in a pretty rural dress of white, a few wild flowers were twisted in her fine hair, a fresh bloom was on her cheek, her whole countenance beamed with smile—I have never seen her look so lovely." To complete the pastoral scene, nature has obligingly provided " 'a beautiful tree behind the cottage' " where the threesome picnic on a feast of wild strawberries and thick sweet cream.[17]

The pastoralization of housework was often accomplished without the rendering of entire scenes, fictional or not. So essential a part of the worldview of antebellum northeasterners did it become that mere phrases ("the link of maternal affection," "the sphere illumed by her smile") evoked the image of repose and refuge from labor presumed to reside in Woman's very being. As Daniel Eddy observed of a verse from Judges, "There is a world of domestic meaning treasured up in these few words."[18]

In both its briefer and its more extended forms, in fiction and in exposition, in prescription and in proscription, the pastoralization of housework permeated the culture of the antebellum Northeast. Often, it was expressed simply as a truism, as when the Reverend Hubbard Winslow reminded his Boston congregation that "[t]he more severe manual labors, the toils of the fields, the mechanics, the cares and burdens of mercantile business, the exposures and perils of absence from home, the duties of the learned professions devolve upon man. . . ." As we have seen, he considered women's occupations to be of a "more delicate and retired nature." That same year, the shocked and angered Congregational clergy of Massachusetts drew upon the same assumptions and the same imagery of Womanhood to denounce the abolitionist activities of Sarah and Angelina Grimké. Reminding their female congregants that "the power of woman is in her dependence," the clergy spoke of the "unobtrusive and private" nature of women's "appropriate duties" and directed them to devote their energies to "those departments of life that form the character of individuals" and to embodying "that modesty and delicacy which is the charm of domestic life. . . ."[19]

Throughout the middle and wealthy classes, male family members were inclined to accept the conventions of pastoralization as accurate representations of how their wives and the women they observed spent their time. When George Templeton Strong listed in 1842 the qualities he considered essential in a wife, he included piety, obedience, good humor, beauty, intellect, and wealth—but failed to mention skills in domestic work or household management. Even after marriage, his closest approach to recognizing his wife's contribution to the functioning of the household was to praise her for having "the sound practical sense" to eschew "fashionable extravagance." Calvin Stowe exhibited a similar blindness to the demands of Harriet Beecher Stowe's family responsibilities. Encouraging her in 1842 to "make all your calculations to spend the rest of your life with your pen," he failed to address the matter of who would take care of the cooking, cleaning, mending, and child-rearing, and turned his attention instead to what apparently seemed to him the more serious obstacle to her publishing career: how she should sign her name.[20]

The pastoralization of housework was often expressed during the antebellum period in the romanticization of Womanhood. But the process also had an underside. A creature who did not contribute to the material welfare of those around her, after all, could as easily be represented as a leech as she could as an angel. Reminiscent of the eighteenth-century wags, antebellum writers often depicted women as silly and irresponsible—not quite grasping the full measure of their dependence on men or of the difficulty of maintaining a household. The following sketch in the "Editor's Drawer" of *Harper's* in January of 1854 illustrated the possibilities for satire even as it demonstrated the narrowed definition of "support":

> "Do you support General Pierce?"
> "No."
> "Do you support General Cass?"
> "No."
> "What! do you support Van Buren?"
> "No, sirrr!—I support my wife Betsy and the children; and I tell you it's mighty hard. . . ."[21]

Presumably *Harper*'s readers would all share in the humor of the situation.

As we have seen, working-class husbands appear to have embraced the view that paid labor was economically superior to unpaid labor. They shared, too, a tendency to pastoralize the labor of their wives. The speeches of early labor activists, for example, frequently invoked both the rhetoric of the ideology of spheres and specifically pastoral images of the household, implying a sharp contrast between "the odious, cruel, unjust and tyrannical system" of the factory, which "compels the operative Mechanic to exhaust his physical and mental powers," and the presumably rejuvenating powers of the home. Discouraging women from carrying their labor "beyond the home," working men called upon women to devote themselves to improving the quality of life within their families. When the men described that undertaking, however, they focused, not on the myriad ways wives contributed daily to the material welfare of their households, but on a mission of passive benevolence. The *Maine Washingtonian Journal*, a working-class temperance journal, declared that "[i]t is in the calm and quiet retreat of domestic life that relaxation from toil is obtained. . . ." And there, as William Sylvis put it, it was the proper work of woman "to guide the tottering footsteps of tender infancy in the paths of rectitude and virtue, to smooth down the wrinkles of our perverse nature, to weep over our shortcomings, and make us glad in the days of our adversity, to counsel, comfort, and console us in our declining years."[22]

African-American newspapers of the antebellum Northeast also reflected and reaffirmed the pastoral conventions of women's domestic labor. *The Rights of All* compared women to ornamental creatures of nature, "as various in decorations as the insects, the birds, and the shells. . . ." In 1842, *The Northern Star and Freeman's Advocate* approvingly reprinted an article from the *Philadelphia Temperance Advocate* in which wives were described as deities "who preside over the sanctities of domestic life, and administer its sacred rights. . . ." That this perception ill fit the experiences of those female readers whose homes were also their unpaid workplaces, as well as those women who worked for money in someone else's home, appears not to have disturbed the paper's editors. Rather than as a worker, Woman was represented as a force of nature—and one presumably intended for man's special benefit: "The morning star of our youth—the day star of our manhood—the evening star of our age."[23]

For both middle-class and working-class men, the insecurities of income-earning during the antebellum period struck at the very heart of their traditional roles as husbands and fathers. Particularly since the late eighteenth century, manhood had been identified with wage-earning—with the provision of the cash to make the necessary purchases of the household. In the context of the reorganization of paid work in the antebellum Northeast, the growing dependence of households on cash, and the roller-coaster business cycles during which few families could feel safe, that identification faced almost constant challenge. And as it was challenged, it intensified.

By the antebellum period, the late–eighteenth-century association of manhood with wage-earning had flowered into the cult of the male "breadwinner." A direct response to the unstable economic conditions of early industrialization, this association crossed the lines of the emerging classes, characterizing the self-perceptions and social claims of both laboring and middle-class men.

Among laboring men, the identification of manhood with wage-earning melded easily with the traditional emphasis on the "manliness" of the crafts. Indeed, it was precisely as an attack on their "manliness" that antebellum workers responded to the demise of the old artisan system. Decrying the loss of what he perceived as the "equality of condition among the people" that had characterized the pre-Revolutionary era, Seth Luther focused on the effects of the economy in preventing working men from fulfilling their traditional roles: "It is much more difficult now, for a man to become possessed of a house to shelter his family than it was at that earlier period." An anonymous "mechanic" assumed that it was the work of the husband to "maintain himself and a wife, together with . . . [their] children" and complained that low wages made this virtually impossible. General Trades' Union leader Ely Moore warned that the unchecked industrial avarice of employers would create a class of "breadless and impotent" workers. When they struck for higher wages in 1860, the shoemakers of Massachusetts linked the encroachments of capital with an attack on their manhood; in the "Cordwainers' Song," they called on each other to "stand for your rights like men" and "Resolve by your fathers' graves" to emerge victorious and "like men" to "hold onto the last!"[24] Gender also provided the language for belittling the oppressor, for working men often expressed their rage, and reaffirmed their own manhood, by impugning the masculinity of their employers. The "Mechanic" sneered at "[t]he employers and those who hang on their skirts."[25]

In the midst of the upheavals of the antebellum economy, however, it was not only employers who threatened the old artisan definitions of manhood. Because an entire way of life was being undermined, the dangers seemed to arise from everywhere in the new social order, including from wage-earning women themselves. In fact, women seldom directly imperiled men's jobs. The young women who went to Lowell were entering an essentially new industry. Moreover, in their families and hired out on an individual basis, carding, spinning, fulling, and even, to some extent, weaving had long been a part of women's work. Similarly, in the shoe and garment industries, where they comprised a sizeable segment of the new outworkers, it is more accurate to describe the women as performing traditional work in a new relationship than as taking men's positions. Women had long worked as seamstresses—again, either for pay (hired out to an individual customer) or without pay (in their own families). Prior to the coming of the central shop, wives found time in between their other household duties to stitch the shoes sold by their husband "shoemakers."

But if wage-earning women did not directly challenge men's jobs, their very presence in the new paid labor force may have underscored the precariousness of men's position as wage-earners. Particularly given the post-Revolutionary emphasis on the importance of women's remaining in the home to cultivate the private virtues, females who were visible as outworkers and operatives may have seemed to bespeak an "unnaturalness" in society—an inability of wage-earning men to establish proper households. Like the witches of the seventeenth century, wage-earning women became symbols of the threats posed to a particular concept of manhood—in this instance, a concept that identified male claims to authority and power with the status of sole wage-earner. As they grappled with the precariousness of their own positions, laboring-class men focused their anxieties on the women who were their wives, daughters, and sisters, as well as on the men who were their employers.

They expressed these anxieties in two forms. First, wage-earning men complained that women were taking jobs, and thus the proper masculine role, away from men. An 1836 report of the National Trades' Union charged that because women's wages were so low, a woman's "efforts to sustain herself and family are actually the same as tying a stone around the neck of her natural protector, Man, and destroying him with the weight she has brought to his assistance." Not uncommonly, working men suggested that women did not really need to work for money and castigated "the girl, or the woman, as the case may be, who being in a condition to live comfortably at home by proper economy" selfishly took work from the truly needy. In 1831, the *Working Man's Advocate* called upon "those females who . . . are not dependent on their labor for a living" to withdraw from paid work so that men might have the jobs.[26]

At the same time, as we have seen, working men organized to call for "the family wage," a wage packet for the male "breadwinner" high enough to permit his wife and children to withdraw from paid work. As Martha May has pointed out, the family wage "promised a means to diminish capitalists' control over family life, by allowing workingmen to provide independently for their families." But the demand for the family wage also signaled the *gendering* of the emerging class system, and, in this, the gendering of early industrial culture. Identifying the husband as the proper and "natural" wage-earner, the family-wage ideal reinforced a distinctive male claim to the role of "breadwinner." By nature, women were ill-suited to wage-earning, many laboring-class men insisted. The National Trades' Union called attention to Woman's "physical organization" and "moral sensibilities" as evidence of her unfitness for paid labor, and the anonymous "mechanic" focused on "the fragile character of a girl's constitution, [and] her peculiar liability to sickness."[27] Presumably, only men had the constitution for regular, paid labor.

It is tempting to see in the antebellum ideology of spheres a simple extension of the Puritan injunction to wives to be keepers at home and faithful helpmates to men. Certainly the two sets of beliefs were related. The colonists brought with them a conviction that men and women were socially different beings, so created by God and so designated in the order of nature. Both were meant to labor, but they were meant to labor at different tasks. Perhaps even more important, they were meant to occupy quite different stations in social life and to exercise quite different levels of control over economic life. Women contributed to the household estate, but men were its owners. "Labor" may have been a gender-neutral term in colonial culture, but "authority" and "property" were masculine concepts, while "dependence" and "subordination" were clearly feminine conditions. Insofar as its gendered division of labor was overlaid with a hierarchy of status, seventeenth-century Euro-American culture provided the firm bedrock for the nineteenth-century ideology of spheres—with its attendant convention, the pastoralization of housework.

The origins of the antebellum gender culture were as much in the particular conditions of early industrialization as in the inherited past, however. Moreover, although historians have tended to focus on changes in women's work in accounting for the declining social status of housework, the specific character of the nineteenth-century gender culture was dictated less by transformations in women's experiences than by transformations in men's. To be sure, the principle of male dominance persisted into the nineteenth-century. If anything, the economic developments of the late eighteenth and early nineteenth centuries served to strengthen it. Social power in the antebellum Northeast rested increasingly on the ability to command the instruments of production and to accumulate and reinvest profits. From these activities wives were legally barred, as they were from the formal political processes that established the ground rules for the development of industrial capitalism. While most men were also eliminated from the contest on other grounds (race, class, and ethnicity, primarily), one had to be male to get into the competition at all.

But if early industrialization preserved male dominance, it effectively eroded the material basis for the specific form that male dominance had assumed in the colonial period: patriarchy. Few men could ground their claims to familial (and by extension, social) authority on their capacity to provide the material foundation for the welfare of succeeding generations. This was perhaps most strikingly the case for working-class men. With the demise of the artisan system, and so of a man's hopes to pass along a trade to his sons, the practical grounds on which a laboring man might lay claim to the role of male head-of-household had altered. Increasingly, it was less his position as future benefactor of the next generation than his position as the provider of the present generation (that is, the "breadwinner") that established a man's familial authority.

For men of the emerging middle class, the stakes were equally high but somewhat different. Many of these were the sons and grandsons of middling farmers, forebears who, while not wealthy, had established their adulthood through the ownership of land, and whose role in the family had centrally been that of the "father." Their power residing in their control of the inheritance left to the next generation, these were men who might have been described with some degree of accuracy as "patriarchs." But by the second decade of the nineteenth century, middling farms throughout much of the Northeast were scarcely capable of supporting the present generation; much less were they sizeable or fertile enough to establish patriarchal control of the family. Simultaneously, the emergence of an increasingly urban and industrial society rendered the inheritance of land a less useful and less attractive investment in the future for sons. Even successful businessmen and professionals experienced diminishing control over their sons' economic futures. A son might still read the law with his father, but new law schools, like medical schools, foreshadowed the time when specialized education, rather than on-the-job-training with his father or his father's friends, would offer a young man the best chance for success. As Mary Ryan has pointed out, small businessmen, "struggling to keep their own firms solvent," found it difficult "to put their progeny on a sound economic footing within the middling sort." Young men had to make their own way, Ryan emphasizes; at best, what a father was likely to be able to provide was not "a stock of cash, tools, goods, or real estate," but the "training acquired at secondary schools or colleges"[28]—training purchased by his father, but acquired at someone else's hand.

Early industrialization preserved the principle of male dominance, then, but in a new form: the "husband" replaced the "father." Men claimed social authority—and indeed exercised economic control—not because they owned the material resources upon which subsequent generations would be founded, but because they owned the resources upon which the present generation subsisted. More important, they had established hegemony over the definition of those resources. In the gender culture of the antebellum Northeast, subsistence was purchased by wages—and men were the wage-earners.

Early industrialization had simultaneously redefined the paradigm that guided the social and economic position of women. If the paradigm of manhood shifted from "father" to "husband," the paradigm of womanhood shifted from "goodwife" to "mother"—that is, from "worker" to "nurturer." Certainly, the role of mother carried some forms of cultural authority, but they were forms that derived from, and had practical power only within the context of, a society structured on relations of obligation and dependence. In a society in which power was asserted competitively and tallied by cash profit and loss, those forms seemed (and were) antiquated. Moreover, whatever cultural authority women gained as "mothers" was at the direct cost of a social identity in the terms that most counted in the nineteenth century—that is, as workers. As Caroline Dall noted in 1860, most Americans cherished "that old idea, that all men support all women. . . . " Dall recognized this to be "an absurd fiction," but it was a fiction with enormous social consequences. Even when women did enter paid work, their preeminent social identity as "mothers" (in distinct contrast to "workers") made their status as producers in the economy suspect: the predisposition to consider women "unfit" helped justify underpaying them.[29]

In all of this, the pastoralization of housework implicitly reinforced both the social right and the power of husbands and capitalists to claim the surplus value of women's labor, both paid and unpaid. It accomplished this by rendering the economic dimension of the labor invisible, thereby making pointless the very question of exploitation: one cannot confiscate what does not exist. Since the ideology of spheres made the noneconomic character of housework a simple "fact of nature," few observers in the antebellum Northeast felt compelled to argue the point.

The ideology of spheres did not affect all women the same way, of course. Insisting that the domestic ideal was founded on the nature of Woman (and not in the nature of society), prescriptive writers saw its embodiments everywhere—from the poorest orphan on the streets, to the mechanic's daughter, to the merchant's wife. But their models transparently were meant to be the women of the emerging middle class. It was, after all, in the middle classes that women had presumably been freed from the necessity for labor that had characterized the colonial helpmate; there, that mothers and wives had supposedly been enabled to express their fullest capacities in the service of family formation. Indeed, in the celebrations of middle-class "Motherhood" lay the fullest embodiments of the marginalization of housewives as workers.

But if middle-class women were encased in the image of the nurturant (and nonlaboring) mother, working-class women found that their visible inability to replicate that model worked equally hard against them. As historian Christine Stansell has vividly demonstrated, the inability (or unwillingness) of working-class women to remain in their homes—that is, their need to go out into the streets, as vendors, washerwomen, prostitutes, or simply as neighbors helping a friend out—provided the excuse for a growing middle-class intrusion into working-class households, as reformers claimed that women who could not (or did not wish to) aspire to middle-class standards were poor mothers.[30]

In all of this, the ideology of spheres bespoke the presumed differences between men and women—between ideal manhood and ideal womanhood. And yet, as the foregoing discussion may suggest, its construction as a gender system accounts for only a part of its power in antebellum America, and only a part of its lasting implications for American culture and society. The language of the ideology of spheres was the language of gender, but its essential dualism was less precisely the opposition of "female" and "male" than it was the opposition of "home" and "work," an opposition founded on the gendering of the concept of labor.

In addition to its specific implications for women, the ideology of spheres, and the pastoralization of housework that lay at the heart of that ideology, both represented and supported larger cultural changes attending the evolution of early industrial capitalism. The transition to industrialization was not purely material: it was ideological as well, involving and requiring new ways of viewing the relationship of labor to its products and of the worker to his or her work. In its denial of the economic value of one form of labor, the pastoralization of housework signaled the growing devaluation of labor in general in industrial America. Artisans were discovering, and would continue to discover, what housewives learned early in the nineteenth century: as the old skills were debased and gradually replaced by new ones, workers' social claims to the fruits of their labor would be severely undercut. Increasingly productivity was attributed, not to workers, but to those "most wonderful machines."[31] It was in part against such a redefinition that the craft workers of New York and the shoemakers of Lynn, Massachusetts, struggled.[32]

The denial of the economic value of housework was also one aspect of a tendency, originating much earlier but growing throughout the eighteenth and nineteenth centuries, to draw ever-finer distinctions between the values of different categories of labor, and to elevate certain forms of economic activity to a superior status on the grounds of the income they produced. As with housework, these distinctions were rarely founded on the actual material value of the labor in question. Rather, they were based on contemporary levels of power and wealth, and served to justify those existing conditions. An industrialist or financier presumably deserved to earn very sizeable amounts of money, because in accumulating capital he had clearly contributed more labor and labor of a more valuable kind to society than had, for example, a drayman or a foundry worker. In her *Conversations on Political Economy* (written in England but widely used by colleges and secondary schools in the United States after 1816), Jane Marcet offered what was to become the standard formulation of this argument: civilization originated in private property, and private property was the result of individual industry. Poverty was a sign of indolence and savagery; wealth symbolized the expenditure of labor toward the betterment of society.[33]

Finally, the ideology of spheres functioned to support the emergence of the wage system necessary to the development of industrial capitalism. The success of the wage system depends on a number of factors—among them the perception of money as a neutral index of economic value and the acceptance of the wage as representing a fair "livelihood." The devaluation of housework was part of a larger process of obscuring the continuation of and necessity for barter-based exchanges in the American economy. In this, it veiled the reliance of the family on resources other than those provided through paid labor and heightened the visibility of the wage as the source of family maintenance.

But how did women respond to the growing devaluation of their contributions as laborers in the family economy? As we have seen, in their private letters and diaries, wives quietly offered their own definition of what constituted the livelihood of their families, posing their own perception of the importance of conservation and stewardship against the cash-based index of the marketplace and easily integrating the family's periodic needs for extra cash into their understanding of their own obligations.

Nevertheless, among the public voices affirming that Woman was meant for a different sphere than Man, and that the employments of Woman in the home were of a spiritual rather than an economic nature, were the voices of many women. In *Woman in America*, for example, Mrs. A. J. Graves declared: "[H]ome is [woman's] appropriate sphere of action; and . . . whenever she neglects these duties, or goes out of this sphere . . . she is deserting the station which God and nature have assigned to her." Underscoring the stark contrast between Woman's duties in the household and Man's in "the busy and turbulent world," Graves described the refuge of the home in terms as solemn as any penned by men during the antebellum period: "[O]ur husbands and our sons . . . will rejoice to return to its sanctuary of rest," she averred, "there to refresh their wearied spirits, and renew their strength for the toils and conflicts of life."[34]

Graves was not unusual in her endorsement of the ideology of spheres and of the pastoralization of housework. Even the women who most championed the continuing importance of women's household labor often couched that position in the language of spheres. No one more graphically illustrates this combination than Catharine Beecher, at once probably the most outspoken defender of the importance of women's domestic labor *and* one of the chief proponents of the ideology of female domesticity. As we have seen, Beecher was clear and insistent that housework was hard work, and she did not shrink from suggesting that its demands and obligations were very similar to men's "business." In her *Treatise on Domestic Economy*, Beecher went so far as to draw a specific analogy between the marriage contract and the wage-labor contract:

> No woman is forced to obey any husband but the one she chooses for herself; nor is she obliged to take a husband, if she prefers to remain single. So every domestic, and every artisan or laborer, after passing from parental control, can choose the employer to whom he is to accord obedience, or, if he prefers to relinquish certain advantages, he can remain without taking a subordinate place to any employer.

Nevertheless, Beecher regularly characterized women's work in the home as the occupation merely of administering "the gentler charities of life," a "mission" chiefly of "self-denial" to "lay up treasures, not on earth, but in heaven." This employment she contrasted with the "toils" of Man, to whom was "appointed the out-door labor—to till the earth, dig the mines, toil in the foundries, traverse the ocean, transport the merchandise, labor in manufactories, construct houses . . . and all the heavy work. . . . "[35]

Beecher's apparently self-defeating endorsement of a view that ultimately discounted the value of women's labor arose from many sources, not the least of which was her own identification with the larger middle-class interests served by the ideology of spheres. Beecher enjoyed the new standing afforded middle-class women by their roles as moral guardians of their families and of society, and based much of her own claim to status as a woman on the presumed differences between herself and immigrant and laboring-class women. For example, she ended a lengthy discussion of "the care of Servants" in *The American Woman's Home* with the resigned conclusion that "[t]he mistresses of American families, whether they like it or not, have the duties of missionaries imposed upon them by that class from which our supply of domestic servants is drawn."[36]

But, also like many women in antebellum America, Catharine Beecher was sharply aware of the power difference between males and females. It was a theme she constantly returned to in her writings, especially in her discussions of women's rights, where she warned again and again that the movement for woman suffrage was "unsafe," since men. . . . In her *Essay on Slavery and Abolitionism*, Beecher was quite explicit about the reasons why a woman might cloak herself and her opinions in the language of dependence and subordination:

> [T]he moment woman begins to feel the promptings of ambition, or the thirst for power, her aegis of defence is gone. All the sacred protection of religion, all the generous promptings of chivalry, all the poetry of romantic gallantry, depend upon woman's retaining her place as dependent and defenceless, and making no claims. . . .

It was much the same point that Elizabeth Ellet would later make in her *Practical Housekeeper*: since men had many more alternatives than women, the smart woman made it her "policy" to create an appearance of domestic serenity.[37]

But it would be a mistake to read women's endorsement of the pastoralization of housework purely as a protective strategy. Women were not immune from the values of their communities, and many wives appear to have shared the perception of the larger society that their work had separated from the economic life of the community and that it was, in fact, not really work at all.

Those misgivings were nowhere more evident than in the letter that Harriet Beecher Stowe wrote to her sister-in-law, Sarah Beecher, in 1850. It was the first opportunity Harriet had had to write since the Stowes had moved to Brunswick, Maine, the spring before. Since her arrival with the children, she explained, she had "made two sofas—or lounges—a barrel chair—divers bedspreads—pillowcases—pillows—bolsters—mattresses . . . painted rooms . . . [and] revarnished furniture." She had also laid a month-long seige at the landlord's door, lobbying him to install a new sink. Meanwhile, she had given birth to her eighth child, made her way through the novels of Sir Walter Scott, and tried to meet the obligations of her increasingly active career as an author—all of this while also attending to the more mundane work of running a household: dealing with tradespeople, cooking, and taking care of the children. From delivery bed to delivery cart, downstairs to the kitchen, upstairs to the baby, out to a neighbor's, home to stir the stew, the image of Stowe flies through these pages like the specter of the sorcerer's apprentice.

Halfway through the letter, Stowe paused. "And yet," she confided to her sister-in-law, "I am constantly pursued and haunted by the idea that I don't do anything."[38] It is a jarring note in a letter—and a life—so shaped by the demands of housework. That a skilled and loving mother could impart dignity and a sense of humane purpose to a family otherwise vulnerable to the degradations of the marketplace, Stowe had no doubt. But was that really "work"? She was less certain. In that uncertainty, to borrow Daniel Eddy's words, lay "a world of domestic meaning"—for housewives of the antebellum era, and for women since.

NOTES

Introduction

1. Antoinette Brown Blackwell, "Industrial Reconstruction," *The Woman's Advocate* 1/1 (January 1869): 41–42. I thank Lori D. Ginzberg for bringing this article to my attention.

2. Elizabeth Cady Stanton, Susan B. Anthony, and Matilda Jocelyn Gage, eds., *History of Woman Suffrage* (New York: Arno and The New York Times, 1969; orig. pub. New York: Fowler and Wells, 1881) I:70, 105, and 233.

3. Dolores Hayden, *The Grand Domestic Revolution: A History of Feminist Designs for American Homes, Neighborhoods, and Cities* (Cambridge, Mass.; MIT Press, 1981), p. 1.

4. The character of the "cult of domesticity," coined by Aileen Kraditor (*Up from the Pedestal: Selected Writings in the History of American Feminism* [Chicago: Quadrangle Books, 1968], p. 10), has been well documented by recent women's historians. The classic descriptions are: Barbara Welter, "The Cult of True Womanhood, 1820–1860," *American Quarterly* 18 (Summer 1966): 151–75; Kathryn Kish Sklar, *Catharine Beecher: A Study in American Domesticity* (New Haven, Conn.: Yale University Press, 1973); Nancy F. Cott, *The Bonds of Womanhood: "Woman's Sphere" in New England, 1780–1835* (New Haven, Conn.: Yale University Press, 1977); Barbara Leslie Epstein, *The Politics of Domesticity: Women, Evangelism, and Temperance in Nineteenth-Century America* (Middletown, Conn.: Wesleyan University Press, 1981); Carl N. Degler, *At Odds: Women and the Family from the Revolution to the Present* (New York: Oxford University Press, 1980); and Mary P. Ryan, *Cradle of the Middle Class:*

The Family in Oneida County, New York, 1790–1865 (New York: Cambridge University Press, 1981). A recent study that argues that the "cult of domesticity" was the source of enormously increased power and influence for women is Glenna Matthews' *"Just a Housewife": The Rise and Fall of Domesticity in America* (New York: Oxford University Press, 1987).

5. Juliet Mitchell, "Women: The Longest Revolution," *New Left Review* 40 (November–December, 1966); Selma James and Mariarosa Dalla Costa, *The Power of Women and the Subversion of the Community* (Bristol, England: Falling Wall Press, 1973); Margaret Benston, "The Political Economy of Women's Liberation," *Monthly Review* (September 1969): 13–27.

6. Wally Seccombe, "The Housewife and Her Labour Under Capitalism," *New Left Review* 83 (January–February 1974): 3–24; see esp. pp. 8–13.

7. Margaret Coulson, Branka Magas, and Hilary Wainwright, " 'The Housewife and Her Labour Under Capitalism'—A Critique," *New Left Review* 89 (January–February 1975): 59–72; Jean Gardiner, "Women's Domestic Labour," *New Left Review* 89 (January–February 1975): 47–58. Quotations from Gardiner are from p. 5l.

8. Gayle Rubin, "The Traffic in Women: Notes on the 'Political Economy' of Sex," in Rayna R. Reiter, ed., *Toward an Anthropology of Women* (New York: Monthly Review Press, 1975), pp. 162 (note) and 164.

9. M. Z. Rosaldo, "The Use and Abuse of Anthropology: Reflections on Feminism and Cross-Cultural Understanding," *Signs* 5 (Spring 1980): 399; 400; n. 20, p. 402. Italics added.

10. Linda K. Kerber, "Separate Sphere, Female Worlds, Woman's Place: The Rhetoric of Women's History." *Journal of American History* 75/1 (June 1988): 9-39.

11. Faye E. Dudden, *Serving Women: Household Service in Nineteenth-Century America* (Middletown, Conn.: Wesleyan University Press, 1983); Laurel Thatcher Ulrich, *Good Wives: Image and Reality in the Lives of Women in Northern New England, 1650–1750* (New York: Alfred A. Knopf, 1982); Joan M. Jensen, *Loosening the Bonds: Mid-Atlantic Farm Women, 1750–1850* (New Haven, Conn.: Yale University Press, 1986).

12. Susan Strasser, *Never Done: A History of American Housework* (New York: Pantheon Books, 1982); Ruth Schwartz Cowan, *More Work for Mother: The Ironies of Household Technology from the Open Hearth to the Microwave* (New York: Basic Books, 1983); Annegret S. Ogden, *The Great American Housewife: From Helpmate to Wage Earner, 1776–1986* (Westport, Conn.: Greenwood Press, 1986); Matthews, *"Just a Housewife."*

13. Cowan, *More Work for Mother*, pp. 4 and 7.

14. Karl Marx, *Capital*, trans. Ben Fowkes (New York: Vintage Books, 1977), 1:162, 164–65, 196, 197.

15. See, for example, Peggy Reeves Sanday, *Female Power and Male Dominance: On the Origins of Sexual Inequality* (New York: Cambridge University Press, 1981).

16. As noted by Zulma Recchini de Lattes and Catalina H. Wainerman, this

point is forcefully illustrated in the categories recommended for labor-force analysis by both the Inter-American Statistical Institute and the United Nations Statistical Commission. Based on the model of "the activity of males in developed economies without crisis," the categories undercount the extent of women's economic participation in Latin America and the Caribbean by 12 to 52 percent, according to the authors. See "Unreliable Account of Women's Work: Evidence from Latin American Census Statistics," *Signs* 11/4 (Summer 1986): 740–50.

17. Judith K. Brown, "Iroquois Women: An Ethnohistoric Note," and Patricia Draper, "iKung Women: Contrasts in Sexual Egalitarianism in Foraging and Sedentary Contexts," in Reiter, *Toward an Anthropology of Women*, pp. 77–109 and 235–51. See also Karen Anderson, "Commodity Exchange and Subordination: Montagnais-Naskapi and Huron Women, 1600–1650," *Signs* 11/1 (Autumn 1985): 48–62. Anderson argues that Huron women were better able to resist male domination than were the Algonkian Mantagnais-Naskapi, not because of the nature of their work, but because of the extent of their access to the means of livelihood: "[a]mong the Huron . . . kin-based social relations of production continued to guarantee women, as well as men, the right of unmediated access to the necessities of life" (p. 62).

For a synthesis of the anthropological literature on women's work in preindustrial societies, see Martin King Whyte, *The Status of Women in Pre-Industrial Societies* (Princeton, N.J.: Princeton University Press, 1978).

18. Heidi I. Hartmann, "Capitalism, Patriarchy, and Job Segregation by Sex," *Signs* 1/3 (Spring 1976): 137–70. See also idem, "The Family as the Locus of Gender, Class, and Political Struggle: The Example of Housework," *Signs* 6 (Spring 1981): 366–94. Several review essays have provided overviews of the recent historical treatments of the subject. See especially Martha C. Howell, "Marriage, Property, and Patriarchy: Recent Contributions to the Literature," *Feminist Studies* 13/1 (Spring 1987): 203–24; and Marjorie Murphy, "Work, Protest, and Culture: New York on Working Women's History," *Feminist Studies* 13/3 (Fall 1987): 657–67.

Notes to Chapter I

1. Ann D. Gordon and Mari Jo Buhle, "Sex and Class in Colonial and Nineteenth-Century America," in Berenice A. Carroll, ed., *Liberating Women's History: Theoretical and Critical Essays* (Urbana: University of Illinois Press, 1976), p. 279. The thesis that the colonial period represented a more equitable environment for women was developed by Elisabeth A. Dexter as early as 1924, in her *Colonial Women of Affairs: Women in Business and the Professions in Colonial America Before 1776* (Boston: Houghton Mifflin). The influence of this interpretation on the new field of women's history in the late 1960s and 1970s is visible in such works as: Gerda Lerner, "The Lady and the Mill Girl: Changes in the Status of Women in the Age of Jackson," *Midcontinent American*

Studies Journal X (Spring 1969): 5–15; Mary P. Ryan, *Womanhood in America: From Colonial Times to the Present* (New York: New Viewpoints, 1975); and Joan Hoff Wilson, "The Illusion of Change: Women and the American Revolution," in Alfred F. Young, ed., *The American Revolution: Explorations in the History of American Radicalism* (DeKalb: Northern Illinois University Press, 1976): 383–445.

2. The depiction of colonial farms as largely self-sufficient and non–market-oriented extends as far back as Percy W. Bidwell and Frank I. Falconer's *History of Agriculture in the Northern United States, 1680–1860* (Washington, D.C.: 1925). More recently, the extent of market involvement by eighteenth-century New Englanders has become the stuff of lively debate among historians. For interesting contributions to that discussion, see: Richard L. Bushman, *From Puritan to Yankee: Character and the Social Order in Connecticut, 1690–1765* (New York: W. W. Norton, 1967), especially pp. 107–43; James Henretta, "Families and Farms: *Mentalité* in Pre-Industrial America," *William and Mary Quarterly*, 3rd ser., 35 (January 1978): 3–32; idem, *The Evolution of American Society, 1700–1815: An Interdisciplinary Analysis* (Lexington, Mass.: D. C. Heath, 1973), especially pp. 95–107; Robert E. Mutch, "Colonial America and the Debate about the Transition to Capitalism," *Theory and Society* 9 (1980): 847–63; Michael Merrill, "Cash Is Good to Eat: Self-Sufficiency and Exchange in the Rural Economy of the United States," *Radical History Review* (Winter 1977), 42–71; Christopher Clark, "The Household Mode of Production—A Comment," *Radical History Review* (Fall 1978), 166–71; Winifred Rothenberg, "The Market and Massachusetts Farmers, 1750–1855," *Journal of Economic History* 6 (1981): 283–313; William Cronon, *Changes in the Land: Indians, Colonists, and the Ecology of New England* (New York: Hill and Wang, 1983); and Bettye Hobbs Pruitt, "Self-Sufficiency and the Agricultural Economy of Eighteenth-Century Massachusetts," *William and Mary Quarterly*, 3rd ser., 41 (1984): 333–64.

3. Mary Beth Norton, "The Myth of the Golden Age," in Carol Ruth Berkin and Mary Beth Norton, *Women of America: A History* (Boston: Houghton Mifflin, 1979), p. 42; and Mary Beth Norton, *Liberty's Daughters: The Revolutionary Experience of American Women, 1750–1800* (Boston: Little, Brown, 1980), p. 38.

4. Ulrich, *Good Wives*, pp. 33–34.

5. William Secker, *A Wedding ring for the finger. . . . Directions to those men who want wives, how to choose them* (Boston: Samuel Green, 1690), n.p.; "Church Trial of Mistress Ann Hibbens," in Nancy F. Cott, ed., *Root of Bitterness: Documents of the Social History of American Women* (New York: E. P. Dutton, 1972), p. 55.

6. For general studies of the society and culture of colonial New York, see Patricia U. Bonomi, *A Factious People: Politics and Society in Colonial New York* (New York: Columbia University Press, 1971); and Michael G. Kammen, *Colonial New York: A History* (New York: Scribner's, 1975). Useful discussions of the economic status of women (especially widows) in colonial New York

include Christine H. Tompsett, "A Note on the Economic Status of Widows in Colonial New York," *New York History* 55 (1974): 319–32; and David Narrett, "Preparation for Death and Provision for the Living: Notes on New York Wills (1665–1760)," *New York History* 52 (1976): 417–37.

7. John Winthrop, *The History of New England*, Vol. 2., ed. James Savage (Boston: Little, Brown, 1853), p. 216.

8. Samuel Willard, *A Compleat Body of Divinity* (Boston, 1726).

9. Alexander Niccoles, *Discourse on Marriage and Wiving* (London, 1615).

10. Proverbs 31:30; John Cotton, *A Meet Help. Or, a Wedding Sermon, Preached at New-Castle in New-England, June 19, 1694* (Boston: B. Green and J. Allen, 1699), p. 14; *A Marriage Prayer* (London, 1637); Mary Boutwell, Essex Record, 1640, as quoted in Rosalyn Baxandall, Linda Gordon, and Susan Reverby, eds., *America's Working Women: A Documentary History—1600 to the Present* (New York: Random House, 1976), p. 21. For my interpretation of Cotton's sermon, I am indebted to Carol F. Karlsen.

11. Bartlett Burleigh James and J. Franklin Jameson, eds., *Journal of Jasper Danckaerts, 1679–1680* (New York: Scribner's, 1913), pp. 47, 54, and 215; advertisement for "Tambour Work," *The New York Gazette and the Weekly Mercury*, March 7, 1774, as quoted in *The Arts and Crafts in New York, 1726–1776: Advertisements and News Items from New York City Newspapers*, Vol. 69 (New York Historical Society Collections, 1939), p. 280.

12. Francis Higginson, "New England's Plantation" (London, 1630), in Alexander Young, ed., *Chronicles of the First Planters of the Colony of Massachusetts Bay* (Boston, 1846), pp. 266–67; Order of Fall, 1639, Sudbury Town Book, Office of the Town Clerk, Sudbury, Massachusetts.

13. George Abbott, will, December 21, 1681, Probate Records of Essex County, as quoted in Philip J. Greven, Jr., *Four Generations: Population, Land, and Family in Colonial Andover, Massachusetts* (Ithaca, N.Y.: Cornell University Press, 1970), n. 12, pp. 82–83; William Brigham, *The Compact with the Charter and Laws of the Colony of New Plymouth* (Boston: Dutton and Wentworth, 1836), p. 281.

14. David Pulsifer, ed., *Deeds, &c., 1620–1651*, Vol. 12 of *Records of the Colony of New Plymouth, in New England*, ed. Nathaniel B. Shurtleff and David Pulsifer (Boston: Press of William White, 1855–1861), May 22, 1627, pp. 9–13; Nathaniel B. Shurtleff, ed., *Records of the Governor and Company of the Massachusetts Bay in New England* (Boston: Press of William White, 1853), September 28, 1630, 1:76–77.

15. Shurtleff, *Massachusetts Records*, May 14, 1645, 2:116–17.

16. Ibid., November 4, 1646, 2:180.

17. Bernard Bailyn, ed., *The Apologia of Robert Keayne: The Self-Portrait of a Puritan Merchant* (New York: Harper Torchbooks, 1964), pp. 5 and 79.

18. Alexander Keyssar, "Widowhood in Eighteenth-Century Massachusetts: A Problem in the History of the Family," *Perspectives in American History* 8 (1974): 83–119; Cotton Mather, *Ornaments for the Daughters of Zion. Or The Character and Happiness of a Virtuous Woman* (Boston: S. G[reen] and B.

G[reen], 1692), p. 8; Thomas Foxcroft, *The Character of Anna. . . . In a Sermon Preach'd after the Funeral of . . . Dame Bridget Usher* . . . (Boston: S. Kneeland, 1723), p. 55.

Discussions of widowhood are also found in: Cotton Mather, *Maternal Consolations. An Essay . . . on the Death of Mrs. Maria Mather* . . . (Boston: T. Fleet, 1714), especially p. 9; Increase Mather, *Two Discourses* . . . (Boston: B. Green, 1716), especially pp. 100–101; idem, "Preface" to Cotton Mather, *Marah Spoken to. A Brief Essay to do good unto the Widow* . . . (Boston: S. Kneeland, 1718), especially pp. i–iv.

19. Benjamin Colman, *The Duty and Honour of Aged Women. A Sermon on the Death of Madam Abigail Foster* (Boston: B. Green, 1711), p. ii; I. Mather, "Preface," p. iv; Thomas Foxcroft, *A Sermon Preach'd at Cambridge, After the Funeral of Mrs. Elizabeth Foxcroft* . . . (Boston: B. Green, 1721), p. 7.

20. George Savile, Marquis of Halifax, *Advice to a Daughter* (London: n.p., 1688); Norton, *Liberty's Daughters*, p. 113.

21. Nicholas Noyes, a poem for Mrs. Mary Brown in Cotton E. Mather, *Eureka. Or a Vertuous Woman Found: An Essay on the Death of Mrs. Mary Brown* (Boston: n.p., 1703), p. 3.

22. "A-La-Mode, for the Year 1756," *Boston Evening Post*, supplement, March 8, 1756; untitled poem, *Boston Gazette*, February 9, 1748; "By the Ranger," *Boston Evening Post*, October 16, 1758.

23. *New York Mercury*, October 16, 1758, as quoted in *Arts and Crafts in New York*, pp. 276–77; Christine Stansell, *City of Women: Sex and Class in New York, 1789–1860* (New York: Alfred A. Knopf, 1986); see especially pp. 19–30.

24. For additional discussion of the "notable housewife," see Norton, *Liberty's Daughters*, pp. 4–5 and 38–39.

25. Shurtleff, *Records*, October 1, 1633, 1:109; October 7, 1640, 1:304.

26. This discussion is based on: Cowan, *More Work for Mother*; John Deetz, *In Small Things Forgotten: The Archeology of Early American Life* (Garden City, N.Y.: Anchor Books, 1977); and Alice Morse Earle, *Colonial Dames and Goodwives* (New York: Houghton Mifflin, 1895); Joan M. Jensen, "Cloth, Butter and Boarders: Women's Household Production for the Market," *Review of Radical Political Economics* 12 (Summer 1980): 14–24; idem, *Loosening the Bonds: Mid-Atlantic Farm Women, 1750–1850* (New Haven, Conn.: Yale University Press, 1986); Norton, *Liberty's Daughters*; Laurel Thatcher Ulrich, " 'A Friendly Neighbor': Social Dimensions of Daily Work in Northern Colonial New England," *Feminist Studies* 6 (Summer 1980): 392–405; and idem, *Good Wives*.

27. Henry M. Burt, ed., *The First Century of the History of Springfield: The Official Records from 1636 to 1736* (Springfield, Mass.: H. M. Burt, 1898), January 10, 1644, 1:176–77.

28. Samuel G. Drake, ed., *Annals of Witchcraft in New England and Elsewhere in the United States, from their First Settlement* (Boston: W. E. Woodward, 1864), p. 229; Alice Apsley is cited in Lyle Koehler, *A Search for Power: "The*

Weaker Sex" in Seventeenth-Century New England (Urbana: The University of Illinois Press, 1980), p. 115.

29. *The Diary of Mary Cooper: Life on a Long Island Farm, 1768–1773*, ed. Field Horne (Oyster Bay, N.Y.: Oyster Bay Historical Society, 1981), July 13, 1769, p. 15.

30. Ibid.: March 7, 1769, p. 9; December 24, 1768, p. 5.

31. Ibid.: July 3, 1772, p. 34; October 5, 1772, p. 41; April 14, 1773, p. 56; October 11–13, 1768, p. 1; July 20–21, 24–25, and 28, 1769, pp. 15–16; August 20, 1772, p. 38; October 16, 1772, p. 42; November 2, 1772, p. 43; November 23, 1768, p. 4; June 2, 1769, p. 13; July 6, 1769, p. 15; December 2, 1769, p. 24; December 16, 1772, p. 46; November 6, 1772, p. 43; November 15, 1769, p. 23; November 16, 1769, p. 23; December 12, 1769, p. 25; May 1 and 4, 1771, pp. 31–32.

32. Ibid.: October 11 and 14, 1768, p. 1; February 3, 1769, p. 7; September 25, 1769, p. 19; August 20, 1772, p. 38; August 3, 1772, p. 35; August 22, 1772, p. 38; October 3, 1768, p. 1; March 20, 1769, p. 10; November 18, 1768, p. 3; October 24, 1768, p. 2.

33. Ibid.: August 4, 1772, p. 37; September 1, 1772, p. 39; August 15, 1772, p. 37; August 5, 1772, p. 64; October 16, 1772, p. 42.

34. Benjamin Franklin, *The Autobiography of Benjamin Franklin* (New Haven, Conn.: Yale University Press, 1964), p. 145.

35. Ulrich, *Good Wives*, p. 75.

36. Carol F. Karlsen and Laurie Crumpacker, eds., *The Journal of Esther Edwards Burr, 1754–1757* (New Haven, Conn.: Yale University Press, 1984), pp. 100, 127, and 165.

37. Ibid., pp. 51, 74, and 170.

38. Ibid., pp. 57, 93, and 155.

39. Ulrich, " 'Friendly Neighbor,' " pp. 395–98. In her larger study, Ulrich speculates from the number of beds present in the household that the Grafton family of late-seventeenth-century Salem included both boarders and servants. Joseph Grafton was a young mariner. See idem, *Good Wives*, p. 25.

40. Karlsen and Crumpacker, *Esther Burr*, p. 155.

41. Willard, *Compleat Body of Divinity*, p. 610. For useful discussions of this early view of "economy" and of its subsequent changes, see Bushman, *From Puritan to Yankee*, pp. 135–43; and J. E. Crowley, *This Sheba, Self: The Conceptualization of Economic Life in Eighteenth-Century America* (Baltimore, Md.: Johns Hopkins University Press, 1974), passim.

42. See Herbert Moller, "Sex Composition and Correlated Cultural Patterns in Colonial America," *William and Mary Quarterly*, 3rd ser., 2 (1945): 113–53.

43. Cotton Mather, *Family Religion Urged* (Boston: n.p., 1709), p. 1; Thomas Cobbett, *A Fruitfull and Usefull Discourse touching the Honour due from Children to Parents and the Duty of Parents towards their Children* (London: n.p., 1654), n.p.; William Bradford, *Of Plymouth Plantation*, ed. Harvey Wish (New York: Capricorn Books, 1962), p. 90.

44. Shurtleff, *Massachusetts Records*, June 14, 1642, 2:6–7; Ulrich, " 'Friendly Neighbor,' " pp. 402–3.

45. These similarities are also noted by Cowan in her discussion of preindustrial housework. See *More Work for Mother*, pp. 24–25.

46. Henretta, *Evolution of American Society*, p. 9; Rowland Berthoff, *An Unsettled People: Social Order and Disorder in American History* (New York: Harper and Row, 1971), p. 34.

47. Douglas Lamar Jones, "The Strolling Poor: Transiency in Eighteenth-Century Massachusetts," *Journal of Social History* (Spring 1975), 32–33; Henretta, *Evolution of American Society*, p. 96; idem, "Economic Development and Social Structure in Colonial Boston," *William and Mary Quarterly*, 3rd ser., 22 (1965): 87.

48. Linda Auwers Bissell, "Family, Friends, and Neighbors: Social Interaction in Seventeenth-Century Windsor, Connecticut" (Ph.D. diss., Brandeis University, 1973), p. 33; Kenneth Lockridge, *A New England Town, The First Hundred Years: Dedham, Massachusetts, 1636–1736* (New York: W. W. Norton, 1970), p. 149; Jones, "Strolling Poor," pp. 32–33; Jackson Turner Main, *The Social Structure of Revolutionary America* (Princeton, N.J.: Princeton University Press, 1965), pp. 7–43.

49. Christopher M. Jedrey, *The World of John Cleaveland: Family and Community in Eighteenth-Century New England* (New York: W. W. Norton, 1979), p. 63; Lockridge, *New England Town*, pp. 10 and 71.

50. Greven, *Four Generations*, pp. 57–62; William B. Scott, *In the Pursuit of Happiness: American Conceptions of Property from the Seventeenth to the Twentieth Century* (Bloomington: Indiana University Press, 1977), pp. 15–17.

51. See note 2 of this chapter.

52. Boston *Evening Post*, p. 4. On Northampton, see Patricia J. Tracy, *Jonathan Edwards, Pastor: Religion and Society in Eighteenth-Century Northampton* (New York: Hill and Wang, 1980), p. 97. On Kent, see Bushman, *From Puritan to Yankee*, pp. 74–76. See also Berthoff, *Unsettled People*, p. 74; and Henretta, *Evolution of American Society*, p. 103.

53. Benjamin Franklin, "The Way to Wealth," in *The Works of Benjamin Franklin*, ed. Jared Sparks (Boston: Hilliard, Gray, 1840) 2:96; Tracy, *Jonathan Edwards*, p. 102; *Colonial Currency Reprints, 1682–1751*, ed. Andrew McFarland Davis (Boston: 1910–1911) 2:325; Greven, *Four Generations*, p. 154.

In addition to larger urban areas, these eighteenth-century shifts have been documented for smaller communities such as Dedham, Chebacco, Andover, and Northampton, Massachusetts; and Kent, Windsor, and Norwich, Connecticut. See, respectively: Lockridge, *New England Town*, pp. 145–46; Jedrey, *World of John Cleaveland*, pp. 65–68; Greven, *Four Generations*, pp. 243–53; Tracy, *Jonathan Edwards*, pp. 40–42, 92, and 97; Henretta, *Evolution of American Society*, p. 103; and Bushman, *From Puritan to Yankee*, p. 123.

54. *The Journal of Madame Knight* (Boston: David R. Godine, 1972), pp. 40–41; Main, *Social Structure of Revolutionary America*, pp. 134, 136, and 145—the quotation is from p. 145; Arthur Nussbaum, *A History of the Dollar* (New York: Columbia University Press, 1957), pp. 19–20; Richard Hofstadter, *America at 1750: A Social Portrait* (New York: Alfred A. Knopf, 1971), p. 140.

55. Bernard Bailyn, *The New England Merchants in the Seventeenth Century* (New York: Harper and Row, 1964), p. 187; Edmund S. Morgan and Helen M. Morgan, *The Stamp Act Crisis: Prologue to Revolution* (New York: Collier Books, 1962), p. 48.

56. Carol F. Karlsen, *The Devil in the Shape of a Woman: Witchcraft in Colonial New England* (New York: W. W. Norton, 1987), see especially Chapters III and VI; Keyssar, "Widowhood," pp. 101–11; Tracy, *Jonathan Edwards*, p. 103. Although the evidence has not been examined from precisely this point of view, John Demos' study of Plymouth and Philip Greven's study of Andover suggest that parallel developments may well have occurred in those communities. See Demos, *A Little Commonwealth: Family Life in Plymouth Colony* (New York: Oxford, 1970), pp. 75, 99, and 177–178; and Greven, *Four Generations*, pp. 90, 137, 143, 145–46, and 152–53.

57. Karlsen, *Devil in the Shape of a Woman*, pp. 153–81; Mather, *Ornaments*, pp. 103–4.

58. In Andover, Massachusetts, for example, the average age at first marriage for men rose from 26.7 in the late seventeenth century to 27.1 throughout the first half of the eighteenth century; the corresponding rise for women was from 22.3 to 24.5 (Greven, *Four Generations*, pp. 33–36, 118–22); Colman, *Duty and Honour of Aged Women*, p. 6.

59. Ulrich, " 'Friendly Neighbor,' " pp. 394–95; Mather, *Ornaments*, pp. 42 and 85.

60. Sumner Chilton Powell, *Puritan Village, The Formation of a New England Town* (Middletown, Conn.: Wesleyan University Press, 1963), p. 161.

61. In Boston the rate of warnings-out tripled between 1745 and 1759 and doubled again in the next decade; in Hampshire County, Massachusetts, the proportion of households warned out increased by 75 percent between 1739 and 1754 and by another 250 percent by 1764. See Alan Kulikoff, "The Progress of Inequality in Revolutionary Boston," *William and Mary Quarterly*, 3rd ser., 28 (1971): 400; and Jones, "Strolling Poor," p. 33.

62. Quoted in Koehler, *Search for Power*, p. 137.

63. Quoted in Sylvester Judd, *History of Hadley, including the Early History of Hatfield, South Hadley, Amherst and Granby, Massachusetts* (Springfield, Mass.: H. R. Huntting and Company, 1905), p. 75; Jared Eliot, *Essays upon Field Husbandry in New England and Other Papers, 1748–1762*, ed. Harry J. Carman, Rexford G. Tugwell, and Rodney H. True (New York: Columbia University Press, 1942), p. 187.

64. Crowley, *This Sheba, Self*, p. 65; Cotton, *A Meet Help*, p. 21.

Notes to Chapter II

1. *Boston Evening Post*, July 3 and September 21, 1769.

2. *American State Papers, 1789–1815*, Vol. 2: *Finance* (Washington, D.C.: Gale and Seaton, 1832) Part 1, pp. 10–11.

3. On the nature of particular shortages, see Henretta, *Evolution of American Society*, p. 159. Quotations are from Victor S. Clark, *History of Manufactures in the United States* (New York: McGraw-Hill Book Company, 1929) 1:200 and 212; and Tench Coxe, *A View of the United States of America* (London: J. Johnson, 1795; orig. pub. Philadelphia, 1794), pp. 167–68.

4. Mary Beth Norton, "Eighteenth-Century American Women in Peace and War: The Case of the Loyalists," *William and Mary Quarterly*, 3rd ser., 33 (July 1976): 386–409. The quotation is from p. 387. Elsewhere, Norton has argued that an important dynamic in the new recognition accorded women as economic agents during the Revolution was wives' gradual movement into (and developing competence in) occupations vacated by their soldier-husbands, particularly farming and shopkeeping. For that view, see Norton, *Liberty's Daughters*, especially pp. 214–24.

5. See, for example, the attack on a Boston merchant by patriot women as recounted in Abigail Adams' letter to John Adams, July 31, 1777, in L. H. Butterfield, Marc Friedlander, and Mary-Jo Kline, eds., *The Book of Abigail and John: Selected Letters of the Adams Family* (Cambridge, Mass.: Harvard University Press, 1975), pp. 184–85.

6. Minutes of the Town Meeting, July 21, 1780, in Francis Olcott Allen, ed., *The History of Enfield, Connecticut* (Lancaster, Pa.: The Wickersham Printing Company, 1900) 1:457–58.

7. *Minutes of the Committee and of the First Commission for Detecting and Defeating Conspiracies in the State of New York*, as cited in Linda K. Kerber, *Women of the Republic: Intellect and Ideology in Revolutionary America* (Chapel Hill: University of North Carolina Press, 1980), pp. 43–44. See also Norton, *Liberty's Daughters*, pp. 157–61.

8. Kerber, *Women of the Republic*, pp. 42–43.

9. Henretta, *Evolution of American Society*, p. 160; Abigail Adams to John Adams, June 23, 1777, in Butterfield, et al., *Book of Abigail and John*, p. 177; Rolla Milton Tryon, *Household Manufactures in the United States, 1640–1860: A Study in Industrial History* (Chicago: University of Chicago Press, 1917), p. 114, n. 5.

10. John Adams to Abigail Adams, August 28, 1774, in Butterfield et al., *Book of Abigail and John*, p. 69; *Providence Gazette*, November 7, 1767, quoted in Norton, *Liberty's Daughters*, p. 166.

11. In New Jersey, the exception, unmarried women worth fifty pounds were initially permitted to vote. This oversight in the law was rectified in 1807.

12. For a detailed discussion of these local trading networks, see Christopher

Clark, "The Household Economy, Market Exchange and the Rise of Capitalism in the Connecticut Valley, 1800–1816," *Journal of Social History* 13 (Winter 1979): 169–90.

13. Douglass C. North, *The Economic Growth of the United States, 1790–1860* (New York: W. W. Norton, 1966), pp. 20–51. For examples of the proliferation of local manufactories, see Arthur Harrison Cole, ed., *Industrial and Commercial Correspondence of Alexander Hamilton, Anticipating His Report on Manufactures* (Chicago: A. W. Shaw, 1928), passim; and *The Diary of William Bentley* (Salem, Mass.: Essex Institute, 1905), especially Vol. 1. The quotation is from Coxe, *View of the United States*, p. 260.

14. S. G. Goodrich, *Recollections of a Lifetime, or Things I Have Seen: In a Series of Familiar Letters to a Friend* (New York: Miller, Orton, and Mulligan, 1857) 1:64, 71-72, 74; Douglas S. Robertson, ed., *An Englishman in America, 1785: Being the Diary of Joseph Hadfield* (Toronto: Hunter-Rose, 1933), p. 200; Abigail Lyman, note dated August 31, 1801, entered in *The Ladies' Remembrancer; or, Polite Journal, for the Year 1800* (London: W. Wilson, 1799); Greene-Roelker Papers, Cincinnati, Ohio Historical Society; "Diary of Martha Moore Ballad, 1785–1812," in Charles Elventon Nash, ed., *The History of Augusta [Maine]* (Augusta: Charles Nash and Sons, 1904), entry for May 21, 1787; Mary Ann Archbald to "The Revd Doctor Wodrow," April 19, 1808, the journals and diary of Mary Ann Archbald, Archbald Papers, Schlesinger Library, Radcliffe College (hereafter, Archbald Papers).

Abigail Brackett Lyman's notes are reprinted in Helen Roelker Kessler, "The Worlds of Abigail Brackett Lyman," (M.A. thesis, Tufts University, 1976), Appendix C. I am indebted to Laurie Crumpacker for bringing Abigail Brackett Lyman's journals to my attention.

15. Henry A. Hazen, *History of Billerica, Mass[achusetts]* (Boston: A. Williams, 1883), p. 274; J. P. Brissot de Warville, *New Travels in the United States of America* (London: J. S. Jordan, 1792) 1:127. For a discussion of the proportion of landless men in the late eighteenth century, see Henretta, *Evolution of American Society*, p. 164.

16. Abigail Brackett Lyman to Mrs. [Abigail Pond] Brackett, October 11, 1797, reprinted in Kessler, "Worlds of Abigail Brackett Lyman," Appendix B; *Diary of William Bentley* 2:293.

17. See, for example, Brissot, *New Travels* 1:282–83; Benjamin Rush to Granville Sharp, August 1791, in L. H. Butterfield, ed., *Letters of Benjamin Rush* (Princeton, N.J.: Princeton University Press, 1951), p. 608; Ezra Stiles Ely, *Visits of Mercy*, 6th ed. (Philadelphia: S. F. Bradford, 1829), pp. 154 and 168–69; Henry Bradshaw Fearon, *Sketches of America: A Narrative of a Journey of Five Thousand Miles through the Eastern and Western States of America* (London: Longman, Hurst, Rees, Orme and Brown, 1818), p. 34; Thomas F. DeVoe, *The Market Book, containing a Historical Account of the Public Markets in the Cities of New York, Boston, Philadelphia and Brooklyn* (New York: Burt Franklin, 1969; orig. pub. 1862), pp. 203–4, 229–30, 325, 347, and 391. Quotations are from Brissot, *New Travels* 1:105; and DeVoe, *Market Book*, p. 344.

18. DeVoe, *Market Book*, pp. 217 and 331–32; J. Hector St. John Crevecoeur, *Letters from an American Farmer* (New York: Fox, Duffield, 1904; originally published 1782), p. 209; Charles William Janson, *The Stranger in America, 1793–1806* (New York: Press of the Pioneers, 1935; reprinted from the 1807 London edition), pp. 21 and 44; John M. Duncan, *Travels through Part of The United States and Canada in 1818 and 1819* (New York: W. B. Gilley, 1823), pp. 242–43. The quotation is from DeVoe, *Market Book*, p. 219.

19. Diary of Anna Bryant Smith, January 23, 1807, as quoted in Cott, *Bonds of Womanhood*, p. 42; DeVoe, *Market Book*, p. 345; Tryon, *Household Manufactures*, p. 201.

20. See, for example, Tryon, *Household Manufactures*, pp. 188–241; Judd, *History of Hadley*, pp. 344–87; Richard Osborn Cummings, *The American and His Food: A History of Food Habits in the United States* (Chicago: University of Chicago Press, 1941), p. 25; Frederick Tupper and Helen Tyler Brown, eds., *Grandmother Tyler's Book: The Recollections of Mary Palmer Tyler, 1775–1866* (New York: G. P. Putnam's Sons, 1925), pp. 141–44; DeVoe, *Market Book*, pp. 150, 249; "Diary of Martha Moore Ballard," p. 350.

21. Mary Ann Archbald to Miss Wodrow, March 13, 1815, journals and diary of Mary Ann Archbald, 1762–1840, Archbald Papers; Brissot, *New Travels*, 1:134.

22. "Diary of Martha Moore Ballard," pp. 244 and 248.

23. Ibid., pp. 274, 296, 322; 416; 317, 306, 347, and 374–75.

24. Ibid., p. 349.

25. Ibid., p. 349. For a detailed accounting of cash receipts and expenses for the single year in 1796, see p. 359.

26. Ibid. For examples of these activities, see pp. 238, 247, 251, 254, 256, 279, 296, 326, 339, 341, 346, 348, 374, 390, 397, and 417.

27. Ibid. For examples of these activities, see pp. 271, 303–4, 314, 318, 344, 346, 355, 363, 377, and 392–93.

28. Mary Ann Archbald to Mr. Summervill, 1808, and Mary Ann Archbald to "My Dear Margaret," June 20, 1809, journals and diary of Mary Ann Archbald, 1762–1840, Archbald Papers; "Diary of Elizabeth Fuller," in Francis Everett Blake, *History of the Town of Princeton [Massachusetts]* (Princeton, Mass.: Published by the Town, 1915): see, pp. 303–22, et passim.

For examples and discussions of these various processes and products, see Tryon, *Household Manufactures*, pp. 188–241; Helen M. Morgan, ed., *A Season in New York, 1801: Letters of Harriet and Maria Trumbull* (Pittsburgh, Pa.: University of Pittsburgh Press, 1969), pp. 78–79 and 96; Goodrich, *Recollections of a Lifetime* 1:71–75; Butterfield, *Letters of Benjamin Rush*, pp. 591–92; *Bessie; or, Reminiscences of a Daughter of a New England Clergyman of the Eighteenth Century*, by a Grandmother (New Haven, Conn.: J. H. Benham, 1861), pp. 35, 112–15, and 150; Cole, *Correspondence of Alexander Hamilton*, especially pp. 1–52.

29. Mary Ann Archbald to "My Dear Margaret," June 20, 1809, journals and diary of Mary Ann Archbald, 1762–1840, Archbald Papers; *Letters from*

John Pintard to his Daughter Eliza, 1816–1833 (New York: New York Historical Society, 1940) 1:212.

30. Raymond A. Mohl, *Poverty in New York City, 1783–1825* (New York: Oxford University Press, 1971), p. 24; *Bessie*, pp. 35, 87–88, 93, 107–9. The quotation is from "Diary of Martha Moore Ballard," p. 393.

31. Journal of Abigail Brackett Lyman, February 3 and 18, 1800; Abigail Brackett Lyman to Erastus Lyman, May 29, 1797; Abigail Brackett Lyman to Mrs. [Abigail Pond] Brackett, May 22, 1799, all reprinted in Kessler, "Worlds of Abigail Brackett Lyman," Appendices A and B; *Letters from John Pintard* 1:162, 188, 215, 230, 247–48, 252–53, 288, and 301–2.

32. Mary Ann Archbald to "My Dear Margaret," January 13, 1822, journals and diary of Mary Ann Archbald, 1762–1840, Archbald Papers; *Bessie*, p. 100; "Diary of Martha Moore Ballard," pp. 251, 304, and 370; *Letters from John Pintard* 1:226, 242, 300–301, and 329; Mary Ann Archbald to "My Dear M," January 1, 1821, journals and diary of Mary Ann Archbald, 1762–1840, Archbald Papers.

33. "Diary of Martha Moore Ballard," pp. 319, 329, 363, 367, 370, and 374–75.

34. *New York Magazine*, May 1795, pp. 301–5.

35. Brissot, *New Travels* 1:95; Mary Ann Archbald to "My Dear M," January 1, 1821, journals and diary of Mary Ann Archbald, 1762–1840, Archbald Papers; Ruth H. Bloch, "American Feminine Ideals in Transition: The Rise of the Moral Mother, 1785–1815," *Feminist Studies* 4 (June 1978): 101–27.

For additional discussion of the ideology of republican motherhood, see Kerber, *Women of the Republic*, pp. 189–288 (especially pp. 269–88) and Norton, *Liberty's Daughters*, pp. 228–99.

36. Lisa Norling, " 'I Have Ever Felt Homeless': Mariners' Wives and the Ideology of Domesticity," paper presented at the Society of the History of the Early American Republic, July 17, 1987, p. 5.

37. Mary Lynn Salmon has argued that women experienced significant improvements in their rights to own property in the post-Revolutionary period. See Salmon, *Women and the Law of Property in Early America* (Chapel Hill: University of North Carolina Press, 1986), pp. 189–93. For an earlier, contrasting view, see Wilson, "Illusion of Change," pp. 383–445.

38. Gordon S. Wood, *The Creation of the American Republic, 1776–1787* (Chapel Hill: University of North Carolina Press, 1969). The importance of eighteenth-century "republican" thought in the political and cultural formation of the early republic has been the subject of a rich secondary literature. In addition to Wood, the most useful of these works include: J.G.A. Pocock, "Machiavelli, Harrington, and English Political Ideologies in the Eighteenth Century," *William and Mary Quarterly*, 3rd ser., 22 (1965), and "Virtue and Commerce in the Eighteenth Century," *Journal of Interdisciplinary History* 3 (1972): 119–34; Bernard Bailyn, *Ideological Origins of the American Revolution* (Cambridge, Mass.: Harvard University Press, 1967); Eric Foner, *Tom Paine and Revolutionary America* (New York: Oxford, 1976); Pauline Maier, *From*

Resistance to Revolution (New York: Random House, 1972); Robert Shalhope, "Republicanism in Early America," *William and Mary Quarterly*, 3rd ser., 38 (1982): 334–56; Sean Wilentz, *Chants Democratic: New York City and the Rise of the American Working Class, 1788–1850* (New York: Oxford, 1984).

39. Kerber, *Women of the Republic*, p. 47. For a discussion of the growing disenchantment with the war, see Robert A. Gross, *The Minutemen and Their World* (New York: Hill and Wang, 1976), pp. 160–70.

40. See Henretta, *The Evolution of American Society*, p. 160; and Clark, *History of Manufactures* 1:229–30.

41. Alexander Hamilton, "Plan for the Support of Public Credit," January 14, 1790, in *American State Papers: Finance* 1:15.

42. Peter Colt to John Chester, July 21, 1791, in Cole, *Correspondence of Alexander Hamilton*, p. 3.

43. Alexander Hamilton, "Report on the Subject of Manufactures," in Cole, *Correspondence of Alexander Hamilton*, pp. 251, 256, and 280.

44. Ibid., p. 259. The Boston Society for Encouraging Industry and Employing the Poor is cited in Edith Abbott, *Women in Industry: A Study in American Economic History* (New York: D. Appleton, 1910), p. 22.

45. Coxe, *Views of America*, pp. 46, 55, and 301; "Diary of Martha Moore Ballard," p. 348.

46. John Cosens Ogden, *The Female Guide: or, Thoughts on the Education of that Sex Accommodated to The State of Society, Manners, and Government, in the United States* (Concord, N.H.: George Hough, 1793), pp. 5, 11, and 12.

47. Ibid., pp. 9 and 26.

48. Prices are for Massachusetts and are based on data provided in Carroll D. Wright's *Comparative Wages, Prices, and Cost of Living* (Boston: Wright and Potter Printing Company, 1889), pp. 66, 69, 114, 115, and 124–25. On the distribution of wealth, see Kulikoff, "Progress of Inequality," Table II-b, p. 381.

49. M. L. Davis, *A Brief Account of the Epidemical Fever Which lately prevailed in the City of New York*, as quoted in James Ford, *Slums and Housing* (Cambridge, Mass.: Harvard University Press, 1936) 1:64.

50. In Massachusetts, carpenters' wages rose from 59 cents a day in 1790, to about 91 cents in 1800, to about $1.24 in 1811. Masons received about $1.00 a day in 1788; with the exception of unusually high rates in 1812, their wages did not exceed $1.74 a day throughout the period. See Wright, *Comparative Wages*, pp. 48–49 and 55.

In 1806–1809, journeymen shoemakers were still earning roughly the same rate they had received in 1794. See "Commonwealth *vs.* Pullis" in John R. Commons et al., eds., *A Documentary History of American Industrial Society* (Cleveland, Ohio: Arthur H. Clark, 1910) 3:119.

51. For a discussion of the bakers' strike, see Howard B. Rock, "The Perils of Laissez-Faire: The Aftermath of the New York Bakers' Strike of 1801," *Labor History* 18 (Summer 1976): 372–87. See also Commons et al., *Documentary History* 3:106–7, 119, and 125; and *American State Papers: Finance*, 1:495–96 and 694–95. The quotation is from John Mix, Jr., to John Chester,

September 30, 1791, in Cole, *Correspondence of Alexander Hamilton*, pp. 49–50.

52. Albert Matthews, ed., *Journal of William Loughton Smith, 1790–1791* (Cambridge, Mass.: Harvard University Press, 1917), p. 48; Winifred B. Rothenberg, "The Market and Massachusetts Farmers, 1750–1855," *Journal of Economic History* 41 (June 1981), Table I, p. 291; Nash, *History of Augusta*, pp. 142–46; Blake, *History of Princeton*, pp. 159–61.

53. *American State Papers: Finance* 1:694.

54. Ibid.; George Daitsman, "Labor and the 'Welfare State' in Early New York," *Labor History* 4 (Fall 1963): 252; Commons et al., *Documentary History*, p. 371.

55. Crevecoeur, *Letters from an American Farmer*, p. 73; [Arthur Young], *Rural Economy, or Essays on the Practical Parts of Husbandry* (Burlington, Vt.: Issac Neale, 1792), p. 3; DeVoe, *Market Book*, p. 204.

56. This was not universally the case. In her *Letters Addressed to Young Married Women*, Mrs. Griffith stressed the importance of daily household management: "[W]e all know," she asserted, "that *without* œconomy, the greatest *wealth* will soon dwindle to nothing; but *with it*, a very moderate share of fortune may enable its possessors to live with ease and comfort." Mrs. Griffith, *Letters Addressed to Young Married Women* (Philadelphia, Pa.: John Turner, 1796), p. 55.

57. Blake, "The Diary of Elizabeth Fuller," p. 307; "The Diary of Martha Moore Ballard," p. 257.

58. Lydia Almy diary, typescript copy, Essex Institute; Francis Rollins Morse, ed., *Henry and Mary Lee: Letters and Journals, with Other Family Letters, 1802–1860* (Boston: Thomas Todd Company, 1926), pp. 178, 202, and 214. I am grateful to Lisa Norling for bringing the Almy diary to my attention.

59. *Niles Weekly Register*, January 23, 1813, p. 328.

60. *Niles Weekly Register*: November 2, 1811, p. 138; April 25, 1812, p. 125 (italics added); November 21, 1812, p.189; February 22, 1812, p. 138.

61. *History of the Town of Whateley, Mass[achusetts], 1661–1889*, rev. by James M. Crafts (Orange, Mass.: D. L. Crandall, 1899), pp. 128–29; Adam Hodgson, *Letters from North America, Written During a Tour in the United States and Canada* (London: Hurst, Robinson, 1824), p. 71.

Notes to Chapter III

1. Henretta, *Evolution of American Society*, p. 180. For an overview of this period, see ibid., pp. 179–222.

2. U.S. Bureau of the Census, *Historical Statistics of the United States, Colonial Times to 1970, Bicentennial Edition, Part 1*, Washington, D.C., Series A 195–209, pp. 27 and 33, and Series A 172–194, p. 22. In 1830, the north-central

region included the states of Ohio, Indiana, Illinois, Michigan, and Missouri, and the territories of Wisconsin, Iowa, and Minnesota.

3. Thomas Dublin, *Women at Work: The Transformation of Work and Community in Lowell, Massachusetts, 1826–1860* (New York: Columbia University Press, 1979), pp. 20 and 66 (Table 4.1).

4. Judith A. McGaw, *Most Wonderful Machine: Mechanization and Social Change in Berkshire Paper Making, 1801–1885* (Princeton, N.J.: Princeton University Press, 1987), passim; Paul E. Johnson, *A Shopkeeper's Millennium: Society and Revivals in Rochester, New York, 1815–1837* (New York: Hill and Wang, 1978), p. 39; Wilentz, *Chants Democratic,* p. 404 (Table 11); see also Wilentz's discussion on pp. 112–15.

5. Wilentz, *Chants Democratic*, pp. 115 and 404 (Table 11). Alan Dawley, *Class and Community: The Industrial Revolution in Lynn* (Cambridge, Mass.: Harvard University Press, 1976), p. 47; Thomas Dublin, "Women and Outwork in a Nineteenth-Century New England Town: Fitzwilliam, New Hampshire, 1830–1850," in Steven Hahn and Jonathan Prude, eds., *The Countryside in the Age of Capitalist Transformation: Essays in the Social History of Rural America* (Chapel Hill: University of North Carolina Press, 1985), p. 55.

6. See, for example, the *New York Daily Tribune*, June 8, 1853.

7. Leon F. Litwack, *North of Slavery: The Negro in the Free States, 1790–1860* (Chicago: University of Chicago Press, 1961), pp. 155 and 165–66; Robert Ernst, *Immigrant Life in New York City, 1825–1863* (New York: King's Crown Press, Columbia University, 1949), pp. 61–83. For a discussion of methods used by whites to ensure that the numbers of black draymen and carters would remain small, see Leonard P. Curry, *The Free Black in Urban America, 1800–1850: The Shadow of the Dream* (Chicago: University of Chicago Press, 1981), pp. 18–19.

8. Fred Mitchell Jones, *Middlemen in the Domestic Trade of the United States, 1800–1860* (Urbana: University of Illinois Press, 1937), p. 45; Allan Nevins, ed., *The Diary of Philip Hone, 1828–1851* (New York: Kraus Reprint Company, 1969; orig. pub. New York: Dodd, Mead, 1927) 1:614.

9. Dublin, *Women at Work*, p. 137. For additional discussion of wages, see below.

10. Alonzo Lewis and James R. Newhall, *History of Lynn, Essex County, Massachusetts: Including Lynnfield, Saugus, Swampscot, and Nahant* (Boston: John L. Shorey, 1865), p. 447. My discussion of the central shop is based on Dawley, *Class and Community*, especially pp. 11–72; and Wilentz, *Chants Democratic*, especially pp. 107–42.

11. E. S. Abdy, *Journal of a Residence and Tour in The United States of North America, from April, 1833, to October, 1834* (London: John Murray, 1835) 1:121, 195 and 358. For fuller discussions of whites' unwillingness to work with blacks, see Curry, *Free Black*, pp. 15–36; and Litwack, *North of Slavery*, pp. 151–86.

12. John M. Duncan, *Travels through Part of The United States and Canada in 1818 and 1819* (New York: W. B. Gilley, 1823) 2:339–41.

13. Wages for carpenters, foundrymen, masons, masons' helpers, and labor-

ers are from Wright, *Comparative Wages*, pp. 49, 54, 55, and 56. Railroad wages are from Francis B. C. Bradlee, "The Boston and Lowell Railroad, The Nashua and Lowell Railroad, and the Salem and Lowell Railroad," *Essex Institute Historical Collections*, 54 (1918): 209.

14. Norman Ware, *The Industrial Worker, 1840–1860: The Reaction of American Industrial Society to the Advance of the Industrial Revolution* (New York: Hart, Shaffner, and Marx, 1924; reprinted Gloucester, Mass.: Peter Smith, 1959), p. 7; Wilentz, *Chants Democratic*, pp. 117 and 405 (Table 14); Ryan, *Cradle of the Middle Class*, p. 46; Dublin, *Women at Work*, pp. 159, 185, 186, and 195; and Dawley, *Class and Community*, pp. 53–54.

15. Ernst, *Immigrant Life*, p. 40. See also *The New-York Cries in Rhyme* (New York: Mahlon Day, 1836) and *The Cries of New-York, with Fifteen Illustrations* (New York: John Doggett, Jr., 1846).

16. John H. Griscom, *The Sanitary Condition of the Laboring Population of New York* (1845; reprinted New York: Arno Press, 1970), pp. 10 and 17.

17. *New York Tribune*, April 12, 1841; Charles Dickens, *American Notes for General Circulation* (New York: Harper and Brothers, 1842), p. 36; D. W. Mitchell, *Ten Years in The United States: Being an Englishman's View of Men and Things in the North and South* (London: Smith, Elder and Company, 1862), p. 145.

18. Donald B. Cole, *Immigrant City: Lawrence, Massachusetts, 1845–1921* (Chapel Hill: University of North Carolina Press, 1963), p. 28; Gardner Morse, "Recollections of the Appearance of New Haven and of its Business Enterprises and Movements in Real Estate between 1825 and 1837," Papers of the New Haven Colony Historical Society, 5:98–100.

19. Prices for food and fuel are from Wright, *Wages, Prices, and Cost of Living*, pp. 107–8, 124–25, 133. Rents are from Abdy, *Journal of a Residence*, 1:216–17; and Edgar W. Martin, *The Standard of Living in 1860: American Consumption Levels on the Eve of the Civil War* (Chicago: University of Chicago Press, 1942), p. 172. Martin found $6–$8 to be an average monthly rent for a rear tenement apartment, $4–$6 for a front tenement apartment, and $3 for a basement apartment. D. W. Mitchell cites the *New York Tribune* as suggesting a slightly lower range of $4–$5 for tenement apartments in New York City in the same period: see Mitchell, *Ten Years in the United States*, p. 153. For an excellent study of the changing nature of the housing market in antebellum New York City, see Elizabeth Blackmar, *Manhattan for Rent, 1785–1850* (Ithaca, N. Y.: Cornell University Press, 1989).

20. Martin, *Standard of Living*, pp. 22, 55. See also Cole, *Immigrant City*, pp. 29–30.

21. Ely, *Visits of Mercy* 2:87–88; Martin, *Standard of Living*, pp. 122–23.

22. Seth Luther, *An Address Delivered Before the Mechanics and Working-Men, of the City of Brooklyn, on the Celebration of the Sixtieth Anniversary of American Independence, July 4, 1836* (Brooklyn, N.Y.: Alden Spooner and Sons, 1836), pp. 7 and 10–11.

23. William Henry Channing, "The Temptation in the Wilderness, from the

Harbinger," in John Thomas Codman, *Brook Farm: Historic and Personal Memoirs* (Boston: Arena Publishing, 1894), Appendix, p. 321.

24. Luther, *Address . . . July 4, 1836*, p. 11.

25. Seth Luther, *An Address to the Working Men of New England, on the State of Education, and on the Condition of the Producing Classes in Europe and America* (New York: George H. Evans, 1833; orig. pub. 1832), pp. 17 and 35.

26. George Combe, *Notes on the United States of North America, during a Phrenological Visit in 1838–39–40* (Edinburgh: MacLachan, Stewart, 1841) 3:145.

27. "A Mechanic," *Elements of Social Disorder: A Plea for the Working Classes in the United States* (Providence, R.I.: Benjamin F. Moore, 1844), pp. 69–70. Both of the latter two classes were charged with "responsibility for the poverty, misery, and vice, that so generally prevail" among workers.

28. George G. Foster, *New York by Gas-Light: With Here and There a Streak of Sunshine* (New York: Dewitt and Davenport, 1850), p. 69. For a useful discussion of the emergence of the middle class, and of the term "middle class," see Burton J. Bledstein, *The Culture of Professionalism: The Middle Class and the Development of Higher Education in America* (New York: W. W. Norton, 1976), especially pp. 1–79.

29. Luther, *Address . . . July 4, 1836*, pp. 10–11.

30. "How to Get Rich," *Manual of Self-Education: A Magazine for the Young* 1/1 (August 1842): 66–67.

31. [Samuel G. Goodrich], *Enterprise, Industry, and Art of Man* (Boston: Bradbury, Soden, 1845), p. 335.

32. Stuart M. Blumin, "The Hypothesis of Middle-Class Formation in Nineteenth-Century America: A Critique and Some Proposals," *American Historical Review* 90 (April 1985): 315. I am indebted to Blumin throughout the present discussion of the new "middle-class" occupational patterns.

33. See, for example, Ryan, *Cradle of the Middle Class*, pp. 108 and 254 (Table B.4); and Ernst, *Immigrant Life*, pp. 214–17 (Table 27).

34. A growing secondary literature is helping to illuminate the emergence and importance of this new occupational sector. Especially important among these are Stuart Blumin, "Hypothesis of Middle-Class Formation"; Ryan, *Cradle of the Middle Class*; Johnson, *Shopkeeper's Millennium*; Bledstein, *Culture of Professionalism*; and John G. Cawelti, *Apostles of the Self-Made Man* (Chicago: University of Chicago Press, 1965).

35. James Dawson Burn, *Three Years among the Working-Classes in the United States during the War* (London: Smith, Elder, 1865), pp. 308–9; *Six Hundred Dollars a Year: A Wife's Effort at Low Living, under High Prices* (Boston: Ticknor and Fields, 1867); Charles Edward Stowe and Lyman Beecher Stowe, *Harriet Beecher Stowe: The Story of Her Life* (Boston and New York: Houghton Mifflin, 1911), p. 143; Thomas L. Nichols, *Forty Years of American Life*, Vol. 2 (London: John Maxwell, 1864), pp. 202–3. Although the title of the anonymous *Six Hundred Dollars a Year* would seem to suggest an annual income of that amount, the figure refers to the cash remaining after house rent; the actual income was $800 a year. Grant Thorburn set the annual earnings of

clerks at $500; see Thorburn, *Sketches from the Note-book of Laurie Todd* (New York: D. Fanshaw, 1847), p. 12. On the earnings of lawyers, see Edward Pessen, *Riches, Class, and Power Before the Civil War* (Lexington, Mass.: D.C. Heath, 1973), p. 58. The salary of a typical New York businessman is cited in Martin, *Standard of Living*, p. 12.

36. Herman Melville, "Bartleby," in Jay Leyda, ed., *The Portable Melville* (New York: Viking Press, 1952), p. 475.

37. For an excellent overview of business forms and procedures during the antebellum period, see Alfred D. Chandler, *The Visible Hand: The Managerial Revolution in American Business* (Cambridge, Mass.: Harvard University Press, Belknap Press, 1977), pp. 15–49. It is not my intention here to enter the debate over whether these structures and procedures ultimately hampered the development of early industrialization; for a summary of that discussion, see Judith A. McGaw, "Accounting for Innovation: Technological Change and Business Practice in the Berkshire Paper Industry," *Technology and Culture* 26/4 (October 1985): 703–25. Melville, "Bartleby," pp. 468–69, 472–73.

38. Catharine E. Beecher and Harriet Beecher Stowe, *The American Woman's Home; or, Principles of Domestic Science* (New York: J. B. Ford, 1869; reprint ed. Hartford, Conn.: Stowe-Day Foundation, 1975), pp. 25–42.

39. Among others, John M. Duncan found that living in boardinghouses was "very common" in the United States as early as 1818. See Duncan, *Travels*, 2:249. See also Thomas B. Gunn, *Physiology of New York Boarding Houses* (New York: Mason Brothers, 1857). Gunn was particularly critical of women who sought in this way to relieve themselves of some of their domestic labor; see op. cit., p. 168.

40. For Boston, Pessen identifies as the "upper middle" level, people who owned $6,000–$20,000 worth of taxable property; for New York, he includes in this group people who owned $7,000–$20,000 in taxable property. See Pessen, *Riches, Class, and Power*, pp. 132 and 140; on the upward mobility of this group, see p. 133.

Based on an examination of property ownership in Brooklyn in 1841, Pessen (p. 36) suggested the following distribution of property:

Level of Wealth	*% of Population*
$50,000 or more	1
$15,000 to $50,000	2
$4,500 to $15,000	9
$1,000 to $4,500	15
$100 to $1,000	7
under $100	66

41. Years later, David Wright recalled that when he and Martha Coffin Wright set up housekeeping in Aurora, New York, in 1829, they paid $750 for a house and lot. The purchase was possible only because Martha Coffin Wright had an inheritance of $1,000 from her first marriage. Travelling in Boston in the mid-

1830s, E. S. Abdy noted that a shopkeeper, married and with children, had paid $1,500 for a dwelling. Catharine Beecher suggested in 1841 that a two-story cottage with a porch in a semirural area would cost between $900 and $1,300. See David Wright, "Reminiscences," n.d., Garrison Papers, Sophia Smith Collection, Smith College, Northampton, Massachusetts (hereafter Garrison Papers); Abdy, *Journal of a Residence* 1:180; Catharine E. Beecher, *A Treatise on Domestic Economy*, rev. ed. (Boston: Thomas H. Webb, 1842), p. 265. The propensity of (especially) young couples in the city to take rooms in boardinghouses and hotels rather than go into housekeeping was registered in the anxieties of a number of observers.

42. Mrs. [Lydia Maria] Child, *The American Frugal Housewife*, 12th ed. (Boston: Carter, Hendee, 1833), pp. 111–13; Alexis de Tocqueville, *Democracy in America*, Book II, Chapter 10.

43. Goodrich, *Recollections of a Lifetime* 2:71; William A. Alcott, *Ways of Living on Small Means*, 3rd ed. (Boston: Light and Stearns, 1837), p. 180; Nevins, *Diary of Philip Hone* 1:185; Pessen, *Riches, Class, and Power*, p. 148.

44. Henry Ward Beecher, *Lectures to Young Men* (Boston: J. P. Jewett, 1846), p. 28; Nichols, *Forty Years of American Life* 1:402, 404.

Notes to Chapter IV

1. Martha Coffin Wright to [Lucretia Mott], [January] 23, [1845], Martha Coffin Wright Correspondence, 1825–1841, Garrison Papers, The Sophia Smith Collection, Smith College.

2. Ibid.; Harriet Beecher Stowe to Sarah Buckingham Beecher, December 17, [1850], Beecher–Stowe Family Papers, Schlesinger Library, Radcliffe College (hereafter, Beecher–Stowe Family Papers); Diaries of Sarah Smith Browne, March 27, 1858, Browne Family Papers, Schlesinger Library, Radcliffe College (hereafter, Browne Family Papers); Susan B. Anthony to Antoinette Brown, April 22, 1858, quoted in Alice Stone Blackwell, *Lucy Stone: Pioneer of Women's Rights* (Boston: Little, Brown, 1930), p. 198; George S. Merriam, ed., *Reminiscences and Letters of Caroline C. Briggs* (New York: Houghton, Mifflin, 1897), pp. 22–23.

3. The Reverend Hubbard Winslow, *A Discourse delivered in The Bowdoin Street Church* (Boston: Weeks, Jordan, 1837), p. 8; William A. Alcott, *The Young Wife, or Duties of Woman in the Marriage Relation* (Boston: George W. Light, 1837), p. 86.

4. Virtually the only extended discussion of the unpaid household labor of women of the working classes in the antebellum Northeast is to be found in Stansell, *City of Women*. The quotation on middle-class women is also from Stansell, pp. xii–xiii. Stansell is not alone in depicting antebellum middle-class women as leisured. Julie A. Matthaei asserts that the presence of paid domestic workers "[f]reed [the wife] from the drudgery of housework," and Faye E.

Dudden argues that "[a]s employers demanded longer hours and more stringent work discipline from domestics . . . , they were able to free themselves from a significant part of the burden of household work." See Matthaei, *An Economic History of Women in America: Women's Work, the Sexual Division of Labor, and the Development of Capitalism* (New York: Schocken Books, 1982), p. 157; and Dudden, *Serving Women*, p. 7.

A contrary claim, and one much closer to the argument made here, is offered by Patricia Branca in her examination of middle-class women in Victorian England. Branca contends that the image of the "leisured lady" ill-fit the lives of most middle-class women. See Branca, "Image and Reality: The Myth of the Idle Victorian Lady," in Mary Hartman and Lois W. Banner, eds., *Clio's Consciousness Raised* (New York: Harper and Row, 1974), pp. 170–89.

5. Martha Coffin Wright to Lucretia Mott, November 19, 1841, Martha Coffin Wright Correspondence, 1825–1841, Garrison Papers.

6. Martha Coffin Wright to Lucretia Mott, November 7 and 19, 1841, Sept[ember] 12, 1844, and Jan[uary] 23, [1845], Martha Coffin Wright Correspondence, 1825–1841, Garrison Papers.

7. Martha Coffin Wright to Lucretia Mott, Sept[ember] 12, 1844, and Jan[uary] 23, [1845], Martha Coffin Wright Correspondence, 1825–1841, Garrison Papers.

8. Martha Coffin Wright to Lucretia Mott, Jan[uary] 15, 1845, Martha Coffin Wright Correspondence, 1825–1841, Garrison Papers.

9. Wright's household almanac for 1838 indicates only one payment to a "mantuamaker," for $1.75 in October. This may well have been for a winter cloak. Wright's diary for 1852–1858 includes a March entry for $1.50 payment to a "dressmaker" for three days' work. Almanac, 1838, n.p., Diaries of Martha Coffin Wright, 1856–1874, Garrison Papers.

10. See n. 40, Chapter III. The census evidence is reviewed and evaluated in Dudden, *Serving Women*, pp. 78–79, and notes 19–27, pp. 273–74.

11. Combe, *Notes on the United States* 1:201; Fredrika Bremer, *The Homes of the New World; Impressions of America* (New York: Harper, 1853) 1:111.

12. Elizabeth Cabot to Mrs. Twistleton, November 26, 1860, in *Letters of Elizabeth Cabot* (Boston: privately printed, 1905) 1:232–33 and 261.

13. Merriam, *Briggs*, p. 94. Faye Dudden also notes the changing educational and training goals of middle-class daughters. See Dudden, *Serving Women*, p. 47.

14. See, for example, T. S. Arthur, ed., *The Mother's Rule; or, The Right Way and the Wrong Way* (Philadelphia: Smith and Peters, 1856), passim. *The Ladies Museum* 1/11 (October 8, 1825): 44.

15. For excellent discussions of changes in attitudes toward child-rearing in this period, see Cott, *Bonds of Womanhood*, pp. 19–62, 84–92, and 150–51; and Ryan, *Cradle of the Middle Class*, pp. 145–85.

16. Arthur, *Mother's Rule*, pp. 91–92; Harriet Beecher Stowe to Sarah Buckingham Beecher, December 17, [1850], Beecher-Stowe Family Papers; Abigail

Bradley Hyde to Mr. and Mrs. Bradley, April 5, 1829, Bradley-Hyde Collection, Schlesinger Library, Radcliffe College (hereafter, Bradley-Hyde Collection); *Diary of Sarah Connell Ayer* (Portland, Me.: Lefavor-Tower, 1910), pp. 226 and 237.

17. Francis J. Grund, *The Americans in Their Moral, Social, and Political Relations* (Boston: Marsh, Capen and Lyon, 1837), p. 32; *Six Hundred Dollars a Year*, p. 49.

18. Journal of Sarah M. Munro, 1853–1856, February 9, 1853, Caroline Wells Dall Papers, 1832–1956, Schlesinger Library, Radcliffe College (hereafter, Caroline Wells Dall Papers); Diaries of Mrs. Bardwell of Walpole, Vt., October 3, 1858–June 15, 1860, November 17, 1858, Helen Temple Cooke Papers, 1858–1951, Schlesinger Library, Radcliffe College (hereafter Helen Temple Cooke Papers); Diaries of Sarah Preston Everett Hale, 1859–1861, March 23, 1859, Hale Papers, Sophia Smith Collection, Smith College (hereafter, Hale Papers); Diary of Sarah Smith Browne, October 6, 1860, and May 10 and 13, 1858, Browne Family Papers.

19. Journal of Sarah M. Munro, 1853–1856, April 8, 1853, Caroline Wells Dall Papers. Italics added.

20. Diary of Lydia Maria Child, 1864, Lydia Maria Child Papers, Anti-Slavery Collection, Cornell University Library. Cited in Gerda Lerner, *The Female Experience: An American Documentary* (Indianapolis: Bobbs-Merrill, 1977), pp. 125–26; Diary of Sarah Smith Browne, May 5, 1858, Browne Family Papers; Blackwell, *Lucy Stone*, p. 233; Martha Coffin Wright to Lucretia Mott, February 7, 1847, Martha Coffin Wright Correspondence, 1825–1841, Garrison Papers; Diary of Sarah Mynderse Campbell, April 6, 1824, New-York Historical Society; Beecher and Stowe, *American Woman's Home*, pp. 87–89, 91, 171, 353–59, and 362.

21. Blackwell, *Lucy Stone*, p. 233; Martha Coffin Wright to Lucretia Mott, February 7, 1847, Martha Coffin Wright Correspondence, 1825–1841, Garrison Papers; Diaries of Sarah Preston Everett Hale, 1859–1861, March 24, April 27, May 26, and June 16 and 17, 1859, Hale Papers; Claudia L. Bushman, *"A Good Poor Man's Wife": Being a Chronicle of Harriet Hanson Robinson and Her Family in Nineteenth-Century New England* (Hanover, N.H.: University Press of New England, 1981), p. 108; Strasser, *Never Done*, p. 16; *Six Hundred Dollars a Year*, pp. 22–26.

22. Harriet Beecher Stowe to Sarah Buckingham Beecher, December 17, [1850], Beecher-Stowe Family Papers; *Six Hundred Dollars a Year*, p. 11; Diaries of Mrs. Bardwell, November 15, 1858, Helen Temple Cooke Papers.

23. *Letters from John Pintard* 1:206; Eliza [?] to Mary [B. Kinsley], July 29, 1822, Anne Ware Allen Papers, Schlesinger Library, Radcliffe College (hereafter, Anne Ware Allen Papers).

24. For a fuller discussion of this subject, see Chapter V.

25. Luella Case to Sarah Edgarton, July, 1841, Hooker Collection, Schlesinger Library, Radcliffe College (hereafter, Hooker Collection); Louisa Meigs

to Mrs. John Rodgers, December 17, 1850, Alger Family Papers, Schlesinger Library, Radcliffe College (hereafter, Alger Family Papers); Beecher, *Treatise on Domestic Economy*, p. 162.

26. Diary of Lydia Maria Child, 1864, as cited in Lerner, *Female Experience*, p. 126; Alcott, *Young Wife*, p. 85; Diaries of Sarah Smith Browne, March 27, 1858, Browne Family Papers. For a quite different interpretation of antebellum middle-class women's attitudes toward cooking, see Matthews, *"Just a Housewife."*

27. Diaries of Sarah Smith Browne, April 19, 21–27, and 30, and May 3, 1858, Browne Family Papers; Bushman, *"Good Poor Man's Wife"*, p. 112.

28. *Six Hundred Dollars a Year*, pp. 48–49, 58–59, and 73; Merriam, *Briggs*, p. 89.

29. Diary of Lydia Maria Child, 1864, as cited in Lerner, *Female Experience*, p. 125; Harriet Beecher Stowe to Calvin Stowe, 1850, quoted in Stowe and Stowe, *Harriet Beecher Stowe*, p. 143.

30. E. S. Abdy, *Journal of a Residence* 1:251; Diary of Sarah Mynderse Campbell, July 22, 1826, and November 26, 1824, New-York Historical Society; Sarah Jackson Russell to Hannah Lowell Jackson Cabot, April 25, 1844, Almy Family Papers, Schlesinger Library, Radcliffe College (hereafter, Almy Family Papers).

31. Solon Robinson, *Hot Corn: Life Scenes in New York Illustrated* (New York: Dewitt and Davenport, 1854), pp. 31 and 198; DeVoe, *Market Book*, pp. 219, 331–32, 370, 391, 408, 409, and 499; *New-York Cries in Rhyme*, pp. 6, 8, 13, and 14; Blackwell, *Lucy Stone*, p. 78.

32. Ernst, *Immigrant Life*, pp. 66–68; DeVoe, *Market Book*, pp. 463 and 573; Litwack, *North of Slavery*, p. 155; Abdy, *Journal of a Residence* 2:44.

33. Diary of William H. Bell, 1850–1851, November 6, 1850, New-York Historical Society.

34. See, for example, Burn, *Three Years among the Working-Classes*, pp. 106 and 298. Although Burn contended that laboring-class housewives did little work, his own observations belie the assertion. See also Ernst, *Immigrant Life*, pp. 52 and 86–87.

35. Mary Paul Guild to "Dear Father," April 27, 1862, in Thomas Dublin, ed., *Farm to Factory: Women's Letters, 1830–1860* (New York: Columbia University Press, 1981), p. 129.

36. Mary Paul Guild to "Dear Father," October 27, 1861, in Dublin, *Farm to Factory*, p. 128.

37. One frequently finds these incidents reported in the newspapers of the period. See, for example, the *New York Tribune*, April 12, 14, 19, and 20, and May 17, 1841. The quotation is from April 20, 1841.

38. Ely, *Visits of Mercy* 1:168–69; 2:88; Boston *Evening Transcript*, September 20, 1830. For additional discussion of the significance of these networks in four very different times and places, see: Ulrich, " 'A Friendly Neighbor'," pp. 392–405; Stansell, *City of Women*, pp. 55–62; Judith E. Smith, "Our Own Kind: Family and Community Networks in Providence," *Radical History Review*

17 (Spring 1968): 99–120; and Ellen Ross, "Survival Networks: Women's Neighbourhood Sharing in London before World War One," *History Workshop* 15 (Spring 1983): 4–27.

39. Boston *Evening Transcript*, July 27, 1830.

40. Diary of William H. Bell, 1850–1851, July 31, 1851, New-York Historical Society; Ely, *Visits of Mercy* 1:169.

41. Diary of Phebe Orvis Eastman, St. Lawrence County Historical Center, Canton, New York. Cited in Dudden, *Serving Women*, pp. 17–18.

42. Nichols, *Forty Years of American Life* 1:23; Blackwell, *Lucy Stone*, p. 10; Sarah Smith to Josiah Smith, in letter of Linus Smith to Josiah Smith, Feb[ruary] 7, 1845, and Philena Thorp to Mrs. Joseph [Sally] Smith, July 31, 1851, Hooker Collection; Tryon, *Household Manufactures*, Table XVI, pp. 304–5.

43. Mary Ann Archbald to "My Dear Margaret," January 13, 1822, the journals and diary of Mary Ann Archbald, 1762–1840, Archbald Papers.

44. Cynthia [H. Allen] to Mary Goodridge, Jan[uary] 8, 1848, Gilbert-Cheever Family Papers, Manuscript Room, Sterling Memorial Library, Yale University (hereafter, Gilbert-Cheever Family Papers).

45. Blanche Brown Bryant and Gertrude Elaine Baker, eds., *The Diaries of Sally and Pamela Brown, 1832–1838, and Hyde Leslie, 1887* (Springfield, Vt.: William L. Bryant Foundation, 1970), pp. 11, 13, 16–18, and 24; Diary of Phebe Orvis Eastman, cited in Dudden, *Serving Women*, p. 17; Nichols, *Forty Years of American Life* 1:23.

46. Nichols, *Forty Years of American Life* 1:33; DeVoe, *Market Book*, pp. 408 and 450; Abdy, *Journal of a Residence* 1:132; *Six Hundred Dollars a Year*, p. 11.

47. See, for example, Thomas Dublin, "Women and Outwork in a Nineteenth-Century New England Town: Fitzwilliam, New Hampshire, 1830–1850," in Hahn and Prude, *Countryside in the Age of Capitalist Transformation*, pp. 51–69.

48. Merriam, *Briggs*, pp. 4 and 7; Mary Ann Archbald to "My Dear Margaret," January 13, 1822, the journals and diary of Mary Ann Archbald, 1762–1840; Bryant and Baker, *Diaries of Sally and Pamela Brown*, p. 12; Diary of Phebe Eastman, cited in Dudden, *Serving Women*, pp. 15–17. Dudden provides a detailed examination of the relationships between mistresses and hired workers in rural families; see especially pp. 17–18, 30–32, and 76–77.

49. Jane Swisshelm, *Letters to Country Girls* (New York: J. C. Riker, 1853), p. 75; Merriam, *Briggs*, p. 15; Blackwell, *Lucy Stone*, p. 19.

50. Caroline H. Gilman, *The Lady's Annual Register and Housewife's Memorandum-Book* (Boston: T. H. Carter, 1838), p. 80.

51. For an interesting discussion of these changes as reflected in plans for farmhouses, see Sally McMurry, *Families and Farmhouses in Nineteenth-Century America* (New York: Oxford University Press, 1988).

52. George S. Boutwell, *Reminiscences of Sixty Years in Public Affairs* (New York: McClure, Phillips, 1902), pp. 2–5.

53. Mary Wilkins Freeman, "The Revolt of 'Mother'," in Barbara H. Sol-

omon, ed., *Short Fiction of Sarah Orne Jewett and Mary Wilkins Freeman* (New York: Signet, 1979), p. 423.

54. Dudden, *Serving Women*, pp. 14–16.

55. Beecher, *Treatise on Domestic Economy*, p. 29.

Notes to Chapter V

1. Helen Sumner, *Report on the Condition of Women and Child Wage-Earners in the United States*, Vol. 9: *History of Women in Industry in the United States* (Washington, D.C.: 1910), p. 29. Jesse T. Peck, *The True Woman; or, Life and Happiness at Home and Abroad* (New York: Carlton and Porter, 1857), p. 243.

2. Paul Johnson discusses these changing residential patterns in *Shopkeeper's Millenium*, pp. 48–55.

3. L[ydia] Maria Child, *Letters from New York*, 1st series (New York: C. S. Francis, 1845), pp. 14–15 and 69. The street lives of city women have been richly documented by Christine Stansell in *City of Women*.

4. The only major study of women's domestic lives to argue that housework underwent a historical process of "industrialization" is Ruth Schwartz Cowan's *More Work for Mother*. The view that women's household experiences remained essentially distinct from the processes of industrialization has informed most examinations of the nineteenth-century cult of domesticity. See, for example, Cott, *Bonds of Womanhood*.

5. Child, *American Frugal Housewife*, p. 113.

6. Griscom, *Sanitary Condition*, pp. 8, 9, and 13.

7. Diary of Sarah Smith Browne, February 8, 1858, Browne Family Papers; Diaries of Mrs. Bardwell, October 13, 1858, Helen Temple Cooke Papers; Diary of Lucretia Warner Hall, March 25 [1834?] and May 19 [1835], New-York Historical Society; Journal of Sarah M. Munro, 1853–1856, January 17, March 7, and April 11, 1853, Caroline Wells Dall Papers; Gunn, *Physiology of New-York Boarding-Houses*, p. 33.

8. Mrs. [Elizabeth] Ellet, ed., *The Practical Housekeeper; A Cyclopædia of Domestic Economy* (New York: Stringer and Townsend, 1857), p. 33.

9. Arthur, *The Mother's Rule*, p. 79.

10. Alcott, *Young Wife*, p. 247.

11. "Cleo Dora," letter to the editor, *Anti-Slavery Bugle*, August 21, 1846, as quoted in Lerner, *Female Experience*, pp. 119–20.

12. Alcott, *Young Wife*, pp. 129 and 134.

13. "Cleo Dora," as quoted in Lerner, *Female Experience*, p. 119; Gilman, *Lady's Annual Register*, pp. 39–40; Christopher Crowfield [Harriet Beecher Stowe], *House and Home Papers* (Boston: Fields, Osgood, 1869), p. 125.

14. Dudden, *Serving Women*, p. 134.

15. Several of the recent studies of the history of housework have focused

especially on domestic technology. See Strasser, *Never Done*, and Cowan, *More Work for Mother*. The classic source on new domestic technologies of the nineteenth century is Siegfried Giedion's *Mechanization Takes Command* (New York: Oxford University Press, 1948). Based largely on an analysis of patents, Giedion's conclusion was that the nineteenth century witnessed an explosion of new domestic inventions. William D. Andrews and Deborah C. Andrews concurred in this. More recently, Susan Strasser has pointed out that scholars should be seeking to learn "when things became commonplace, not when they were invented," and has argued that, for most women, housework remained comparatively *un*mechanized through the nineteenth century. William D. Andrews and Deborah C. Andrews, "Technology and the Housewife in Nineteenth-Century America," *Women's Studies* 2 (1974): 321–23; Strasser, *Never Done*, p. xiv.

16. *Ladies' Literary Cabinet*, New Series, IV (July 21, 1821), p. 85; Burn, *Three Years among the Working-Classes*, p. 298.

17. Jane Sophia Appleton, "Sequel to the 'Vision of Bangor in the Twentieth Century,' " in Arthur Orcutt Lewis, ed., *American Utopians: Selected Short Fiction* (New York: Arno Press, 1971), p. 256. The story was originally published in 1848.

18. See, for example, Amelia Simmons, *Amercian Cookery* (New York: Oxford University Press, 1958; orig. pub. 1796). On the diet of New Englanders, see also: Waverly Root and Richard de Rochemont, *Eating in America: A History* (New York: William Morrow, 1976); John L. Hess and Karen Hess, *The Taste of America* (New York: Grossman, 1977); and Sarah Frances McMahon, " 'A Comfortable Subsistence': A History of Diet in New England," (Ph.D. diss., Brandeis University, 1982).

19. Diaries of Sarah Smith Browne, September 25 and November 21, 1860, Browne Family Papers.

20. Martha Coffin Wright to Lucretia Mott, November 7, 1841, Martha Coffin Wright Correspondence, 1825–1841, Garrison Papers; [Stowe], *House and Home Papers*, p. 140.

21. Stansell, *City of Women*, pp. 11–12.

22. Combe, *Notes on the United States* 3:206.

23. Zephaniah W. Pease, ed., *The Diary of Samuel Rodman: A New Bedford Chronicle of Thirty-Seven Years, 1821–1859* (New Bedford, Mass.: Reynolds Printing Company, 1927), p. 203; Beecher and Stowe, *American Woman's Home*, p. 175.

24. Elizabeth Cabot to Ellen Twistleton, March 27, 1860, in *Letters of Elizabeth Cabot* 1:237. Cabot's household income, which was approximately $6,000 in 1860, placed her well above the "middle class" as defined in this study.

25. Susan Warner, *The Wide, Wide World* (New York: Feminist Press, 1987), p. 103.

26. Glenna Matthews offers a rather different reading of the importance of housework in *The Wide, Wide World* (and other domestic novels of the period). Although she also finds in Warner's depiction of Aunt Fortune a deep respect

for "a female craft tradition," she sees the recurrent discussion of housewifery in early nineteenth-century women's novels as evidence of the continued vitality of that tradition. Indeed, Matthews argues that the pre–Civil War era was "the golden age of domesticity." As I argue throughout this chapter as well as in Chapters IV and VI, the evidence seems to me considerably more complicated and contradictory.

27. Burn, *Three Years among the Working-Classes*, p. 81.

28. Mrs. L[ouisa] C[aroline] Tuthill, *Reality; or, The Millionaire's Daughter* (New York: Charles Scribner, 1856), p. 297; Caroline H. Gilman, *Recollections of a Housekeeper* (New York: Harper and Brothers, 1836), p. 152; Ellet, *Practical Housekeeper*, p. 15.

29. Beecher and Stowe, *American Woman's Home*, p. 175; Anonymous, *Women's Influence and Woman's Mission* (Philadelphia: Willis P. Hazard, 1854), pp. 57–58.

The prolific Catharine Beecher, whose *Treatise on Domestic Economy* went through fifteen printings in as many years, called attention again and again to the poor preparation of housewives for their tasks. See Beecher, *Treatise on Domestic Economy*, pp. 140–42; and idem, *Suggestions Respecting Improvements in Education, Presented to the Trustees of the Hartford Female Seminary* (Hartford, Conn.: Packard and Butler, 1829), pp. 7–9.

30. Diaries of Sarah Smith Browne, July 6, 1859, Browne Family Papers. See also Beecher and Stowe, *American Woman's Home*, pp. 66–83 and 403–18.

31. [Stowe], *House and Home Papers*, pp. 281–82; Bremer, *Homes of the New World*, p. 230. For additional discussion of the dangers of the new lamps, see Dudden, *Serving Women*, p. 129.

32. Beecher, *Treatise on Domestic Economy*, pp. 142, 143, 171, 175, and 176; U.S. Secretary of the Treasury, *Documents Relating to the Manufactures in the U.S.*, House Doc. 308, 22nd Cong., 2nd sess. (1833), 2:844.

33. Sarah Smith to Josiah Smith in letter of Linus Smith to Josiah Smith, February 7, 1845, Hooker Collection.

34. Dudden, *Serving Women*, p. 156. See pp. 154–92.

35. Household account book of Ann (Lyon) Garfield, 1821–1825 [May 17, 1825], John Metcalf Garfield Papers, Sterling Memorial Library, Yale University (hereafter, John Metcalf Garfield Papers).

36. Diaries of Sarah Smith Browne, January 7, 9, and 20, 1858, Browne Family Papers. The quotation is from January 20, 1858.

37. Quotation from "Eliza" to Mary [B. Kinsley], July 29, 1822, Anne Ware (Winsor) Allen Papers, Schlesinger Library, Radcliffe College (hereafter, Anne Ware [Winsor] Allen Papers). See also Mary [Lovell Pickard Ware] to Mary [Kinsley], March 22, 1827, Anne Ware (Winsor) Allen Papers.

38. M. A. S[carborough?] to W. B. [Weltha Brown], May, 1818, Hooker Collection.

39. Louisa [?] to W. B. [Weltha Brown?], n.d., Hooker Collection.

40. Child, *American Frugal Housewife*, pp. 14, 16, and 22; Merriam, *Briggs*, p. 89.

41. Lydia D. Pierce to Sally Smith, December 4, 1836, Hooker Collection.

42. Child, *American Frugal Housewife*, p. 3; [Stowe], *House and Home Papers*, p. 175; Gilman, *The Lady's Annual Register*, p. 57.

43. [Stowe], *House and Home Papers*, p. 175; Martha Coffin Wright to [Lucretia Mott], [December] 18, [1841], Martha Coffin Wright Correspondence, 1825–1841, Garrison Papers.

44. Gilman, *Recollections*, pp. 152–55. The quotation is from p. 152.

45. Appleton, "Sequel," pp. 254–58. The quotation is from page 258.

46. Mary Antoinette Doolittle, *Autobiography of Mary Antoinette Doolittle* (Mount Lebanon, N.Y.: 1880), pp. 35–36. The status of women in American Fourierist communities is examined in Kathryn M. Tomasek, "Fourierist Association in Theory and in Practice: Women, the Family, and Social Change" (Master's thesis, University of Wisconsin, 1989).

47. Doolittle, *Autobiography*, pp. 35–36; Edward D. Andrews, *The Community Industries of the Shakers* (Albany: University of the State of New York, 1932; reprinted Philadelphia: Porcupine Press, 1972), pp. 40–44.

48. Beecher, *Treatise on Domestic Economy*, pp. 151 and 152; Ellet, *Practical Housekeeper*, pp. 16 and 17.

Notes to Chapter VI

1. Griscom, *Sanitary Condition*, pp. 2, 10, and 17.

2. Ibid., p. 39.

3. Ibid., pp. 10 and 17.

4. These include: Ware, *Industrial Worker*; Dawley, *Class and Community*; Johnson, *Shopkeeper's Millennium*; Dublin, *Women at Work*; Wilentz, *Chants Democratic*.

Included among those studies that have paid some attention to the relationship between household life and the transformation of the paid economy are Hahn and Prude, *Countryside in the Age of Capitalist Transformation*; and McGaw, *Most Wonderful Machine*.

5. *Six Hundred Dollars a Year*, pp. 28–29.

6. [Stowe], *House and Home Papers*, pp. 184–85.

7. Martha Coffin Wright to Lucretia Mott, February 7, 1847, Martha Coffin Wright Correspondence, 1825–1841, Garrison Papers.

8. *Six Hundred Dollars a Year*, pp. 49, 58, 68–69, 73, and 117.

9. Paul Smith argues that it is especially inappropriate to include work like cooking in the concept of productive labor, arguing that "there is no social mechanism which defines the necessary tasks which are supposed to contribute to the value of labour power." "If cooking meals is necessary for its production,"

he asks, "why not eating them?" He concludes that, "[o]ne might as well argue that since sleeping is necessary for the replenishment of the capacity for labour, it too is value creating labour." Smith fails to take cognizance of the important difference between cooking and either eating or sleeping: women's cooking is a part of the marital exchange. Men do not require that their wives either eat or sleep *for* them. See Paul Smith, "Domestic Labour and Marx' Theory of Value," in Annette Kuhn and AnnMarie Wolpe, eds., *Feminism and Materialism: Women and Modes of Production* (London: Routledge and Kegan Paul, 1978), p. 208.

10. Journal of Sarah M. Munro, 1853–1856, April 18, 1853, Caroline Wells Dall Papers; *Diary of Sarah Connell Ayer*, p. 259; Diaries of Mrs. Bardwell, November 2, 1858, Helen Temple Cooke Papers; *Six Hundred Dollars a Year*, p. 83.

11. Child, *American Frugal Housewife*, pp. 4 and 7.

12. Merriam, *Briggs*, p. 7; Child, *American Frugal Housewife*, p. 6.

13. Beecher, *Treatise on Domestic Economy*, p. 65.

14. Cowan, *More Work for Mother*, pp. 40–68.

15. [Stowe], *House and Home Papers*, p. 65. See Luke 10:38–42 for the story of Martha.

16. Ellet, *Practical Housekeeper*, p. 16.

17. See Stansell, *City of Women*, pp. 48–49 and 193–216.

18. Alcott, *Young Wife*, p. 247.

19. Using the wages of paid household workers as a basis for imputing a market value to unpaid domestic labor does not raise for the antebellum period the methodological probiems that it has raised in some contemporary studies. For a detailed analysis of existing techniques for evaluating the economic worth of housework, see Luisella Goldschmidt-Clermont, *Unpaid Work in the Household: A Review of Economic Evaluation Methods* (Geneva: International Labour Office, 1982).

20. Wages are from Martin, *Standard of Living*, p. 177; and Dudden, *Serving Women*, p. 149. These figures are supported by my own research. On seamstresses, see: entry for October, 1838, Almanac, Diaries of Martha Coffin Wright, 1856–1874, Garrison Papers. For the wages of nurses, see, for example, the household account book of Ann (Lyon) Garfield, 1821–1825, n.d., John Metcalf Garfield Papers.

21. This is calculated on the basis of an average weekly budget for a working-class family of five, as itemized in the *New York Daily Tribune*, May 27, 1851. According to that budget, flour could be bought in bulk at $5 a barrel, a barrel lasting a family of five about eight weeks. Since the *Tribune* budget assumes a family with an annual income over $500 (and therefore able to benefit from the savings of buying in bulk), I have increased the cost by 30%. On savings from buying in bulk, see Griscom, *Sanitary Condition*, p. 8. For additional discussions of food prices, see Martin, *Standard of Living*, p. 122; and Cummings, *American and His Food*, pp. 75–78.

22. The *New York Daily Tribune*, May 27, 1851.

23. Martin, *Standard of Living*, p. 168.

24. Ibid., p. 177.

25. This calculation is based on wages in Wright, *Comparative Wages*, pp. 47 and 55. It provides a very conservative index for wives' work; wives frequently had skills far beyond the "helper" level.

26. Thorburn, *Sketches*, p. 12. Thorburn recommended marriage as a sensible economic decision for young men earning as little as $500 a year—more than males of the laboring poor, but within the range of better-paid workingmen.

27. See, for example, household receipts, 1844, Almy Family Papers.

28. This estimate is based on expenditures recorded by Martha Coffin Wright for December, 1825, and January, February, and April, 1826. See diary of 1825, Diaries of Martha Coffin Wright, 1856–1874, Garrison Papers.

29. Alice Kessler-Harris, *Out to Work: A History of Wage-Earning Women in the United States* (New York: Oxford University Press, 1982), pp. 56–57.

30. See Martin, *Standard of Living*, p. 168, for the average weekly cost of room and board for a single, adult male living in New York City.

31. Ibid.

32. In her study of working-class families in late-nineteenth- and twentieth-century England, Laura Owen has concluded that women's inferior power in the family often resulted in their existing at a lower standard of maintenance than their husbands. See Owen, "The Welfare of Women in Laboring Families: England, 1860–1950," *Feminist Studies* 1/3–4 (Winter–Spring 1973): 107–25.

33. On the rhetoric of the "family wage" in antebellum America, see Martha May, "Bread before Roses: American Workingmen, Labor Unions and the Family Wage," in Ruth Milkman, ed., *Women, Work, and Protest* (Boston: Routledge and Kegan Paul, 1985), pp. 1–21. For an illuminating analysis of the assertion of the prerogatives of the male "breadwinner" by working-class men in Victorian England, see Wally Seccombe, "Patriarchy Stabilized: The Construction of the Male Breadwinner Wage Norm in Nineteenth-Century Britain," *Social History* 2/1 (January 1986): 53–76.

34. Ely, *Visits of Mercy* 1:98 and 193–94.

35. The most complete analysis to date of married women's property rights in the nineteenth century is Norma Basch's *In the Eyes of the Law: Women, Marriage, and Property in Nineteenth-Century New York* (Ithaca, N.Y.: Cornell University Press, 1982).

36. Alice Kessler-Harris and Karen Brodlin Sacks make this point in their examination of the contemporary effects of de-industrialization in the United States. They note, "For most of the American working class for most of its history, the wage of even the principal (male) earner was inadequate to raise a family." See "The Demise of Domesticity in America" in Lourdes Beneria and Catharine R. Stimpson, eds., *Women, Households and the Economy* (New Brunswick, N.J.: Rutgers University Press, 1987), p. 67.

37. See Dublin, *Women at Work*, p. 20; and Clark, *History of Manufactures* 1:374.

38. Wilentz, *Chants Democratic*, p. 117, n. 20.

39. Quoted in Ware, *Industrial Worker*, p. 77. Italics added.

40. John McVickar, *Outlines of Political Economy* (New York: Wilder and Campbell, 1825), p. 107.

41. Theodore Sedgwick, *Public and Private Economy* (New York: Harper and Brothers, 1836), pp. 30 and 225.

42. Harriet A. Weed, ed., *Life of Thurlow Weed, including His Autobiography and A Memoir* (Boston: Houghton, Mifflin, 1883), pp. 74–75.

43. Reported in the *New York Times*, November 15, 1861. I am indebted to Lori Ginzberg for bringing this item to my attention.

Notes to Chapter VII

1. Peck, *True Woman*, p. 245.

2. *The Ladies Museum*, July 16, 1825, p. 3; Beecher, *Lectures to Young Men*, pp. 87 and 91.

3. Ann Douglas, *The Feminization of American Culture* (New York: Alfred A. Knopf, 1977), p. 12.

4. Peck, *True Woman*, pp. 242–43.

5. Arthur, *Mother's Rule*, p. 261; Alcott, *Young Wife*, p. 149.

6. Daniel C. Eddy, *The Young Woman's Friend; or, the Duties, Trials, Loves, and Hopes of Woman* (Boston: Wentworth, 1857), p. 23.

7. Alcott, *Young Wife*, p. 265.

8. Peck, *True Woman*, p. 243–44.

9. Although he does not discuss women's labor, Raymond Williams' explication of the "pastoralization" of the labor of the English peasants in the seventeenth century provides a model for deciphering the discontinuity in the status and value of housework in industrial societies. I am indebted to him for this concept. See Raymond Williams, *The Country and the City* (London: Chatto and Windus, 1973), p. 31.

10. Ibid., p. 32.

11. Alcott, *Young Wife*, pp. 84–85.

12. Journal of Sarah M. Munro, 1853–1856, January 20, 1853, Caroline Wells Dall Papers; Mary Ann Archbald to "My Dear M[argaret]," January 1, 1821, the journals and diary of Mary Ann Archbald, 1762–1840.

13. J. H. Agnew, "Woman's Offices and Influence," *Harper's New Monthly Magazine* 3/17 (October 1851): 654–57.

14. For an excellent discussion of the meaning and importance of the concept of female "influence," see Lori D. Ginzberg, *Women and the Work of Benevolence: Morality, Politics, and Class in the Nineteenth-Century United States* (New Haven, Conn.: Yale University Press, 1990).

15. Agnew, "Woman's Offices," p. 657.

16. Mary Bushnell Cheney, *Life and Letters of Horace Bushnell* (New York: Harper and Brothers, 1880), p. 27.

17. Washington Irving, "The Wife," *Ladies Literary Cabinet*, July 4, 1819, pp. 82–84. Quotations are from Washington Irving, *The Sketch Book of Geoffrey Crayon, Gent.* (New York: Signet Classic, 1961), pp. 34–36.

18. These examples are taken from Thorburn, *Sketches*, p. 8; and Beecher, *Treatise on Domestic Economy*, p. 149, respectively. Eddy, *Young Woman's Friend*, p. 28.

19. "Pastoral Letter of the Massachusetts Congregationalist Clergy (1837)," in Kraditor, *Up from the Pedestal*, pp. 51–52; Winslow, *Discourse*, p. 8.

20. Allan Nevins and Milton Malsey Thomas, eds., *The Diary of George Templeton Strong* 1:179–80 and 325; Calvin Stowe to Harriet Beecher Stowe, quoted in Catherine Gilbertson, *Harriet Beecher Stowe* (New York: D. Appleton-Century Company, 1937), p. 105.

21. "Editor's Drawer," *Harper's New Monthly Magazine* 8/44 (January 1854): 282.

22. *The Man*, May 13, 1835; *Maine Washingtonian Journal* as quoted in *The Northern Star and Freeman's Advocate*, January 2, 1843; James C. Sylvis, ed., *Life, Speeches, Labors, and Essays of William H. Sylvis* (Philadelphia: Claxton, Remsen, and Haffelfinger, 1872), p. 120.

23. *The Rights of All*, June 12, 1829; *The Northern Star and Freeman's Advocate*, December 8, 1842, and January 2, 1843.

24. Luther, "Address . . . July 4, 1836," p. 10; "Mechanic," *Elements of Social Disorder*, p. 51. Moore is quoted in Wilentz, *Chants Democratic*, p. 239. The "Cordwainers' Song" is printed in Dawley, *Class and Community*, pp. 82–83.

25. "Mechanic," *Elements of Social Disorder*, p. 96.

26. Quoted in John Andrews and W. D. P. Bliss, *A History of Women in Trade Unions*, Vol. 10 of *Report on Condition of Woman and Child Earners in the United States*, Senate Doc. 645, 61st Cong., 2nd sess. (Washington, D.C.: Government Printing Office, 1911; reprint, New York: Arno Press, 1974), p. 48; "Mechanic," *Elements of Social Disorder*, p. 45; *Working Man's Advocate*, June 11, 1831.

27. May, "Bread before Roses," p. 4; Commons et al., *Documentary History* 6:281; "Mechanic," *Elements of Social Disorder*, p. 42.

28. Ryan, *Cradle of the Middle Class*, pp. 152 and 169.

29. Caroline Dall, *"Woman's Right to Labor"; or, Low Wages and Hard Work* (Boston: Walker, Wise, 1860), p. 57. Veronica Beechey discusses the function of this assumption in lowering women's wages in "Women and Production: A Critical Analysis of Some Sociological Theories of Women's Work," in Kuhn and Wolpe, *Feminism and Materialism*, pp. 156–97.

30. Stansell, *City of Women*, pp. 193–216.

31. The phrase is from the title of Judith McGaw's study, *Most Wonderful Machine*. McGaw has adapted the phrase from Melville's "most wonderful factory" in his tale "The Tartarus of Maids."

32. Wilentz, *Chants Democratic*; Dawley, *Class and Community*.

33. Mrs. [Jane] Marcet, *Conversations on Political Economy; in which the*

Elements of that Science are Familiarly Explained, 7th ed. (London: Longman, Orme, Brown, Green, & Longmans, 1839), especially pp. 25–72.

34. Mrs. A. J. Graves, *Woman in America: Being an Examination into the Morals and Intellectual Condition of American Female Society* (New York: Harper and Brothers, 1841), p. 156.

35. Beecher, *Treatise on Domestic Economy*, p. 26; Catharine E. Beecher, *An Essay on Slavery and Abolitionism, with reference to the Duty of American Females* (Philadelphia, Pa.: Henry Perkins, 1837), p. 128; Beecher and Stowe, *American Woman's Home*, p. 19.

36. Beecher and Stowe, *American Woman's Home*, p. 327.

37. Beecher, *Essay on Slavery*, pp. 101–2; Ellet, *Practical Housekeeper*, p. 17.

38. Harriet Beecher Stowe to Sarah Buckingham Beecher, December 17, [1850], Beecher–Stowe Family Papers.

Bibliography

Archival Collections

Beinecke Rare Book and Manuscript Library, Yale University, New Haven, Connecticut:
- American Literature Collection

Arthur and Elizabeth Schlesinger Library on the History of Women in America, Radcliffe College, Cambridge, Massachusetts:
- Almy Family Papers
- Anne Ware (Winsor) Allen Papers
- Archbald Papers
- Beecher-Stowe Family Papers
- Bradley-Hyde Collection
- Browne Family Papers
- Caroline Wells Dall Papers
- Helen Temple Cooke Papers
- Hooker Collection

Sophia Smith Collection, Smith College, Northampton, Massachusetts:
- Garrison Family Papers
- Hale Family Papers

The New York Historical Society, New York City, New York

Sterling Memorial Library, Yale University, New Haven, Connecticut:
- Beecher Family Papers
- Gilbert-Cheever Family Papers
- John Metcalf Garfield Papers

Stowe-Day Foundation, Hartford, Connecticut:
- Acquisitions

Katharine S. Day Collection
Foote Collection

Primary Sources

Abdy, E. S. *Journal of a Residence and Tour in the United States of North America, from April, 1833, to October, 1834.* London: John Murray, 1835.

Advocate of Moral Reform. New York, 1836.

Alcott, William A. *The Young Wife, or Duties of Woman in the Marriage Relation.* Boston: George W. Light, 1837.

———. *Ways of Living on Small Means.* 3rd ed. Boston: Light and Stearns, 1837.

American State Papers, 1789–1815. Vol. 2, *Finance.* Washington, D.C.: Gale and Seaton, 1832.

Appleton, Jane Sophia. "Sequel to the 'Vision of Bangor in the Twentieth Century.' " In *American Utopias: Selected Short Fiction.* Edited by Arthur Orcutt Lewis. New York: Arno Press, 1971.

Arthur, T. S., ed. *The Mother's Rule; or, The Right Way and the Wrong Way.* Philadelphia: Smith and Peters, 1856.

Bailyn, Bernard, ed. *The Apologia of Robert Keayne: The Self-Portrait of a Puritan Merchant.* New York: Harper Torchbooks, 1964.

Baxandall, Rosalyn, Linda Gordon, and Susan Reverby, eds. *America's Working Women: A Documented History—1600 to the Present.* New York: Random House, 1976.

Bayles, James C. *House Drainage and Water Service: In Cities, Villages, and Rural Neighborhoods, with Incidental Consideration of Causes Affecting the Healthfulness of Dwellings.* New York: David Williams, 1878.

Beecher, Catharine E. *A Treatise on Domestic Economy.* Rev. ed. Boston: Thomas H. Webb, 1842.

———. *An Essay on Slavery and Abolitionism, with Reference to the Duty of American Females.* Philadelphia: Henry Perkins, 1837.

Beecher, Catharine, and Harriet Beecher Stowe. *The American Woman's Home, or Principles of Domestic Science.* Hartford, Conn.: Stowe-Day Foundation, 1975. Originally published 1869.

Beecher, Henry Ward. *Lectures to Young Men.* Boston: J.P. Jewett, 1846.

Bessie; or, Reminiscences of a Daughter of a New England Clergyman of the Eighteenth Century. New Haven: J. H. Benham, 1861.

Boston Evening Post. 1740–1760.

Boston Evening Transcript. 1830–1840.

Boston-Gazette. 1720–1760.

Boutwell, George S. *Reminiscences of Sixty Years in Public Affairs.* New York: McClure, Phillips, 1902.

Bradford, William. *Of Puritan Plantation.* Edited by Harvey Wish. New York: Capricorn Books, 1962.

Bremer, Fredrika. *The Homes of the New World: Impressions of America.* New York: Harper, 1853.

Brigham, William. *The Compact with the Charter and Laws of the Colony of New Plymouth.* Boston: Dutton and Wentworth, 1836.

Brissot de Warville, J. P. *New Travels in the United States of America.* London: J. S. Jordan, 1792.

Brown, Antoinette Blackwell. "Industrial Reconstruction." *The Woman's Advocate* 1/1 (January 1869), 41–42.

Bryant, Blanche Brown, and Gertrude Elaine Baker, eds. *The Diaries of Sally and Pamela Brown, 1832–1838, and Hyde Leslie, 1887.* Springfield, Vt.: William L. Bryant Foundation, 1970.

Burn, James Dawson. *Three Years among the Working-Classes in the United States During the War.* London: Smith, Elder, 1865.

Burt, Henry M., ed. *The First Century of the History of Springfield: The Official Records from 1636 to 1736.* Springfield, Mass.: H. M. Burt, 1898.

Bushnell, Horace. *Work and Play: or, Literary Varieties.* New York: C. Scribner, 1864.

Butterfield, L. H., ed. *Letters of Benjamin Rush.* Princeton, N.J.: Princeton University Press, 1951.

Butterfield, L. H., Marc Friedlander, and Mari-Jo Kline, eds. *The Book of Abigail and John: Selected Letters of the Adams Family, 1762–1784.* Cambridge, Mass.: Harvard University Press, 1975.

Child, Lydia Maria. *The American Frugal Housewife.* Boston: American Stationers' Company, 1836.

———. *Letters from New York.* New York: C. S. Francis, 1845.

———. *The Mother's Book.* Boston: Carter and Hendee, 1831.

Cobbett, Thomas. *A Fruitfull and Usefull Discourse Touching the Honour Due from Children to Parents and the Duty of Parents towards Their Children.* London, 1654.

Cole, Arthur Harrison, ed. *The Industrial and Commercial Correspondence of Alexander Hamilton, Anticipating His Report on Manufactures.* Chicago: A. W. Shaw, 1928.

Colman, Benjamin. *The Duty and Honour of Aged Women. A Sermon on the Death of Madam Abigail Foster.* Boston: B. Green, 1711.

Combe, George. *Notes on the United States of North America, During a Phrenological Visit in 1838–9–40.* 3 vols. Edinburgh: MacLachan, Stewart, 1841.

Cott, Nancy F., ed. *Root of Bitterness: Documents of the Social History of American Women.* New York: E. P. Dutton, 1972.

Cotton, John. *A Meet Help. Or, a Wedding Sermon, Preached at New-Castle in New-England, June 19, 1694.* Boston: B. Green and J. Allen, 1699.

Coxe, Tench. *A View of the United States of America.* London: J. Johnson, 1795.

Crevecoeur, J. Hector St. John. *Letters from an American Farmer*. New York: Fox, Duffield, 1904. Originally published 1782.

The Cries of New-York, with Fifteen Illustrations. New York: John Doggett, Jr., 1846.

Cummings, Abbott Lowell, ed. *Rural Household Inventories, 1675–1775*. Boston: Society for the Preservation of New England Antiquities, 1964.

Dall, Caroline. *Women's Right to Labor*. Boston: Walker, Wise, 1860.

Davis, Andrew McFarland. *Colonial Currency Reprints, 1682–1751*. Boston: 1910–1911.

Demos, John, ed. *Remarkable Providences, 1600–1760*. New York: George Braziller, 1972.

DeVoe, Thomas F. *The Market Book, Containing a Historical Account of the Public Markets in the Cities of New York, Boston, Philadelphia and Brooklyn*. New York: Burt Franklin, 1862.

Diary of Sarah Connell Ayer. Portland, Maine: Lefavor-Tower, 1910.

The Diary of William Bentley. 4 vols. Salem, Mass.: Essex Institute, 1905.

Dickens, Charles. *American Notes for General Circulation*. New York: Harper and Brothers, 1842.

Doolittle, Mary Antoinette. *Autobiography of Mary Antoinette Doolittle*. Mount Lebanon, New York: 1880.

Drake, Samuel G., ed. *Annals of Witchcraft in New England and Elsewhere in the United States, from Their First Settlement*. Boston: W. E. Woodward, 1864.

Duncan, John M. *Travels through Part of the United States and Canada in 1818 and 1819*. New York: W. B. Gilley, 1823.

Eddy, Daniel C. *The Young Woman's Friend; or the Duties, Trials, Loves, and Hopes of Woman*. Boston: Wentworth, 1857.

Eliot, Jared. *Essays upon Field Husbandry in New England and Other Papers, 1748–1762*. Ed. Harry J. Carman and Rexford G. Tugwell. New York: Columbia University Press, 1942.

Ellet, Mrs. (Elizabeth), ed. *The Practical Housekeeper; A Cyclopaedia of Domestic Economy*. New York: Stringer and Townsend, 1857.

Ely, Ezra Stiles. *Visits of Mercy*. 6th ed. Philadelphia: S. F. Bradford, 1829.

Fearon, Henry Bradshaw. *Sketches of America: A Narrative of a Journey of Five Thousand Miles through the Eastern and Western States of America*. London: Longman, Hurst, Rees, Orme and Brown, 1818.

Foster, George G. *New York by Gas-Light: With Here and There a Streak of Sunshine*. New York: Dewitt and Davenport, 1850.

Foxcroft, Thomas. *The Character of Anna. . . . In a Sermon Preach'd after the Funeral of . . . Dame Bridget Usher. . . .* Boston: S. Kneeland, 1723.

———. *A Sermon Preach'd at Cambridge, After the Funeral of Mrs. Elizabeth Foxcroft. . . .* Boston: B. Green, 1721.

Franklin, Benjamin. *The Autobiography of Benjamin Franklin*. New Haven: Yale University Press, 1964.

———. "The Way of Wealth," *The Works of Benjamin Franklin*. Edited by Jared Sparks. Boston: Hilliard, Gray, 1840.

Freeman, Mary Wilkins. "The Revolt of 'Mother,' " Barbara H. Solomon, ed. *Short Fiction of Sarah Orne Jewett and Mary Wilkins Freeman*. New York: Signet, 1979.

Gallatin, Albert. "Report on Manufactures," *American State Papers, 1789–1815: Finance*. 3 vols. Washington, D.C.: Gales and Seaton, 1832.

Gilman, Caroline Howard. *The Lady's Annual Register and Housewife's Memorandum-Book*. Boston: T. H. Carter, 1838.

———. *The Lady's Annual Register and Housewife's Memorandum-Book*. Boston: T. H. Carter, 1839.

———. *Recollections of a Housekeeper*. New York: Harper and Brothers, 1836.

Goodrich, S. G. *Recollections of a Lifetime, or Men and Things I Have Seen*. 2 vols. New York: Miller, Orton and Mulligan, 1857.

———. *Enterprise, Industry and Art of Man*. Boston: Bradbury, Soden, 1845.

Graves, Mrs. A. J. *Woman in America: Being an Examination into the Moral and Intellectual Condition of American Female Society*. New York: Harper and Brothers, 1841.

Griffith, Mrs. *Letters Addressed to Young Married Women*. Philadelphia: John Turner, 1796.

Griscom, John H. *The Sanitary Condition of the Laboring Population of New York*. New York: Arno Press, 1970.

Grund, Francis J. *The Americans in Their Moral, Social, and Political Relations*. Boston: Marsh, Capen and Lyon, 1837.

Gunn, Thomas B. *Physiology of New York Boarding Houses*. New York: Mason Brothers, 1857.

Harper's New Monthly Magazine. 1850–1853.

Higginson, Francis. "New England Plantation," Alexander Young, ed., *Chronicles of the First Planters of the Colony of Massachusetts Bay*. Boston, 1846.

Hodgson, Adam. *Letters from North America, Written During a Tour in the United States and Canada*. London: Hurst, Robinson, 1824.

Irving, Washington. *The Sketch Book of Geoffrey Crayon, Gent*. New York: Signet Classic, 1961.

James, Bartlett Burleigh, and J. Franklin Jameson, eds. *Journal of Jasper Danckaerts, 1679–1680*. New York: Scribner's, 1913.

Janson, Charles William. *The Stranger in America, 1793–1806*. New York: Press of the Pioneers, 1935. Originally published London, 1807.

"Journal of Abigail Brackett Lyman." Helen Roelker Kessler, "The Worlds of Abigail Brackett Lyman." M.A. thesis, Tufts University, 1976.

"The Journal of William Wheeler." In *Black Rock: Seaport of Old Fairfield, Connecticut, 1644–1870*. Edited by Cornelia Penfield Lathrop. New Haven: Tuttle, Morehouse and Taylor, 1930.

Karlsen, Carol F., and Laurie Crumpacker, eds. *The Journal of Esther Edwards Burr, 1754–1757*. New Haven: Yale University Press, 1984.

[Knight, Sarah]. *The Journal of Madam Knight.* Boston: David R. Godine, 1972.

Kraditor, Aileen S., ed. *Up from the Pedestal: Selected Writings in the History of American Feminism.* Chicago: Quadrangle Books, 1968.

Ladies' Literary Cabinet. New York: 1819–1822.

The Ladies Museum. Philadelphia, 1800.

The Ladies Museum. Providence, 1825–1826.

Larcom, Lucy. *A New England Girlhood.* Boston: Houghton Mifflin, 1889.

Lerner, Gerda. *The Female Experience: An American Documentary.* Indianapolis: Bobbs-Merrill, 1977.

Letters of Elizabeth Cabot. Boston: privately printed, 1905.

Letters from John Pintard to His Daughter Eliza, 1816–1833. 4 vols. New York: New-York Historical Society, 1940–1941.

Luther, Seth. *An Address Delivered before the Mechanics and Working-Men of the City of Brooklyn, on the Celebration of the Sixtieth Anniversary of American Independence, July 4, 1836.* Brooklyn: Alden Spooner and Sons, 1836.

———. *An Address to the Working Men of New England, on the State of Education, and on the Condition of the Producing Classes in Europe and America.* Revised edition. New York: George H. Evans, 1833. Originally published 1832.

McLane, Louis. Secretary of the Treasury. *Documents Relative to the Manufactures in the United States, Collected and Transmitted to the House of Representatives in Compliance with a Resolution of January 19, 1832.* New York: Burt Franklin, 1969.

McVickar, John. *Outlines of Political Economy: Being a Republication of the Article upon That Subject Contained in the Edinburgh Supplement to the Encyclopaedia Britannica.* New York: Wilder and Campbell, 1825.

The Man. New York, 1834–35.

Manual of Self-Education: A Magazine for the Young. 1842.

Marcet, Mrs. [Jane]. *Conversations on Political Economy; in Which the Elements of That Science Are Familiarly Explained.* 7th ed. London: Longman, Orme, Brown, Green, and Longmands, 1839.

A Marriage Prayer. London, 1637.

Mather, Cotton. *Bonifacius: An Essay upon the Good.* Edited by David Levin. Cambridge, Mass.: Belknap Press, 1966.

———. *Eureka. Or a Vertuous Woman Found: An Essay on the Death of Mrs Mary Brown.* Boston: n.p., 1703.

———. *Family Religion Urged.* Boston: 1709.

———. *Marah Spoken to. A Brief Essay to Do Good unto the Widow. . . .* Preface by Increase Mather. Boston: S. Kneeland, 1718.

———. *Maternal Consolations. An Essay . . . on the Death of Mrs. Maria Mather. . . .* Boston: T. Fleet, 1714.

———. *Ornaments for the Daughters of Zion. Or the Character and Happiness of a Virtuous Woman.* Boston: S. Green and B. Green, 1692.

Matthews, Albert, ed. *Journal of William Loughton Smith, 1790–1791*. Cambridge, Mass.: Harvard University Press, 1917.

"Mechanic, A." *Elements of Social Disorder: A Plea for the Working Classes in the United States*. Providence, R.I.: Benjamin F. Moore, 1844.

Melville, Herman. "Bartleby the Scrivener," Jay Leyda, ed., *The Portable Melville*. New York: Viking Press, 1952.

Merriam, George S., ed. *Reminiscences and Letters of Caroline C. Briggs*. New York: Houghton, Mifflin, 1897.

Mitchell, D. W. *Ten Years in the United States: Being an Englishman's View of Men and Things in the North and South*. London: Smith, Elder, 1862.

Morgan, Helen M., ed. *A Season in New York, 1801: Letters of Harriet and Maria Trumbull*. Pittsburgh: University of Pittsburgh Press, 1969.

Morse, Francis Rollins, ed. *Henry and Mary Lee: Letters and Journals, with Other Family Letters, 1802–1860*. Boston: Thomas Todd, 1926.

Morse, Gardner. "Recollections of the Appearance of New Haven and of Its Business Enterprises and Movements in Real Estate between 1825 and 1837." *Papers of the New Haven Colony Historical Society* 5:97–100.

Nevins, Allan, ed. *The Diary of Philip Hone, 1828–1851*. New York: Kraus Reprint Company, 1969.

Nevins, Allan, and Milton Halsey Thomas, eds. *The Diary of George Templeton Strong*. 4 vols. New York: Macmillan, 1952.

The New-York Cries in Rhyme. New York: Grosset and Dunlap, 1939.

New York Times. 1855–1865.

New York Tribune. 1841–1851.

Nichols, Thomas L. *Forty Years of American Life*. 2 vols. London: John Maxwell, 1864.

Niles' Weekly Register. Baltimore, 1811–1818.

The Northern Star and Freeman's Advocate. Albany, 1842–1843.

Ogden, John Cosens. *The Female Guide: or, Thoughts on the Education of That Sex Accommodated to the State of Society, Manners, and Government in the United States*. Concord, N.H.: George Hough, 1793.

Pease, Zephaniah W., ed. *The Diary of Samuel Rodman: A New Bedford Chronicle of Thirty-Seven Years, 1821–1859*. New Bedford, Mass.: Reynolds Printing Company, 1927.

Peck, Jesse T. *The True Woman; or, Life and Happiness at Home and Abroad*. New York: Carlton and Porter, 1857.

The Rights of All. New York, 1829.

Robertson, Douglas S., ed. *An Englishman in America, 1785: Being the Diary of Joseph Hadfield*. Toronto: Hunter-Rose, 1933.

Robinson, Solon. *Hot Corn: Life Scenes in New York Illustrated*. New York: Dewitt and Davenport, 1854.

Secker, William. *A Wedding Ring for the Finger. . . . Directions to Those Men Who Want Wives, How to Choose*. Boston: Samuel Green, 1690.

Sedgwick, Theodore. *Public and Private Economy*. New York: Harper and Brothers, 1836.

Shurtleff, Nathaniel B., ed. *Records of the Governor and Company of the Massachusetts Bay in New England.* Boston: Press of William White, 1853.

Shurtleff, Nathaniel B., and David Pulsifier, eds. *Records of the Colony of New Plymouth, in New England.* Boston: Press of William White, 1855–1861.

Simmons, Amelia. *American Cookery.* New York: Oxford University Press, 1958. Originally published 1796.

Six Hundred Dollars a Year: A Wife's Effort at Low Living, under High Prices. Boston: Ticknor and Fields, 1867.

Solomon, Barbara H., ed. *Short Fiction of Sarah Orne Jewett and Mary Wilkins Freeman.* New York: Signet, 1979.

Sparks, Jared, ed. *The Works of Benjamin Franklin.* Boston: Hilliard, Gray, 1840.

Stanton, Elizabeth Cady, Susan B. Anthony, and Matilda Jocelyn Gage, eds. *The History of Woman Suffrage.* 6 vols. New York: Arno and the *New York Times*, 1969. Originally published New York: Fowler and Wells, 1881.

[Stowe, Harriet Beecher]. *House and Home Papers.* Boston: Fields, Osgood, 1869.

———. *Oldtown Folks.* Boston: Fields, Osgood, 1869.

———. *Uncle Tom's Cabin, or Life among the Lowly.* New York: Pocket Books, 1971.

Swisshelm, Jane. *Letters to Country Girls.* New York: J. C. Riker, 1853.

Sylvis, James C., ed. *Life, Speeches, Labors, and Essays of William H. Sylvis.* Philadelphia: Claxton, Remsen, and Haffelfinger, 1872.

Thorburn, Grant. *Sketches from the Note-book of Laurie Todd.* New York: D. Fanshaw, 1847.

Tupper, Frederick, and Helen Tyler Brown, eds. *Grandmother Tyler's Book: The Recollections of Mary Palmer Tyler, 1775–1866.* New York: G. P. Putnam's Sons, 1925.

Tuthill, Mrs. L[ouisa] C[aroline]. *Reality; or, The Millionaire's Daughter.* New York: C. Scribner, 1856.

U.S. Secretary of the Treasury. *Documents Relating to the Manufactures in the U.S.* House Doc. 308, 22nd Cong., 2nd sess. (1833).

Warner, Susan. *The Wide, Wide World.* New York: Feminist Press, 1987.

Wayland, Francis. *The Elements of Political Economy.* 3rd ed. Boston: Gould, Kendall, and Lincoln, 1837.

Weed, Harriet A., ed. *Life of Thurlow Weed, Including His Autobiography and a Memoir.* Boston: Houghton, Mifflin, 1883.

Williard, Samuel. *A Compleat Body of Divinity.* Boston, 1726.

Wilson, Harriet E. *Our Nig; or, Sketches from the Life of a Free Black.* New York: Vintage Books, 1983. Originally published 1859.

Winslow, Hubbard. *A Discourse Delivered in the Bowdoin Street Church.* Boston: Weeks, Jordan, 1837.

Winthrop, John. *The History of New England.* Edited by James Savage. Boston: Little, Brown, 1853.

Women's Influence and Women's Mission. Philadelphia: Willis P. Hazard, 1854.
Working Man's Advocate. Lowell, Mass., 1863–1865.
[Young, Arthur]. *Rural Economy, or Essays on the Practical Parts of Husbandry*. Burlington, Vt.: Issac Neale, 1792.

Secondary Sources

Abbott, Edith. *Women in Industry: A Study in American Economic History*. New York: D. Appleton, 1910.

Allen, Francis Olcott, ed. *The History of Enfield, Connecticut*. 3 vols. Lancaster, Pa.: Wickersham Printing Company, 1900.

Althusser, Louis, and Etienne Balibar. *Reading Capital*. London: National Labour Board, 1970.

Anderson, Karen. "Commodity Exchange and Subordination: Montagnais-Naskapi and Huron Women, 1600–1650." *Signs*, 11/1 (Autumn 1985), 48–62.

Andrews, Edward E. *The Community Industries of the Shakers*. Albany: University of the State of New York, 1932. Reprinted Philadelphia: Porcupine Press, 1972.

Andrews, John, and W.D.P. Bliss. *A History of Women in Trade Unions*. Vol. 10 of *Report on Condition of Woman and Child Earners in the United States*, Senate Doc. 645, 61st Cong., 2nd sess. Washington, D.C.: Government Printing Office, 1911. Reprint ed. New York: Arno Press, 1974.

Andrews, William D., and Deborah C. Andrews. "Technology and the Housewife in Nineteenth-Century America." *Women's Studies* 2 (1974).

The Arts and Crafts in New York, 1726–1776: Advertisements and News Items from New York City Newspapers, Vol. 69. New York: New-York Historical Society Collections, 1939.

Bailyn, Bernard. *The New England Merchants in the Seventeenth Century*. New York: Harper and Row, 1964.

Basch, Norma. *In the Eyes of the Law: Women, Marriage, and Property in Nineteenth-Century New York*. Ithaca, N.Y.: Cornell University Press, 1982.

Beneria, Lourdes, and Catharine R. Stimpson, eds. *Women, Households, and the Economy*. New Brunswick, N.J.: Rutgers University Press, 1987.

Benston, Margaret. "The Political Economy of Women's Liberation." *Monthly Review* (September 1969), pp. 13–27.

Berg, Barbara J. *The Remembered Gate: Origins of American Feminism—The Woman and the City, 1800–1860*. New York: Oxford University Press, 1978.

Berk, Sarah Fenstermaker, ed. *Women and Household Labor*. Beverly Hills, Calif.: Sage Publications, 1980.

Berthoff, Rowland. *An Unsettled People: Social Order and Disorder in American History*. New York: Harper and Row, 1971.

Bidwell, Percy W., and Frank I. Falconer. *History of Agriculture in the Northern United States, 1680–1860*. Washington, D.C., 1925.

Bissell, Linda Auwers. "Family, Friends, and Neighbors: Social Interaction in Seventeenth-Century Windsor, Connecticut." Ph.D. dissertation, Brandeis University, 1973.

Blackmar, Elizabeth. *Manhattan for Rent, 1785–1850*. Ithaca, N.Y.: Cornell University Press, 1989.

Blackwell, Alice Stone. *Lucy Stone: Pioneer of Woman's Rights*. Boston: Little, Brown, 1930.

Blake, Francis Everett. *History of the Town of Princeton, in the County of Worchester and Commonwealth of Massachusetts, 1759–1915*. 2 vols. Princeton, Mass.: published by the town, 1915.

Blake, Nelson. *Water for the Cities*. Syracuse, N.Y.: Syracuse University Press, 1956.

Bledstein, Burton J. *The Culture of Professionalism: The Middle Class and the Development of Higher Education in America*. New York: W. W. Norton, 1976.

Bloch, Ruth. "American Feminine Ideals in Transition: The Rise of the Moral Mother, 1785–1815." *Feminist Studies* 6 (June 1978): 101–127.

Blumin, Stuart M. "The Hypothesis of Middle-Class Formation in Nineteenth-Century America: A Critique and Some Proposals." *American Historical Review* 90 (April 1985).

Bonomi, Patricia U. *A Factious People: Politics and Society in Colonial New York*. New York: Columbia University Press, 1971.

Bradlee, Francis B. C. "The Boston and Lowell Railroad, the Nashua and Lowell Railroad, and the Salem and Lowell Railroad." *Essex Institute Historical Collections* 54 (1918): 208–210.

Branca, Patricia. "Image and Reality: The Myth of the Idle Victorian Lady," Mary Hartman and Lois W. Banner, eds. *Clio's Consciousness Raised*. New York: Harper and Row, 1974.

Bridenbaugh, Carl. *Cities in Revolt: Urban Life in America, 1743–1776*. New York: Alfred A. Knopf, 1968.

———. *Vexed and Troubled Englishmen, 1590–1642*. New York: Oxford University Press, 1968.

Brown, Judith K. "Iroquois Women: An Ethnohistoric Note," Rayna Reiter, ed. *Toward an Anthropology of Women*. New York: Monthly Review Press, 1975.

Brown, Richard D. *Modernization: The Transformation of American Life, 1600–1865*. New York: Hill and Wang, 1976.

Bruchey, Stuart. *The Roots of American Economic Growth, 1607–1861*. New York: Harper Torchbooks, 1968.

Burns, Rex. *Success in America: The Yeoman Dream and the Industrial Revolution*. Amherst: University of Massachusetts Press, 1976.

Bushman, Claudia L. *"A Good Poor Man's Wife": Being a Chronicle of Harriet Hanson Robinson and Her Family in Nineteenth-Century New England.* Hanover, N.H.: University Press of New England, 1981.

Bushman, Richard L. *From Puritan to Yankee: Character and the Social Order in Connecticut, 1690–1765.* New York: W. W. Norton, 1967.

Byington, Margaret. *Homestead: The Households of a Mill Town.* New York: Russell Sage Foundation, 1910.

Cawelti, John G. *Apostles of the Self-Made Man.* Chicago: University of Chicago Press, 1965.

Chandler, Alfred D. *The Visible Hand: The Managerial Revolution in American Business.* Cambridge, Mass.: Harvard University Press, The Belknap Press, 1977.

Cheney, Mary Bushnell. *Life and Letters of Horace Bushnell.* New York: Harper and Brothers, 1880.

Clark, Alice. *Working Life of Women in the Seventeenth Century.* London: G. Routledge and Sons, 1919.

Clark, Christopher. "The Household Economy, Market Exchange and the Rise of Capitalism in the Connecticut Valley, 1800–1816." *Journal of Social History* 13 (Winter 1979): 169–190.

———. "The Household Mode of Production—A Comment." *Radical History Review* (Fall 1978), 166–171.

Clark, Victor S. *History of Manufactures in the United States.* 3 vols. New York: McGraw-Hill, 1929.

Codman, John Thomas. *Brook Farm: Historic and Personal Memoirs.* Boston: Arena Publishing, 1894.

Cole, Donald B. *Immigrant City: Lawrence, Massachusetts, 1845–1921.* Chapel Hill: University of North Carolina Press, 1962.

Commons, John R., David J. Saposs, Helen L. Sumner, E. B. Mittleman, H. E. Hoagland, John B. Andrews, and Selig Perlman. *History of Labour in the United States.* New York: Macmillan, 1918.

Cott, Nancy F. *The Bonds of Womanhood: "Woman's Sphere" in New England, 1780–1835.* New Haven: Yale University Press, 1977.

———. "Eighteenth-Century Family and Social Life Revealed in Massachusetts Divorce Records." *Journal of Social History* (Fall 1976), 20–43.

Coulsen, Margaret, Branka Magas, and Hilary Wainwright. " 'The Housewife and Her Labour under Capitalism'—a Critique." *New Left Review* 89 (January–February 1975): 59–72.

Cowan, Ruth Schwartz. "The Industrial Revolution in the Home: Household Technology and Social Change in the Twentieth Century." *Technology and Culture* 17 (1976): 1–23.

———. *More Work for Mother: The Ironies of Household Technology from the Open Hearth to the Microwave.* New York: Basic Books, 1983.

Cronon, William. *Changes in the Land: Indians, Colonists, and the Ecology of New England.* New York: Hill and Wang, 1983.

Crowley, J. E. *This Sheba, Self: The Conceptualization of Economic Life in Eighteenth-Century America.* Baltimore: Johns Hopkins University Press, 1974.

Cummings, Richard Osborn. *The American and His Food: A History of Food Habits in the United States.* Chicago: University of Chicago Press, 1941.

Curry, Leonard P. *The Free Black in Urban America, 1800–1850: The Shadow of the Dream.* Chicago: University of Chicago Press, 1981.

Daitsman, George. "Labor and the 'Welfare State' in Early New York." *Labor History* 4 (Fall 1963): 248–256.

Dalla Costa, Mariarosa. *The Power of Women and the Subversion of the Community.* Bristol, England: Falling Wall Press, 1972.

Dawley, Alan. *Class and Community: The Industrial Revolution in Lynn.* Cambridge, Mass.: Harvard University Press, 1976.

Deetz, John. *In Small Things Forgotten: The Archeology of Early American Life.* Garden City, N.Y.: Anchor Books, 1977.

Degler, Carl N. *At Odds: Women and the Family in America from the Revolution to the Present.* New York: Oxford University Press, 1980.

Demos, John. *A Little Commonwealth: Family Life in Plymouth Colony.* New York: Oxford University Press, 1970.

Dexter, Elisabeth A. *Colonial Women of Affairs: Women in Business and the Professions in Colonial America before 1776.* Boston: Houghton Mifflin, 1924.

Douglas, Ann. *The Feminization of American Culture.* New York: Alfred A. Knopf, 1977.

Draper, Patricia. "!Kung Women: Contrasts in Sexual Egalitarianism in Foraging and Sedentary Contexts," Rayna Reiter, ed. *Toward an Anthropology of Women.* New York: Monthly Review Press, 1975.

Dublin, Thomas, ed. *Farm to Factory: Women's Letters, 1830–1860.* New York: Columbia University Press, 1981.

———. *Women at Work: The Transformation of Work and Community in Lowell, Massachusetts, 1826–1860.* New York: Columbia University Press, 1979.

Dudden, Faye E. *Serving Women: Household Service in Nineteenth-Century America.* Middletown, Conn.: Wesleyan University Press, 1983.

Earle, Alice Morse. *Colonial Dames and Goodwives.* New York: Houghton, Mifflin, 1895.

Eisenstein, Zillah R., ed. *Capitalist Patriarchy and the Case for Socialist Feminism.* New York: Monthly Review Press, 1979.

Epstein, Barbara Leslie. *The Politics of Domesticity: Women, Evangelism, and Temperance in Nineteenth-Century America.* Middletown, Conn.: Wesleyan University Press, 1981.

Ernst, Robert. *Immigrant Life in New York City, 1825–1863.* New York: King's Crown Press, 1949.

Faragher, Johnny, and Christine Stansell. "Women and their Families on the

Overland Trail to Oregon and California, 1849–1860." *Feminist Studies* 2 (1975): 150–166.

Ford, James. *Slums and Housing*. 2 vols. Cambridge, Mass.: Harvard University Press, 1936.

Gadt, Jeanette Carter. "Women and Protestant Culture: The Quaker Dissent from Puritanism." Ph.D. dissertation, University of California, 1974.

Gardiner, Jean. "Women's Domestic Labour." *New Left Review* 89 (January–February 1975): 47–58.

Genovese, Eugene D. *Roll, Jordon, Roll: The World the Slaves Made*. New York: Vintage Books, 1976.

Giedion, Siegfried. *Mechanization Takes Command*. New York: Oxford University Press, 1948.

Gilbertson, Catherine. *Harriet Beecher Stowe*. New York: D. Appleton-Century, 1937.

Ginzberg, Lori D. *Women and the Work of Benevolence: Morality, Politics, and Class in the Nineteenth-Century United States*. New Haven: Yale University Press, 1990.

Glasco, Laurence A. "The Life Cycles and Household Structure of American Ethnic Groups: Irish, Germans, and Native-born Whites in Buffalo, New York, 1855." *Journal of Urban History* 1 (May 1975): 339–364.

Goldschmidt-Clermont, Luisella. *Unpaid Work in the Household: A Review of Economic Evaluation Methods*. Geneva: International Labour Office, 1982.

Gordon, Ann D., Mari Jo Buhle. "Sex and Class in Colonial and Nineteenth-Century America," *Liberating Women's History: Theoretical and Critical Essays*. Edited by Berenice A. Carroll. Urbana: University of Illinois Press, 1976.

Greven, Philip, Jr. *Four Generations: Population, Land, and Family in Colonial Andover, Massachusetts*. Ithaca, N.Y.: Cornell University Press, 1970.

Gross, Robert A. *The Minutemen and Their World*. New York: Hill and Wang, 1976.

Guettel, Charnie. *Marxism and Feminism*. Toronto: Canadian Women's Educational Press, 1974.

Hahn, Steven, and Jonathan Prude, eds. *The Countryside in the Age of Capitalist Transformation: Essays in the Social History of Rural America*. Chapel Hill: University of North Carolina Press, 1985.

Hareven, Tamara. "Family Time and Industrial Time: Family and Work in a Planned Corporation Town, 1900–1924." *Journal of Urban History* 1 (1975): 365–389.

Hartmann, Heidi I. "Capitalism, Patriarchy, and Job Segregation by Sex." *Signs* 1/3 (Spring 1976), 137–170.

———. "The Family as the Locus of Gender, Class, and Political Struggle: The Example of Housework." *Signs* 6 (Spring 1981): 366–394.

Hayden, Dolores. *The Grand Domestic Revolution: A History of Feminist De-*

signs for American Homes, Neighborhoods, and Cities. Cambridge, Mass.: MIT Press, 1981.

Hazen, Henry A. *History of Billerica, Mass[achusetts].* Boston: A. Williams, 1883.

Henretta, James A. "Economic Development and Social Structure in Colonial Boston." *William and Mary Quarterly*, 3rd ser., 22 (1965): 75–92.

———. *The Evolution of American Society, 1700–1815: An Interdisciplinary Analysis.* Lexington, Mass.: D. C. Heath, 1973.

———. "Families and Farms; *Mentalité* in Pre-Industrial America." *William and Mary Quarterly*, 3rd ser., 35 (January 1978): 3–32.

Hess, John L., and Karen Hess. *The Taste of America.* New York: Grossman, 1977.

History of the Town of Whateley, Mass[achusetts], 1661–1899. Revised by James M. Crafts. Orange, Mass.: D. L. Crandall, 1899.

Hofstadter, Richard. *America at 1750: A Social Portrait.* New York: Alfred A. Knopf, 1971.

Horne, Field, ed. *The Diary of Mary Cooper: Life on a Long Island Farm, 1768–1773.* Oyster Bay, N.Y.: Oyster Bay Historical Society, 1981.

Howell, Martha C. "Marriage, Property, and Patriarchy: Recent Contributions to the Literature." *Feminist Studies* 13/1 (Spring 1987), 203–224.

Illich, Ivan. *Shadow Work.* Boston: M. Boyars, 1981.

James, Edward T. *Notable American Women: A Biographical Dictionary.* Cambridge, Mass.: The Belknap Press of Harvard University, 1971.

James, Selma, and Mariarosa dalla Costa. *The Power of Women and the Subversion of the Community.* Bristol, England: Falling Wall Press, 1973.

Jedrey, Christopher M. *The World of John Cleaveland: Family and Community in Eighteenth-Century New England.* New York: W. W. Norton, 1979.

Jensen, Joan M. "Cloth, Butter and Boarders: Women's Household Production for the Market." *Review of Radical Political Economics* 12 (Summer 1980): 14–24.

———. *Loosening the Bonds: Mid-Atlantic Farm Women, 1750–1850.* New Haven: Yale University Press, 1986.

Johnson, Paul E. *A Shopkeeper's Millennium: Society and Revivals in Rochester, New York, 1815–1837.* New York: Hill and Wang, 1978.

Jones, Douglass Lamar. "The Strolling Poor: Transiency in Eighteenth-Century Massachusetts." *Journal of Social History* (Spring 1975), 28–54.

Jones, Fred Mitchell. *Middlemen in the Domestic Trade of the United States, 1800–1860.* Urbana: University of Illinois Press, 1937.

Judd, Sylvester. *History of Hadley, Including the Early History of Hatfield, South Hadley, Amherst, and Granby, Massachusetts.* Springfield, Mass.: H. R. Huntting, 1905.

Kammen, Michael G. *Colonial New York: A History.* New York: Scribner's, 1975.

Karlsen, Carol F. *The Devil in the Shape of a Woman: Witchcraft in Colonial New England.* New York: W. W. Norton, 1987.

Kerber, Linda K. "Separate Spheres, Female Worlds, Woman's Place: The Rhetoric of Women's History." *Journal of American History* 75/1 (June 1988), 9–39.

———. *Women of the Republic: Intellect and Ideology in Revolutionary America.* Chapel Hill: University of North Carolina Press, 1980.

Kessler, Helen Roelker. "The Worlds of Abigail Brackett Lyman." M.A. thesis, Tufts University, 1976.

Kessler-Harris, Alice. *Out to Work: A History of Wage-Earning Women in the United States.* New York: Oxford University Press, 1982.

———. " 'Where Are the Organized Women Workers?' " *Feminist Studies* 3 (Fall 1975): 92–110.

Keyssar, Alexander. "Widowhood in Eighteenth-Century Massachusetts: A Problem in the History of the Family." *Perspectives in American History* 7 (1974): 83–119.

Kleinberg, Susan J. "Technology and Women's Work, 1870–1920." *Labor History* 17 (Winter 1976): 58–72.

Koehler, Lyle. *A Search for Power: "The Weaker Sex" in Seventeenth-Century New England.* Urbana: University of Illinois Press, 1980.

Kraditor, Aileen. *Up from the Pedestal: Selected Writings in the History of American Feminism.* Chicago: Quadrangle Books, 1968.

Kuhn, Annette, and AnnMarie Wolpe, eds. *Feminism and Materialism: Women and Modes of Production.* Boston: Routledge and Kegan Paul, 1978.

Kulikoff, Alan. "The Progress of Inequality in Revolutionary Boston." *William and Mary Quarterly*, 3rd ser., 28 (1971): 375–412.

Lattes, Zulma Recchini de, and Catalina H. Wainerman. "Unreliable Account of Women's Work: Evidence from Latin American Census Statistics." *Signs* 11/4 (Summer 1986), 740–750.

Lerner, Gerda. "The Lady and the Mill Girl: Changes in the Status of Women in the Age of Jackson." *Midcontinent American Studies Journal* X (Spring 1969): 5–15.

Lewis, Alonzo, James R. Newhall. *History of Lynn, Essex County, Massachusetts: including Lynnfield, Saugus, Swampscot, and Nahant.* Boston: John L. Shorey, 1865.

Litwack, Leon F. *North of Slavery: The Negro in the Free States, 1790–1860.* Chicago: University of Chicago Press, 1961.

Lockridge, Kenneth. *A New England Town, The First Hundred Years: Dedham, Massachusetts, 1636–1736.* New York: W. W. Norton, 1970.

McGaw, Judith A. "Accounting for Innovation: Technological Change and Business Practice in the Berkshire Paper Industry." Technology and Culture 26/4 (October 1985), 703–725.

———. *Most Wonderful Machine: Mechanization and Social Change in Berkshire Paper Making, 1801–1885.* Princeton: Princeton University Press, 1987.

McMahon, Sarah Frances. " 'A Comfortable Subsistence': A History of Diet in New England." Ph.D. dissertation, Brandeis University, 1982.

McMurry, Sally. *Families and Farmhouses in Nineteenth-Century America.* New York: Oxford University Press, 1988.

Main, Jackson Turner. *The Social Structure of Revolutionary America.* Princeton, N.J.: Princeton University Press, 1965.

Malmsheimer, Lonna Myers. "New England Funeral Sermons and Changing Attitudes Toward Woman, 1672–1792." Ph.D. dissertation, University of Minnesota, 1973.

Malos, Ellen, ed. *The Politics of Housework.* London: Allison and Busby, 1980.

Martin, Edgar W. *The Standard of Living in 1860: American Consumption Levels on the Eve of the Civil War.* Chicago: University of Chicago Press, 1942.

Marx, Karl. *Capital.* Translated by Ben Fowkes. 3 vols. New York: Vintage Books, 1977.

Matthaei, Julie. *An Economic History of Women in America: Women's Work, the Sexual Division of Labor, and the Development of Capitalism.* New York: Shocken Books, 1982.

Matthews, Glenna. *"Just a Housewife": The Rise and Fall of Domesticity in America.* New York: Oxford University Press, 1987.

May, Martha. "Bread before Roses: American Workingmen, Labor Unions and the Family Wage," Ruth Milkman, ed. *Women, Work, and Protest.* Boston: Routledge and Kegan Paul, 1985, pp. 1–21.

Merrill, Michael. "Cash Is Good to Eat: Self-Sufficiency and Exchange in the Rural Economy of the United States." *Radical History Review* (Winter 1977), 42–71.

Milkman, Ruth. "Women's Work and the Economic Crisis: Some Lessons from the Great Depression." *Review of Radical Political Economics* 8 (Spring 1976), 73–97.

Mitchell, Juliet. "Women: The Longest Revolution." *New Left Review* 40 (November–December 1966).

Moers, Ellen. *Literary Women.* Garden City, N.Y.: Anchor Doubleday, 1977.

Mohl, Raymond A. *Poverty in New York, 1783–1825.* New York: Oxford University Press, 1971.

Morgan, Edmund S. *The Puritan Family: Religion and Domestic Relations in Seventeenth-Century New England.* New York: Harper and Row, 1966.

Morgan, Edmund S. and Helen M. Morgan. *The Stamp Act Crisis: Prologue to Revolution.* New York: Collier Books, 1962.

Murphy, Marjorie. "Work, Protest, and Culture: New York on Working Women's History." *Feminist Studies* 13/3 (Fall 1987), 657–667.

Mutch, Robert E. "Colonial America and the Debate about the Transition to Capitalism." *Theory and Society* 9 (1980), 847–63.

Narrett, David. "Preparation for Death and Provision for the Living: Notes on New York Wills (1665–1760)." *New York History* 52 (1976), 417–37.

Nash, Charles Elventon, ed. *The History of Augusta [Maine].* Augusta: Charles Nash and Sons, 1904.

Nettels, Curtis P. *The Emergence of a National Economy, 1775–1815.* New York: Holt, Rinehart and Winston, 1962.

Norling, Lisa. "I Have Ever Felt Homeless: Mariners' Wives and the Ideology of Domesticity." Unpublished paper presented at the Society on the History of the Early American Republic, July 17, 1987.

North, Douglass C. *The Economic Growth of the United States, 1790–1860*. New York: W. W. Norton, 1966.

Norton, Mary Beth. "Eighteenth-Century American Women in Peace and War; The Case of the Loyalists." *William and Mary Quarterly*, 3rd ser., 33 (July 1976): 386–409.

———. *Liberty's Daughters: The Revolutionary Experience of American Women, 1750–1800*. Boston: Little, Brown, 1980.

Norton, Mary Beth. "The Myth of the Golden Age," Carol Ruth Berkin and Mary Beth Norton, eds., *Women of America: A History*. Boston: Houghton Mifflin, 1979.

Nussbaum, Arthur. *A History of the Dollar*. New York: Columbia University Press, 1957.

Oakley, Ann. *Woman's Work: The Housewife, Past and Present*. New York: Vintage Books, 1976.

Ogden, Annegret S. *The Great American Housewife: From Helpmate to Wage Earner, 1776–1986*. Westport, Conn.: Greenwood Press, 1986.

Oren, Laura. "The Welfare of Women in Laboring Families: England, 1860–1950." *Feminist Studies* 1/3–4 (Winter–Spring 1973), 107–125.

Papashvily, Helen. *All the Happy Endings*. New York: Harper and Row, 1956.

Pessen, Edward. *Riches, Class, and Power before the Civil War*. Lexington, Mass.: D. C. Heath, 1973.

Pinchbeck, Ivy. *Women Workers and the Industrial Revolution, 1750–1850*. London: Cass, 1969.

Pleck, Elizabeth. "Two Worlds in One: Work and Family." *Journal of Social History* 10 (1976/1977): 178–195.

Powell, Sumner Chilton. *Puritan Village: The Formation of a New England Town*. Garden City, N.Y.: Anchor Books, 1965.

Pruitt, Bettye Hobbs. "Self-Sufficiency and the Agricultural Economy of Eighteenth-Century Massachusetts." *William and Mary Quarterly*, 3rd ser., 41 (1984): 333–364.

Reiter, Rayna R., ed. *Toward an Anthropology of Women*. New York: Monthly Review Press, 1975.

Rock, Howard B. "The Perils of Laissez-Faire: The Aftermath of the New York Bakers' Strike of 1801." *Labor History* 18 (Summer 1976): 372–387.

Root, Waverly, and Richard de Rochemont. *Eating in America: A History*. New York: William Morrow, 1976.

Rosaldo, M. Z. "The Use and Abuse of Anthropology: Reflections on Feminism and Cross-cultural Understanding." *Signs* 5 (Spring 1980): 389–417.

Rosaldo, Michele, and Louise Lamphere, eds. *Woman, Culture, and Society*. Stanford, Calif.: Stanford University Press, 1974.

Ross, Ellen. "Survival Networks: Women's Neighborhood Sharing in London before World War One." *History Workshop* 15 (Spring 1983): 4–27.

Rothenberg, Winifred B. "The Market and Massachusetts Farmers, 1750–1855." *The Journal of Economic History* 41 (June 1981): 283–287.

Rubin, Gayle. "The Traffic in Women: Notes on the 'Political Economy' of Sex," Rayna Reiter, ed., *Toward an Anthropology of Women*. New York: Monthly Review Press, 1975.

Ryan, Mary P. *Cradle of the Middle Class: The Family in Oneida County, New York, 1790–1865*. New York: Cambridge University Press, 1981.

———. *Womanhood in America: From Colonial Times to the Present*. New York: New Viewpoints, 1975.

Salmon, Marylynn. *Women and the Law of Property in Early America*. Chapel Hill: University of North Carolina Press, 1986.

Sanday, Peggy Reeves. *Female Power and Male Dominance: On the Origins of Sexual Inequality*. New York: Cambridge University Press, 1981.

Scott, William B. *In Pursuit of Happiness: American Conceptions of Property from the Seventeenth to the Twentieth Century*. Bloomington: Indiana University Press, 1977.

Seccombe, Wally. "The Housewife and Her Labour under Capitalism." *New Left Review* 83 (January–February 1974): 3–24.

Sklar, Kathryn Kish. *Catharine Beecher: A Study in American Domesticity*. New Haven, Conn.: Yale University Press, 1973.

Smith, Judith E. "Our Own Kind: Family and Community Networks in Providence." *Radical History Review* 17 (Spring 1978): 99–120.

Smith Rosenberg, Carroll. *Religion and the Rise of the American City: The New York City Mission Movement, 1812–1870*. Ithaca, N.Y.: Cornell University Press, 1971.

Stack, Carol B. *All Our Kin: Strategies for Survival in a Black Community*. New York: Harper and Row, 1974.

Stansell, Christine. *City of Women: Sex and Class in New York, 1789–1860*. New York: Alfred A. Knopf, 1986.

Stowe, Charles Edward. *Life of Harriet Beecher Stowe, Compiled from Her Letters and Journals by Her Son*. Detroit: Gale Research Company, 1967.

Stowe, Charles Edward, and Lyman Beecher Stowe. *Harriet Beecher Stowe: The Story of Her Life*. Boston and New York: Houghton Mifflin, 1911.

Strasser, Susan May. *Never Done: A History of American Housework*. New York: Pantheon, 1982.

Sumner, Helen. *History of Women in Industry in the United States*. Vol. 9, *Report on Condition of Women and Child Earners in the United States*. Washington, D.C.: Government Printing Office, 1910.

Tiffany, Sharon W., ed. *Women and Society: An Anthropological Reader*. St. Albans, Vt.: Eden Press Women's Publications, 1979.

Tomasek, Kathryn M. "Fourierist Association in Theory and In Practice: Women, the Family, and Social Change." M.A. thesis, University of Wisconsin, 1989.

Tompsett, Christine H. "A Note on the Economic Status of Widows in Colonial New York." *New York History* 55 (1974): 319–32.

Tracy, Patricia J. *Jonathan Edwards, Pastor: Religion and Society in Eighteenth-Century Northampton*. New York: Hill and Wang, 1980.

Tryon, Rolla Milton. *Household Manufactures in the United States, 1640–1860*. Chicago: University of Chicago Press, 1917.

Ulrich, Laurel Thatcher. " 'A Friendly Neighbor': Social Dimensions of Daily Work in Northern Colonial New England." *Feminist Studies* 6 (Summer 1980): 392–405.

———. *Good Wives: Image and Reality in the Lives of Women in Northern New England, 1650–1750*. New York: Alfred A. Knopf, 1982.

———. "Vertuous Women Found: New England Ministerial Literature, 1668–1735." *American Quarterly* 28 (Spring 1976): 20–40.

U.S. Bureau of the Census, *Historical Statistics of the United States, Colonial Times to 1970, Bicentennial Edition*.

Wallace, Anthony F. C. *Rochdale: The Growth of an American Village in the Early Industrial Revolution*. New York: W. W. Norton, 1978.

Warden, G. B. "The Distribution of Property in Boston, 1692–1775." *Perspectives in American History* 10 (1976): 81–130.

Ware, Norman. *The Industrial Worker, 1840–1860: The Reaction of American Industrial Society to the Advance of the Industrial Revolution*. Chicago: Quadrangle Books, 1964.

Waring, George E., Jr. *Draining for Profit and Draining for Health*. Rev. ed., New York: Orange Judd, 1911.

Welter, Barbara. "The Cult of True Womanhood, 1820–1860." *American Quarterly* 18 (Summer 1966): 151–75.

Wertheimer, Barbara Mayer. *We Were There: The Story of Working Women in America*. New York: Pantheon Books, 1977.

Whyte, Martin King. *The Status of Women in Preindustrial Societies*. Princeton, N.J.: Princeton University Press, 1978.

Wilentz, Sean. *Chants Democratic: New York City and the Rise of the American Working Class, 1788–1850*. New York: Oxford University Press, 1984.

Williams, Raymond. *The Country and the City*. New York: Oxford University Press, 1973.

Wilson, Joan Hoff. "The Illusion of Change: Women and the American Revolution," Alfred F. Young, ed., *The American Revolution: Explorations in the History of American Radicalism*. DeKalb: Northern Illinois University Press, 1976.

Wood, Gordon S. *The Creation of the American Republic, 1776–1787*. Chapel Hill: University of North Carolina Press, 1969.

Wright, Carroll D. *Comparative Wages, Prices, and Cost of Living*. Boston: Wright and Potter, 1889.

Yans-McLaughlin, Virginia. *Family and Community: Italian Immigrants in Buffalo*. Ithaca, N.Y.: Cornell University Press, 1977.

Index